'TRUE BIOGRAPHIES OF NATIONS?'

THE CULTURAL JOURNEYS OF DICTIONARIES OF NATIONAL BIOGRAPHY

'TRUE BIOGRAPHIES OF NATIONS?'

THE CULTURAL JOURNEYS OF DICTIONARIES OF NATIONAL BIOGRAPHY

EDITED BY KAREN FOX

PRESS

Published by ANU Press
The Australian National University
Acton ACT 2601, Australia
Email: anupress@anu.edu.au

Available to download for free at press.anu.edu.au

ISBN (print): 9781760462741
ISBN (online): 9781760462758

WorldCat (print): 1097202530
WorldCat (online): 1097202413

DOI: 10.22459/TBN.2019

This title is published under a Creative Commons Attribution-NonCommercial-NoDerivatives 4.0 International (CC BY-NC-ND 4.0).

The full licence terms are available at creativecommons.org/licenses/by-nc-nd/4.0/legalcode

The ANU.Lives Series in Biography is an initiative of the National Centre of Biography at The Australian National University, ncb.anu.edu.au.

Cover design and layout by ANU Press

This edition © 2019 ANU Press

CONTENTS

Acknowledgements. vii
1. The Cultural Journeys of Dictionaries of Biography. 1
   Karen Fox

PART I: THE DIGITAL AGE

2. Individual Lives and National Truths: Locating Biographies within a National Encyclopedia. 21
   Jock Phillips

3. The Irish World: How to Revise a Long-Standing Dictionary Project. 37
   Turlough O'Riordan

4. What is National Biography For? Dictionaries and Digital History. 57
   Philip Carter

5. Using Lives: The *Australian Dictionary of Biography* and Its Related Corpora. 79
   Melanie Nolan

PART II: THE REPRESENTATIONAL CHALLENGE

6. Why Gender Matters: Fostering Diversity in the *American National Biography* with Lessons Learned from *Notable American Women*. 101
   Susan Ware

7. Women and the Biographies of Nations: *The Biographical Dictionary of Scottish Women*. 119
   Elizabeth Ewan

8. An Indigenous Australian Dictionary of Biography 139
   Shino Konishi

9. Writing the Nation in Two Languages: The *Dictionary of Welsh Biography* 159
   Dafydd Johnston

PART III: THE TRANSNATIONAL DIMENSION

10. Writing a Dictionary of World Biography 179
    Barry Jones

11. British National Biography and Global British Lives: From the *DNB* to the *ODNB*—and Beyond?................. 193
    David Cannadine

12. The *Dictionary of Canadian Biography* and the Irish Diaspora 209
    David A. Wilson

Contributors 225

ACKNOWLEDGEMENTS

This book had its genesis in a conference held in Canberra in 2016. Titled '"True Biographies of Nations"? Exploring the Cultural Journeys of Dictionaries of National Biography', it was organised by the National Centre of Biography (NCB) at The Australian National University (ANU) and supported by the National Library of Australia (NLA), and it sought to bring together practitioners working on national dictionaries of biography, along with librarians, archivists, fellow researchers, and others interested or involved in biographical dictionary enterprises. Heartfelt thanks are due to my fellow conference organisers, Melanie Nolan and Christine Fernon; to Scott Yeadon, Karen Ciuffetelli, and all my colleagues at the NCB; to the National Library of Australia, particularly to Margy Burn and Kathryn Favelle; to the ANU College of Arts and Social Sciences, which provided funding; to the volunteers, who helped things run so smoothly; and to all the speakers and attendees, who made the two days of the conference so stimulating and enjoyable.

A great many debts have also been incurred in the preparation of this book. First and foremost, I am grateful to all the contributors: Jock Phillips, Turlough O'Riordan, Philip Carter, Melanie Nolan, Susan Ware, Elizabeth Ewan, Shino Konishi, Dafydd Johnston, Barry Jones, David Cannadine, and David A. Wilson. It has been a pleasure to work with each of them, and I am lucky to have had such a gentle introduction to the art of editing a collection. My sincere thanks to you all.

I am most grateful to Melanie Nolan, the chair of the editorial board for the ANU.Lives Series in Biography, who has been a source of guidance and support from the moment this project was conceived. I thank the reviewers of the manuscript, and the members of the ANU.Lives editorial board, for their suggestions and feedback, which was much appreciated. Thanks are also due to the staff of ANU Press, especially Emily Hazlewood, for all their help and support as this book was in preparation, and to Geoff Hunt, whose fine copyediting has greatly benefited the final work. Financially, the production of this book was assisted by an ANU Publication Subsidy, for which I am very grateful.

Every effort has been made to locate the copyright holders for material that has been quoted. I offer my apologies to any copyright holders I have been unable to identify or trace. Any individual or organisation that may have been overlooked or misattributed may contact the publisher.

I wish also to record my gratitude to my colleagues and friends at the National Centre of Biography/*Australian Dictionary of Biography* and the School of History at ANU. It is a delight to be part of such a warm and lively scholarly community, and to share in the triumphs and tribulations of historical research and writing with you all. I am especially grateful to Christine Fernon for her support and advice during the preparation of this manuscript.

No acknowledgements would be complete without mention of my family. During the preparation of this book we have welcomed its newest member, Carlin Eric McDonald, and his smile and giggle shared across the Tasman in photos and videos have helped to remind me of the joy and wonder in discovery that is so central to human life, as it is to historical research. And, as always, I thank Jamie, my beloved partner and friend. Mere words can never capture what you are to me.

Karen Fox
March 2019

1

THE CULTURAL JOURNEYS OF DICTIONARIES OF BIOGRAPHY

KAREN FOX

Fifty years after the publication of the first volume of the *Australian Dictionary of Biography*, in mid-2016 participants from around the English-speaking world gathered in Canberra for the conference '"True Biographies of Nations"? Exploring the Cultural Journeys of Dictionaries of National Biography'.[1] Organised by the National Centre of Biography at The Australian National University (ANU) and supported by the National Library of Australia (NLA), the conference provided a rare opportunity for those involved in the production of dictionaries of national biography to come together, along with archivists, librarians, fellow researchers, and members of the public, to reflect on the purpose and place of national biographies in the twenty-first century. The aim was to explore the cultural journeys taken by dictionaries of national biography, to consider the challenges and opportunities facing such projects today, and to gauge the extent of their development into truly national biographies.

Thematically and institutionally the 2016 gathering was the sequel to an earlier conference on national biographies, organised by the Humanities Research Centre and the Australian Dictionary of Biography at ANU, and the NLA, and held in Canberra in 1995. Setting out to 'explore the literary and historical character of the genre' of national biography, and to

---

1 The term 'cultural journey' is also used in relation to dictionaries of national biography by Marcello Verga. Marcello Verga, 'The Dictionary is Dead, Long Live the Dictionary! Biographical Collections in National Contexts', in *Setting the Standards: Institutions, Networks and Communities of National Historiography*, eds Ilaria Porciani and Jo Tollebeek (Houndmills and New York: Palgrave Macmillan, 2012), 89.

'compare a variety of its modern manifestations', it took place over three days, with the proceedings published as *National Biographies and National Identity: A Critical Approach to Theory and Editorial Practice*.[2] Musing on the genre in the introduction to the collection, Iain McCalman suggested that the genre of the national biographical dictionary stood 'at the heart of the most ferocious and divisive contemporary debates about the epistemology and hermeneutics of knowledge'.[3] In the late twentieth-century context of fracturing national identities and the assertion of multiculturalism and multilingualism in Europe and the antipodes, he stated, '[m]akers of national biographies stand in the front line of these identity wars'.[4]

McCalman's characterisation of dictionaries of national biography as prisms through which debates over identity—national, global, or even individual—are refracted remains pertinent 20 years later. Many of the issues discussed at the earlier conference, and in the resulting collection of papers, involved questions about the nation: its composition, its meanings, or its future. James Walter asked 'seven questions' of national biography, including how well such works could encapsulate 'the imaginative life of the nation' or embody the whole community rather than merely elites within a society, and what role collective biography plays in nation building.[5] Focusing on female lives, Patricia Grimshaw too considered 'the tradition of nation-making', suggesting that recording women's significance in these processes required understanding 'the racial and gender dimensions of the construction of the idea of "nation"', as well as the ways in which women were themselves 'enmeshed in' that idea.[6] Elizabeth Baigent reflected upon the nation not only as the 'subject matter' of dictionaries of national biography, but also as its 'audience' and 'sponsor', exploring not only 'how ideas of the nation, nationality and national life are constructed [and] reconstructed', but also how those same ideas and processes can restrict possibilities for dictionary producers.[7]

---

2   Iain McCalman, 'Introduction', in *National Biographies and National Identity: A Critical Approach to Theory and Editorial Practice*, eds Iain McCalman with Jodi Parvey and Misty Cook (Canberra: Humanities Research Centre, The Australian National University, 1996), iii.
3   McCalman, 'Introduction', i.
4   McCalman, 'Introduction', i.
5   James Walter, 'Seven Questions About National Biography', in McCalman with Parvey and Cook, *National Biographies and National Identity*, 21–22, 31–34.
6   Patricia Grimshaw, 'Female Lives and the Tradition of Nation-Making', in McCalman with Parvey and Cook, *National Biographies and National Identity*, 53.
7   Elizabeth Baigent, 'Nationality and Dictionaries of National Biography', in McCalman with Parvey and Cook, *National Biographies and National Identity*, 63.

And, as is always the case when those involved in biographical dictionary projects congregate, there was discussion of the numerous practical difficulties involved in such work—among them issues of selectivity and space, editorial decisions, funding, and revisions. Each of these matters, in different ways, finds resonance in the present book.

In a sense, the question that lay behind the 1995 conference was one recently highlighted by Marcello Verga: what is a dictionary of national biography for? According to Verga, the genre has been 'undergoing a steady transformation', from being 'an instrument designed to vindicate past glories and national supremacy', to developing as 'a learned and specialised work without the earlier ideological overtones'.[8] Certainly, dictionaries of national biography have changed significantly over time. Since the emergence of these works in the Western world in the eighteenth century, the cultural, social, and political landscapes in which they are produced have shifted dramatically. The assertion of national glories and the delineation of national identities—a key if never the sole driving force behind these vast publications—seemed not only outdated by the late twentieth century, but unenlightened, if not positively dangerous. Such a destabilisation of the imperatives that had brought national biographical dictionaries into being necessitated a rethinking of their role and purpose. Yet the history of dictionaries of national biography is not simply a journey from unreflective vessel of national supremacy to multiethnic reflection of national diversity. Dictionaries of national biography have always been reference works, serious, scholarly, and factual, as well as works of literature, able to provide readers with diversion and entertainment. Nor is their relationship with the nations they represent either settled or obvious in the twenty-first century. The cultural journey they have taken has been traversed in tandem with that of the nation itself, and that journey continues today.

Collective Biography and Dictionaries of National Biography

Collective biography has a long history, as Keith Thomas has reminded us. Well before the emergence of dictionaries of national biography as we understand them today, group biography was a flourishing genre in the Western world, produced in ancient Greece and Rome, and later in

---

8 Verga, 'The Dictionary is Dead', 102.

Renaissance Europe. Such works often collected the lives of leaders (military, political, or religious), saints, or those engaged in a particular profession.[9] Another form of collective biography, conceived in early modern Europe, was universal biography, an enterprise seeking to assemble 'the lives of all the notable people who had ever lived'.[10] These works were sometimes very large, as was the *Biographie Universelle*, produced in France from 1810 by Louis-Gabriel Michaud, with numerous collaborators, and in its first edition (including supplements) spanning 85 volumes.[11] National biography, as such, grew out of the development of nationalist ideas, and began with the 1662 publication *Worthies of England*, by Thomas Fuller.[12]

Though by no means a new development, collective national biography experienced a boom in the nineteenth century as nationalism flowered in Europe. As Thomas put it, during this period dictionaries of national biography became 'an obligatory accompaniment to the process of European state formation' and 'a stock way of forging national identity and generating national pride'.[13] Beginning with Sweden from 1835, national biographical dictionaries were produced across Europe, including in the Netherlands, Austria, Belgium, Germany, and Denmark, as well as on the other side of the Atlantic in the United States of America.[14] For Verga, these works began with the commissioning of Belgium's *Biographie Nationale* in 1845. In this publication, he posited, could be seen 'a new way of writing national history' that required the production of biographies which both profiled individuals 'worth recalling for their personal merits', and 'provided an effective illustration of the Belgian national character'.[15] The *Biographie Nationale* was, in his view, 'the first approach to writing the biography of a nation' via the lives of individuals selected to represent that national community.[16] Dictionaries of national biography such as

---

9   Keith Thomas, *Changing Conceptions of National Biography: The* Oxford DNB *in Historical Perspective* (Cambridge: Cambridge University Press, 2005), 2–3. doi.org/10.1017/CBO97805 11497582; Julie F. Codell, 'Biographical Dictionaries', in *Encyclopedia of Life Writing: Autobiographical and Biographical Forms*, ed. Margaretta Jolly, vol. 1, *A–K* (Chicago and London: Fitzroy Dearborn Publishers, 2001), 107.
10 Thomas, *Changing Conceptions*, 4.
11 Thomas, *Changing Conceptions*, 8; Christopher Smith, 'Biographie universelle; Dictionnaire de biographie française', in Jolly, *Encyclopedia of Life Writing*, 1:109.
12 Thomas, *Changing Conceptions*, 9–11.
13 Thomas, *Changing Conceptions*, 14.
14 Thomas, *Changing Conceptions*, 15.
15 Verga, 'The Dictionary is Dead', 90–91. Colin Matthew also identified the *Biographie Nationale de Belgique* as 'the first large scale [dictionary of national biography] in a recognizably modern format'. Colin Matthew, 'Dictionaries of National Biography', in McCalman with Parvey and Cook, *National Biographies and National Identity*, 3.
16 Verga, 'The Dictionary is Dead', 91.

these displayed 'an unconcealed nationalist agenda', in Thomas's words, although their creators were also driven by other motives, such as 'the commemoration of the virtuous dead', the provision of exemplary lives to inspire people, and the entertainment and education of readers.[17]

Britain's *Dictionary of National Biography* (*DNB*), published from 1885, has been described as 'a belated response' to this nineteenth-century literary phenomenon.[18] Yet for its first editor, Leslie Stephen, a dictionary of national biography was not merely a product of 'the "commemorative instinct"' (as the next editor, Sidney Lee, would see it), but a boon to learning at a moment when scholarship was greatly expanding.[19] Moreover, the *DNB* was, in the words of Colin Matthew—the founding editor of its successor, the *Oxford Dictionary of National Biography* (*ODNB*)— 'dramatically eclectic'.[20] It included eccentrics and notorious figures as well as eminences, and it was vague and nonprescriptive about the precise contours of the nation it depicted. Such a lack of jingoism was perhaps a result of the dominant global position held by the United Kingdom at the time. As Thomas contended, '[t]ranquil consciousness of Britain's world superiority made [the *DNB*] less obviously chauvinistic than its European counterparts, for whom national independence was newer and less secure'.[21] Lawrence Goldman, the third editor of the *ODNB*, similarly argued that 'the *DNB* was not a characteristic work of its age, but something much more eclectic, broad, independent and ultimately unclassifiable'.[22]

Many countries outside Europe have also produced their own dictionaries of national biography. In the United States, the *Dictionary of American Biography* was published between 1927 and 1936, with supplements appearing until 1985; its successor, the *American National Biography*, appeared in 24 volumes in 1999 and is now published online and

---

17 Thomas, *Changing Conceptions*, 15–24.
18 Alison Booth, 'Fighting for Lives in the *ODNB*, or Taking Prosopography Personally', *Journal of Victorian Culture* 10, no. 2 (2005): 273–74. doi.org/10.3366/jvc.2005.10.2.267.
19 David Amigoni, 'Distinctively Queer Little Morsels: Imagining Distinction, Groups, and Difference in the *DNB* and the *ODNB*', *Journal of Victorian Culture* 10, no. 2 (2005): 280. doi.org/10.3366/jvc.2005.10.2.279.
20 Matthew, 'Dictionaries of National Biography', 7.
21 Thomas, *Changing Conceptions*, 26–27.
22 Lawrence Goldman, 'A Monument to the Victorian Age? Continuity and Discontinuity in the Dictionaries of National Biography 1882–2004', *Journal of Victorian Culture* 11, no. 1 (2006): 118. doi.org/10.3366/jvc.2006.11.1.111.

regularly updated.[23] Established through a bequest and first published in 1966, Canada's *Dictionary of Canadian Biography/Dictionnaire biographique du Canada* is produced in both English and French, and to date comprises 15 print volumes and an online edition that also contains additional biographies, including from the volume currently in progress.[24] The *Australian Dictionary of Biography* (*ADB*) was founded in the 1950s, with its first volume also appearing in 1966. Extending thus far to 18 volumes and a supplement, the *ADB* went online in 2006, and entries are now published first online.[25] On the other side of the Tasman, the *Dictionary of New Zealand Biography* (*DNZB*) was published in five print volumes, plus a parallel series in the Māori language, between 1990 and 2000, and has since been digitised and integrated into the online resource *Te Ara—The Encyclopedia of New Zealand*.[26]

These examples, and indeed all the dictionaries discussed in this book, are located in the English-speaking world. While several of those considered in this volume are not English language–only publications, those that are bilingual are all produced in English as well as another language. Other national dictionary projects might have been chosen for inclusion, and would have provided valuable contrasts to those discussed in these pages. The *Dictionary of Swedish National Biography* (*Svenskt biografiskt lexicon*), for example, began publication in 1917, and includes individuals 'active in Sweden, or who have acted for Sweden abroad', while in Switzerland biographies form one part of the *Historical Dictionary of Switzerland* (*Historisches Lexikon der Schweiz/Dictionnaire historique de la Suisse/Dizionario storico della Svizzera*), along with families, geographical entries, and thematic or subject articles.[27] Like the *ODNB*, the *Neue deutsche Biographie* is the successor to an earlier national biographical dictionary, the *Allgemeine deutsche Biographie*. Produced by the Historical Commission of the Bavarian Academy of Sciences, it focuses on 'people

---

23 'About the *ANB*' and 'Frequently Asked Questions', *American National Biography Online*, accessed 4 January 2017, www.anb.org/aboutanb.html and www.anb.org/qa.html.
24 'About Us', *Dictionary of Canadian Biography*, accessed 4 January 2017, www.biographi.ca/en/about_us.php.
25 For the history of the *ADB*, see Melanie Nolan and Christine Fernon, eds, *The ADB's Story* (Canberra: ANU E Press, 2013). doi.org/10.22459/ADBS.10.2013.
26 '*Dictionary of New Zealand Biography*', Ministry for Culture and Heritage, accessed 4 January 2017, www.mch.govt.nz/what-we-do/websites-we-run/dictionary-new-zealand-biography.
27 'What is the Dictionary of Swedish National Biography?' *Dictionary of Swedish National Biography*, accessed 21 August 2018, sok.riksarkivet.se/Sbl/OmSBL.aspx; 'The History of the *Historical Dictionary of Switzerland*', *Historisches Lexikon der Schweiz/Dictionnaire historique de la Suisse/Dizionario storico della Svizzera*, accessed 21 August 2018, www.hls-dhs-dss.ch/d/english.

from the German-speaking areas whose achievements have influenced developments in politics, the economy, social sciences, technical fields, and the arts'.[28] In Spain, meanwhile, the release of the first volumes of the *Spanish Dictionary of Biography* (*Diccionario biográfico español*) in 2011 was accompanied by criticism of its treatment of General Francisco Franco, among others, and it was later announced that Franco's entry would be amended in the online edition.[29] Further afield, illuminating contrasts might be made with biographical traditions in Asia, Africa, or Latin America. Biography in China, for example, was for centuries an important part of dynastic histories and developed as a means of 'transmitting to posterity certain aspects of a life'.[30] New trends emerged from the late nineteenth century, while since 1949 biographical writing in China has been 'shaped by the political and ideological movements' engulfing the country.[31]

To some extent the selection of dictionary projects discussed in this volume is accidental, shaped by practical limitations of funding, scale, and contacts, which constrained the scope of the conference from which it arises. The English-language format of the conference, and my own English-speaking background, likewise restricted the ambit of both event and book. Indeed, as evident elsewhere in this volume, issues of language can pose their own challenge for national dictionary projects, especially in nations where a variety of languages are spoken. As Barry Jones's chapter makes clear, questions of language would pose a significant difficulty for any project to produce a truly global or universal dictionary of biography. Yet there is also an intellectual reason to consider this particular group of dictionary projects together. The histories of each of the nations whose dictionaries feature in this collection are intertwined with the history of the British Empire. This historical connection to the British Empire adds

---

28   Gregor Hens, 'Neue Deutsche Biographie', in *Encyclopedia of Life Writing: Autobiographical and Biographical Forms*, ed. Margaretta Jolly, vol. 2, *L–Z* (Chicago and London: Fitzroy Dearborn Publishers, 2001), 649.
29   Giles Tremlett, 'Spaniards Outraged Over Favourable Franco Biography', *Guardian*, 1 June 2011, accessed 23 August 2018, www.theguardian.com/world/2011/may/31/spaniards-outraged-favourable-franco-biography; 'Minister Tells Academy to Alter Biography After Row Over Franco Entry', *El Pais*, 13 June 2011, accessed 27 August 2018, elpais.com/elpais/2011/06/13/inenglish/1307942450_850210.html; James Badcock, 'General Franco to be Officially Defined by Spain as a Dictator', *Telegraph*, 8 April 2015, accessed 23 August 2018, www.telegraph.co.uk/news/worldnews/europe/spain/11519691/General-Franco-to-be-officially-defined-by-Spain-as-a-dictator.html.
30   Pei-Yi Wu, 'China: to the 19th Century', in Jolly, *Encyclopedia of Life Writing*, 1:206–7.
31   Shao Dongfang, 'China: 19th Century to 1949', in Jolly, *Encyclopedia of Life Writing*, 1:208–10; Shao Dongfang, 'China: 1949 to the Present', in Jolly, *Encyclopedia of Life Writing*, 1:210–11.

an additional layer—the imperial or colonial—to the national/global framework that underlies this book. To some degree, each of the projects discussed here has arguably to wrestle with the imperial strand in the history of the nation with which it deals, and each faces the question of how best to treat that imperial past in a dictionary of national biography. Such resonances between this set of dictionary ventures make them an ideal group for exploring comparatively the evolution of national biographical dictionary projects into the twenty-first century.

Dictionaries of national biography take the form of collections of concise biographies, and generally span both well-known or major historical figures, on which much has previously been written, and more minor or less well-known individuals, on whom there may be nothing previously written, or even relatively few biographical details easily available. Entries usually have a specific and at times quite prescriptive format, in order to meet the needs of a reference work to provide accurate information that is as comprehensive as possible, and which is presented in a consistent manner. At the same time, they are also literary works, and as such their producers generally seek to make them lively and readable, entertaining as well as informative. Like biography itself—as Virginia Woolf so memorably put it—they are caught between the 'granite-like solidity' of fact and the 'rainbow-like intangibility' of personality, attempting to accurately record all the salient features of a person's life and activities, and also to capture something of the spark of their personality or character, perhaps in just a few well-chosen words or a revealing anecdote.[32] Despite their implication in issues of nationalism and national identity, for many of those who work in their production, it is their purpose as works of reference that is of greatest significance, shaping both broad strategic decisions such as selection choices, and editorial interventions in the articles themselves. According to Thomas, for example, the *ODNB* has been produced primarily as 'a neutral work of reference', with subjects 'chosen for their historical importance' rather than through prisms such as nationalism or the commemoration of exemplary lives.[33] Likewise, addressing the challenges of selecting 'missing persons' to be added to an existing dictionary, Christine Nicholls (the editor of the *DNB*'s *Missing Persons* volume) emphasised the importance of whom readers—in that

---

32 Virginia Woolf, *Granite and Rainbow: Essays by Virginia Woolf* (London: Hogarth Press, 1958), 149.
33 Thomas, *Changing Conceptions*, 36–37.

case, people of the late twentieth century—sought to find among the entries. 'We dictionary editors', she said, 'should never forget that we are the servants of the enquirer'.³⁴

An Ever-Changing Genre

Dictionaries of national biography may be seen as part of a wider genre of collective biographies about a nation's greats, and they share with the works in that wider genre a number of characteristic challenges, as well as displaying similar patterns of change over time. In Australia, as in other parts of the world, the current *ADB* project was preceded by earlier efforts in collective national biography. Looking at these publications alongside the evolution of the *ADB* can reveal something further of the cultural journeys that dictionaries of national biography have taken during the past two centuries.³⁵ Biographical dictionaries of various kinds have been published in Australasia since the latter part of the nineteenth century. Prior to the establishment of the *ADB* venture in 1958, these works tended to be produced by a sole author, and to focus upon individuals who held official positions or could be said in some way to represent established authority, or who produced literary or artistic works.

From the 1960s, there was a noticeable increase in the number of books published about 'famous Australians', and an even greater expansion is evident in this broad genre from the 1990s. While many of these works are not biographical dictionaries per se, and are not necessarily conceived as such, they may be understood as being part of a general category of texts about famous, significant, or influential Australians. Within this explosion of publishing on 'famous Australians', there has also been a diversification. Works produced have varied in terms of their focus, with some limited to particular occupational groups, and others seeking to highlight the

---

34   Christine Nicholls, 'Missing Lives: An Editor's Perspective', in McCalman with Parvey and Cook, *National Biographies and National Identity*, 55.
35   For a more detailed discussion of the changing nature of Australian biographical dictionaries, see Karen Fox, 'Heroes, Legends and Divas: Framing Famous Lives in Australia', in *Migrant Nation: Australian Culture, Society and Identity*, ed. Paul Longley Arthur (London and New York: Anthem Press, 2018), 213–34. doi.org/10.2307/j.ctt1xhr5j8.15. My discussion in this section draws on this chapter. On the history of biography and biographical dictionaries in Australia, see also Melanie Nolan, 'Country and Kin Calling? Keith Hancock, the National Dictionary Collaboration, and the Promotion of Life Writing in Australia', in *Clio's Lives: Biographies and Autobiographies of Historians*, eds Doug Munro and John G. Reid (Canberra: ANU Press, 2017), 247–72. doi.org/10.22459/CL.10.2017.11; Nolan and Fernon, *The ADB's Story*.

achievements and contributions to the nation of individuals from specific demographic groups, such as women or Indigenous Australians. They have varied in their audience: some have been popular works aimed at the general public, some scholarly works, and others addressed to children, often presenting those included as role models. And they have varied in authorship and production processes, encompassing both single-authored volumes in which decisions on selection and interpretation appear to have been made by one individual, and multiauthored works with more complex methods of selection, such as the *Monash Biographical Dictionary of 20th Century Australia* or the Bicentennial publication *The People Who Made Australia Great*.[36] Alongside this slew of print publications have also appeared a range of web resources, often innovative and of high quality.

Inevitably, one of the most common questions fielded by those who work on biographical dictionary projects is: who gets in? Choices about selection and representation in Australian dictionaries of biography have changed significantly as Australia's place in the world has changed. Intricate interactions of nationalism and imperialism in the country's history, as well as shifting understandings of particular strands of identity—such as Britishness or Australian nationalism—have shaped these works in distinctive ways. The earliest biographical dictionaries in Australia were produced before Federation in 1901, and as such display a fluid approach to questions of inclusion related to nationality. Both J. H. Heaton's *Australian Dictionary of Dates and Men of the Time* (1879) and Philip Mennell's *Dictionary of Australasian Biography* (1892) included New Zealand as well as the six Australian colonies, a reflection of New Zealand's status as a potential partner in a federated nation.[37] These works also had an imperial flavour, showcasing the achievements and development of these far-flung portions of the British Empire.

Works produced after Federation, and especially from the middle of the twentieth century following a nationalist awakening in literary and historical circles, often displayed a more overt nationalism and a greater degree of wrestling with the issue of who ought to be considered adequately

---

36   John Arnold and Deirdre Morris, eds, *Monash Biographical Dictionary of 20th Century Australia* (Port Melbourne: Reed Reference Publishing, 1994); Simon Blackall, ed., *The People Who Made Australia Great* (Sydney: Collins Australia, 1988).

37   J. H. Heaton, *Australian Dictionary of Dates and Men of the Time: Containing the History of Australasia from 1542 to Date* (London: S. W. Silver, 1879); Philip Mennell, *The Dictionary of Australasian Biography, Comprising Notices of Eminent Colonists from the Inauguration of Responsible Government Down to the Present Time* (London: Hutchinson, 1892).

Australian to include.[38] In the 1960s cooperation among historians on either side of the Tasman began to dissipate, as both Australia and New Zealand began to focus more closely upon teaching, researching, and writing their own national histories. Their respective national biographical dictionaries—one beginning in the 1950s and the other in the 1980s—though not without cross-fertilisation, thus developed as largely individual national projects.[39] Perhaps surprisingly, the *ADB* has been an exception to this general tendency towards increased reflection on the nation, and on how selection choices relate to that nation; the *ADB* provided no specific comment on the issue of who counted as 'Australian' before the publication of volume 18 in 2012.[40] In the twenty-first century, this issue has taken a different cast, as questions have arisen over the place of national dictionaries in a globalised world, where transnational history has become a popular historical framework. This interplay of the national and the global or transnational is one of the themes of this book.

The issue of selection which has, perhaps, provoked most discussion and criticism for dictionaries of national biography has been that relating to demographics. Australia was remade demographically during the twentieth century, as the White Australia immigration policy was dismantled and replaced by a multicultural ideal, while other social and political currents—such as the so-called 'second wave' of feminism and the intensification of Indigenous rights movements—have also transformed the country. Historiographical developments arising out of and alongside these cultural and political changes have, meanwhile, radically reshaped the disciplines of history and biography. In particular, biographical dictionaries have come under pressure to engage with and respond to the insights of new subfields such as women's history and Indigenous history. Dictionaries produced in the nineteenth and early twentieth centuries, predictably, included small numbers of women, and even fewer figures

---

38   See for examples, Fred Johns, *Johns's Notable Australians: Who They Are and What They Do: Brief Biographies of Men and Women of the Commonwealth* (Melbourne: George Robertson, 1906); Fred Johns, *An Australian Biographical Dictionary* (Melbourne: Macmillan, 1934); Percival Serle, *Dictionary of Australian Biography*, 2 vols (Sydney: Angus and Robertson, 1949); *1000 Famous Australians* (Adelaide: Rigby, 1978); Ann Atkinson, *The Dictionary of Famous Australians* (St Leonards: Allen and Unwin, 1992).
39   Melanie Nolan, 'The Politics of Dictionaries of Biography in New Zealand', in *After the Treaty: The Settler State, Race Relations and the Exercise of Power in Colonial New Zealand: Essays in Honour of Ian McLean Wards*, eds Brad Patterson, Richard S. Hill, and Kathryn Patterson (Wellington: Steele Roberts Publishers, 2016), 52–54, and an earlier version of this chapter kindly provided to the author.
40   Melanie Nolan, ed., *Australian Dictionary of Biography*, vol. 18, *1981–1990, L–Z* (Carlton: Melbourne University Press, 2012), viii.

not of European descent. Significant change to these patterns waited several decades, but, particularly from the 1960s and 1970s, biographical dictionaries began to feature larger numbers of women, and more entries on Indigenous Australians.[41] Dictionary producers were, however, to some extent limited in their ability to remedy these imbalances, which are the product of past social and political circumstances as well as of current historical blindness. As Claudia Orange, the second general editor of the *DNZB*, pointed out in relation to the fifth volume of the dictionary (covering the years 1941–60), the shortage of women in the book was 'probably indicative of the social conditions of the period'.[42] A similar point could be made about the representation of non-European populations in national biographical dictionaries in Australia, New Zealand, or other settler colonial countries.

Although there has undoubtedly been an increase in the numbers of women and Indigenous Australians included in Australian biographical dictionaries, the issue of appropriate levels of representation has by no means been resolved. As *ADB* general editor Nolan has observed, from the 1970s the *ADB* has been subject to critiques regarding groups underrepresented in the dictionary—including, besides women and Indigenous Australians, the working class—as well as to complaints that other groups are overrepresented.[43] One response to such perceived flaws in general biographical dictionaries has been the production of targeted works focused on these groups. Such works are not new. Collective biographies of historical women in English, for example, may be traced to at least to the mid-eighteenth century.[44] Both in Australia and internationally, however, collections of women's lives flourished in the

---

41 For a more detailed numerical analysis of the changing proportions of women and non-European subjects included in Australian biographical dictionaries since the 1870s, see Fox, 'Heroes, Legends and Divas', 222–26.
42 Claudia Orange, ed., *The Dictionary of New Zealand Biography*, vol. 5, *1941–1960* (Auckland and Wellington: Auckland University Press and the Department of Internal Affairs, 2000), ix.
43 Melanie Nolan, '"Insufficiently Engineered": A Dictionary Designed to Stand the Test of Time?' in Nolan and Fernon, *The ADB's Story*, 23. doi.org/10.22459/ADBS.10.2013.01.
44 Alison Booth, 'The Lessons of the Medusa: Anna Jameson and Collective Biographies of Women', *Victorian Studies* 42, no. 2 (1999/2000): 261. doi.org/10.2979/VIC.1999.42.2.257; Barbara Caine, *Biography and History* (Houndmills: Palgrave Macmillan, 2010), 54–56; Susan E. Searing, 'Biographical Reference Works For and About Women, from the Advent of the Women's Liberation Movement to the Present: An Exploratory Analysis', *Library Trends* 56, no. 2 (Fall 2007): 470. doi.org/10.1353/lib.2008.0009.

wake of the revitalisation of the feminist movement from the late 1960s.[45] Large numbers of publications focusing on the lives of Indigenous Australians have also been produced, especially from the 1990s.[46] These works too have parallels elsewhere, such as the eight-volume *African American National Biography* in the United States.[47] Targeted works have also appeared for particular occupational areas, although not necessarily in response to perceived inadequacies of representation elsewhere.

In the preceding discussion I have focused upon issues of selection and representation as they unfolded in the past, but of course these are not the only issues facing national biographical dictionary ventures in the twenty-first century. There are a host of others, many of which were not such issues—or at least, not in the same way—for the corpus of nineteenth- and twentieth-century works mentioned above. Perhaps most obviously, in the twenty-first century dictionary projects operate in a digital environment, unlike many of the endeavours discussed above. This shift to the digital has brought a range of new opportunities, but also new challenges. Sustainability is one; revisions another. Dictionary projects today often face the need not only to be funded and resourced to produce an output—one or more print volumes, or a web-based resource—but also to secure the resources needed to maintain and sustain that output. The ease of access to information, and its ever-expanding nature, as well as the ease of interaction with the public brought about by the web, have created increasing pressures to revisit and revise existing material in the light of new research, fresh interpretations, and public expectations.

---

45   Caine, *Biography and History*, 58–59; Searing, 'Biographical Reference Works', 475. Searing discusses English-language publications broadly, but the Australian subset displays a similar pattern. Examples of collective biographies of women published in Australia from the 1970s include *A Sense of Purpose: Great Australian Women of the 20th Century* (Port Melbourne: Reed Reference Australia, 1996); Andrea Lofthouse, *Who's Who of Australian Women* (North Ryde: Methuen Australia, 1982); Heather Radi, *200 Australian Women* (Broadway: Women's Redress Press, [1988]).
46   For example, Alex Barlow and Marji Hill, *Indigenous Heroes and Leaders* (Port Melbourne: Heinemann Library, 2003); Linda Bruce, John Hilvert, and Alan Hilvert-Bruce, *Indigenous Australians: Artists* (South Yarra: Macmillan Education, 2004); Linda Bruce, John Hilvert, and Alan Hilvert-Bruce, *Indigenous Australians: Entertainers* (South Yarra: Macmillan Education, 2004); Linda Bruce, John Hilvert, and Alan Hilvert-Bruce, *Indigenous Australians: Leaders* (South Yarra: Macmillan Education, 2004); Linda Bruce, John Hilvert, and Alan Hilvert-Bruce, *Indigenous Australians: Sportspeople* (South Yarra: Macmillan Education, 2004).
47   Henry Louis Gates Jr and Evelyn Brooks Higginbotham, eds, *African American National Biography*, 8 vols (Oxford: Oxford University Press, 2008).

Challenges for the Twenty-First Century

If the context for national biographical dictionaries had changed considerably by the time of the first Canberra conference in 1995, it has changed still further in the years since. In 1995 it might still have been conceivable for dictionary projects to have a future as hard copy–only publications. In 2016 it is much less so, and most dictionary projects in the English-speaking world have become online repositories as well as, or instead of, being produced as physical books. This transition to the digital is one kind of cultural journey taken by dictionaries of national biography since their emergence during the flowering of nationalism in nineteenth-century Europe. Another has resulted in changing demographic profiles in many of these works, as their producers have become ever more alert to the need for national dictionaries to appropriately represent the diversity of the nations thus biographied. A third type of cultural journey has been driven by globalisation and the turn to transnational history writing in the academy. Although still existing as dictionaries of *national* biography, these projects have not entirely escaped this change in scholarly focus, and ideas for greater cooperation between them, or even for a return to the ideal of universal biography, have been raised periodically. At the 1995 conference, for example, Baigent asked whether online publishing offered the chance to bring together the various national dictionaries into a 'universal biographical dictionary'.[48]

All three of these cultural journeys—or we might equally describe them as challenges for the future—were discussed at the conference in Canberra in 1995, and each of them is revisited and developed in new ways in this book. Penned from different perspectives by scholars from various locations in the English-speaking world, the chapters of this book address these three key areas of challenge for national biographical dictionary projects in the twenty-first century. The book is divided into three sections: the digital challenge, the representational or diversity challenge, and the transnational or global challenge. Each chapter deals with a particular aspect of one of those cultural journeys, while also illuminating the specific situations of different dictionary endeavours around the world, and revealing the interconnected nature of these challenges, and, perhaps, the solutions to them. Most were originally presented in shorter form at the conference in Canberra in 2016, but some have been produced for this

---

48 Baigent, 'Nationality and Dictionaries of National Biography', 72.

collection. All demonstrate the rich possibilities, deep scholarship, and lively humanism involved in producing dictionaries of national biography, and collectively they form a powerful argument for the continued value and importance of this kind of large-scale collaborative research. In 2012, Verga questioned whether or not the genre of the national biographical dictionary 'really respond[ed] to pressing historiographical issues, and our present concerns'.[49] The papers gathered together in this book, delving with seriousness of thought into three key concerns of both scholars and wider society today, suggest that they do.

To begin with the digital challenge, it is clear that 20 years on from the first Canberra conference, the digital revolution that was then only nascent has now transformed scholarship, both in the ways it is conducted and in the ways it is encountered and consumed. In his chapter on the integration of the *Dictionary of New Zealand Biography* with the digital resource *Te Ara—The Encyclopedia of New Zealand*, Jock Phillips reveals how the biographies included in national dictionaries of biography can be given wider significance through linking with other online resources, such as the contextual essays contained in an encyclopedia project, as well as how the inclusion of those biographies in an encyclopedia can add depth and human richness to the stories of the nation contained in such a work. Turlough O'Riordan discusses the production of the *Dictionary of Irish Biography*, focusing on the transformations in both research methods and editorial and publishing practices wrought by the digital revolution. He suggests that the growth of digital resources for research, and increasing moves to present scholarly outputs online, introduce new issues that many scholars have yet to fully consider. Paradoxically, he argues that the way forward for dictionaries of national biography in this digital world is to be guided by past practices perfected in the era of hard-copy, analogue-only research and publication.

Philip Carter considers the 'purpose of national biography', presenting a positive vision of the future for dictionaries of national biography, and suggesting that these venerable reference works are 'on the cusp of significant development and opportunity'. He emphasises the significance of a curated, scholarly collection of biographies in an era of 'information overload', and argues that the function of national biographical dictionaries as platforms for presenting and enabling original research—including

---

49   Verga, 'The Dictionary is Dead', 100–101.

through methods made possible by a new digital environment—ought to be more widely acknowledged and promoted. In her chapter, *Australian Dictionary of Biography* general editor Melanie Nolan discusses the extent to which the digital challenge, with all the new possibilities offered by digital tools, has transformed the project of producing a national biographical dictionary. She too provides an optimistic view of the potential of such technological advances, suggesting that far from undermining dictionary projects, the move to new 'digital environment[s]' may assist in meeting old challenges.

Moving to the challenge of diversity, or representation, Susan Ware draws on the lessons she learned as editor of a specialist biographical dictionary of women's lives to outline how in practical terms an editor might act on his or her commitment to increasing the gender balance of a dictionary of national biography, stressing in particular the importance of continually keeping that aim in view, given the range of pressures that may tend in the direction of the status quo. She points out that the same lessons might equally apply to the task of improving the coverage of other underrepresented groups, including ethnic minorities, as well as suggesting an aspect of the challenge of diversity that is yet to be fully comprehended—that of the inclusion of Trans* individuals. In discussing the specialist dictionary *Notable American Women* alongside her experiences as general editor of the *American National Biography*, Ware asks whether the need for such specialist dictionaries will be obviated if national dictionaries do succeed in the task of improving their representation of women's lives. This question is at the heart of Elizabeth Ewan's chapter, which considers the part that biographical dictionaries of women may play in constructing biographies of nations, through a detailed study of the case of Scotland. She argues that biographical dictionaries of women can raise questions about 'what it has meant to be a woman in a society in the past', as well as about the ways in which those meanings have shifted over time. At the same time, in a context where no recent large-scale national biographical dictionary has been produced, she suggests that 'a wide-ranging women's biographical dictionary' can influence approaches to the history of that nation in a range of ways.

Shino Konishi takes up the issue of diversity in relation to Indigenous Australia, discussing the representation of Indigenous Australians in the *Australian Dictionary of Biography*, and the development of a project to produce a specialist dictionary of Indigenous Australian biography. Her chapter also raises questions as to how such a dictionary might depart from the conventions of national biography as practised in the past, and what implications such departures might have for the genre as a whole. Finally in this section, Dafydd Johnston examines the relationship between the Welsh and the English languages in the *Y Bywgraffiadur Cymreig/ Dictionary of Welsh Biography* project, from its beginnings in print up to its current online incarnation. Exploring language as a central aspect of Welsh identity, and thus of national identity, he shows how important language, and choices around it, may be for the task of writing a true national biography.

Dictionaries of national biography are of course not only a European or English-speaking world phenomenon, although for reasons of practicality it is projects in those parts of the globe upon which this book focuses. Drawing on his own lifetime experience of writing, and revising, a *Dictionary of World Biography*, Barry Jones considers some of the challenges involved in producing such a work. His considered experience of a lifetime's thought about such a project, and reflections on the differences between his work and that of the *Chambers Biographical Dictionary*, suggest that if a national biographical dictionary is difficult, a global one is even more so. In his chapter, David Cannadine reflects upon the history of the British *Dictionary of National Biography*, and its twenty-first-century reincarnation as the *Oxford Dictionary of National Biography*, revealing the ways in which both projects have showcased global or transnational lives alongside those more firmly located in place, be that local, regional, or national. He concludes that the task of global biography remains crucial today, despite both the difficulties of the task and the present 'backlash' towards globalisation. Discussing the *Dictionary of Canadian Biography/Dictionnaire biographique du Canada*, David A. Wilson also considers the issue of transnationalism in the production of a national biographical dictionary, and the relationship of such endeavours to global or transnational history. As a case study, he examines the Irish diaspora, demonstrating how transnational links may be both revealed and obscured in a national biographical dictionary. While recognising the difficulties of creating links between such projects, he encourages the growth of an awareness of the international contexts of both subjects' lives and dictionary production.

The 2016 Canberra conference set out to assess the extent to which dictionaries of national biography had risen to the challenge posed in 2004 by Thomas, who was then the chairman of the supervisory committee of the new *ODNB*. Since historians no longer restricted their attention to particular sections of the population, he suggested, there was 'no reason' why previously 'hidden lives' ought not to be included, while technological advances had removed the practical problem of being unable to encompass much larger numbers of individuals in biographical dictionaries. He raised the tantalising possibility that, therefore, '[o]ne day … we may have a database so vast that its claim to be a true national biography will be incontrovertible'.[50] Taken together, the chapters in this collection suggest that this dream is at once closer to achievement and more difficult to accomplish than it may have seemed in 2004.

And yet, even as the 'True Biographies of Nations?' conference was being organised and held in 2016, and the chapters prepared for this book, there were signs of yet another seismic shift in global affairs, which may once again reshape the environment in which dictionaries of national biography are produced. If the movement against globalisation represented by the Brexit vote in the United Kingdom in June 2016 and the election of Donald Trump as United States president in November the same year does indeed indicate a new wave of populist antiglobalisation nationalism, as some have claimed, or even a return to more traditionally nation-focused identities and politics, what are the implications for the venture of the national biographical dictionary? Slowly being transformed in order to take account of the breaking down of national borders and identities, will these projects find it necessary to similarly reassert these markers of nationality? Matthew, the *ODNB*'s founding editor from 1992 to 1999, suggested that, at least in Europe, nationality would yield to European Union citizenship, and that works of reference, such as biographical dictionaries, would follow suit, becoming aggregated into a worldwide dictionary of biography.[51] In the post-Brexit world, this confident assertion of the end of the nation seems, at the least, somewhat unlikely. With national interests and national agendas apparently reasserting themselves, and the whole project of globalisation under attack, the future of national biographical dictionaries may well be strikingly different to that predicted by Matthew. As recently as 2012, Verga proclaimed dead the 'established model' of biographical dictionaries, whereby they were 'identified with the story of the nation-state'.[52] It seems, however, that rumours of its demise may well have been vastly exaggerated.

---

50 Thomas, *Changing Conceptions*, 56.
51 Matthew, 'Dictionaries of National Biography', 17; Thomas, *Changing Conceptions*, 38.
52 Verga, 'The Dictionary is Dead', 92.

PART I: THE DIGITAL AGE

2

INDIVIDUAL LIVES AND NATIONAL TRUTHS: LOCATING BIOGRAPHIES WITHIN A NATIONAL ENCYCLOPEDIA

JOCK PHILLIPS

I must begin with an admission. As a historian I have long held a scepticism about the place of biography in historical studies. My sense of the role of the historian is to present the larger patterns, to paint and explain the huge social forces, the determinative cultural and political ideas, and the economic developments which forged the world of the past. Individual lives are simply the flotsam and jetsam floating above these massive historical waves. Even major political leaders or seminal thinkers need to be explained against wider social and cultural currents. In this view of the historian's mission, dictionaries of national biography become extremely useful reference works, to check the details of particular lives. They are useful for case studies, for providing the telling example. They do not contribute in themselves to the larger generalisations about nations or eras.

That is what I firmly believed until I became involved in the project to digitise the *Dictionary of New Zealand Biography* (*DNZB*). This opened up new ways of using the dictionary and its database, and created the possibility of using the individual biographies in the dictionary to inform the history of the nation itself. What had been a purely reference work, used only by historians to check biographical details, could become a tool for answering new questions central to understanding a national history. A dictionary of biography might become the biography of a nation. This discovery is the major focus of this chapter.

'TRUE BIOGRAPHIES OF NATIONS?'

Although a two-volume *Dictionary of New Zealand Biography* had been published in 1940 under the editorship of the journalist and librarian G. H. Scholefield, a more comprehensive and scholarly *Dictionary of New Zealand Biography* was begun in 1983. Under the editorship of W. H. Oliver and then Claudia Orange, the project published five volumes in English from 1990 to 2000 and five volumes of biographies of Māori subjects in the Māori language. By that stage over 3,000 lives of New Zealanders who had flourished from 1769 to 1960 had been completed. For its time this was an exciting project. The editors decided that 'representative' figures, as well as those of recognised significance, should be included. There was a sustained use of working parties to ensure that there was good representation of Māori and women, and also excellent regional representation. The standards of research and accuracy were impeccable. I was not hugely involved in the project initially. However, I did contribute eight biographies, and from 1989 when I became the nation's chief historian, with a mandate to oversee all government historical projects, I served on the project's policy committee. The project was located within the Department of Internal Affairs, and in 1997 I took over a role as general manager for a heritage group within that department. One of the first issues I faced was the projected end of the dictionary project in 2000. By that stage those people who had flourished up to 1960 would have been covered, but the principle had been established that a person had to be dead to be included in the dictionary. So it was expected that the task of writing new biographies would go into abeyance while we waited for another tranche of significant New Zealanders to die.

In common with others in the department, I decided that we should use that period to explore new uses for the outstanding biographical content. Having already established a history website (www.nzhistory.net.nz) and been astonished at its popular uptake, we decided that digitising the content of the *DNZB* and adding images of the subjects would add a visual richness and make the content more available to those interested in New Zealand history. We did not have any expectations beyond that. So, as a millennium project, we made the digitised material available in both English and, for all Māori subjects, in the Māori language, on a new searchable website. That act obviously made the biographies of individual lives more accessible, and the numbers using the dictionary website rose quickly. However, once the site was up and running, we began to realise that digitisation had made the content more valuable in other ways, particularly for those researching larger social forces. To take a simple example, if a historian were interested in the nature of temperance and prohibition, simply putting those words into the search engine of the new *DNZB* website produced much suggestive information about the type of people involved and why those movements arose. The word 'temperance' leads to more than 200 biographies, and 'prohibition' to more than 100. By reading those biographies you could learn a huge amount about the nature of the temperance movement, and you could conduct a statistical analysis about the age or religious background of the prohibitionists.

The Dictionary Database and the Cultural Contribution of United Kingdom–Born Immigrants

As a result, I became interested in using the digitised *DNZB* content in other ways that might contribute to wider generalisations about the history of New Zealand. I made several efforts in this direction. The first came about because at that time I was deeply engaged in attempting to work out more about the geographical and social origins of the British and Irish settlers to New Zealand. In an essay in 1990 I had argued that New Zealand historical work had been singularly lacking in-depth studies of the rituals and culture (defined in its widest sense) of the society.[1] If you were going to explain such matters as patterns of speech, or dress, or food, or sport, or architecture, then an essential prerequisite was to understand exactly who had settled New Zealand and what was the cultural baggage they had brought with them. The vast majority of those who had migrated to New Zealand until the 1960s came from the United Kingdom. So with Terry Hearn I sought to find out, in as much precision as possible, just who the settlers from that part of the world were from 1800 to 1945. In the absence of census records, which had all been destroyed, the primary methodology was to carry out a one in 10 sample of the death registers of those who had been born in the United Kingdom and died in New Zealand. This would give us information about the place and county of origin of the United Kingdom migrants, their age and the date when they migrated, their religion, their family situation, and the occupation of their father.

---

1   Jock Phillips, 'Of Verandahs and Fish and Chips and Footie on Saturday Afternoon', *New Zealand Journal of History* 24, no. 2 (1990): 124.

Our research in these sources was immensely informative, but what it lacked was a sense of the culture brought by people from particular communities, and how their geographical and occupational origins played out in the new country. Here the resources of the *Dictionary of New Zealand Biography* project came into their own. I realised that the individuals in the *DNZB* formed a relatively small proportion of the country's population and to some extent their selection had been a matter of decision-making by the editors, which might have been arbitrary. Thus simply looking at the few dictionary subjects who had been born in the Highlands of Scotland or Ulster would be a dangerous basis for larger generalisations about the nature of migrants from those areas. However, in preparing the *DNZB* a digital database of individuals who might find inclusion in the dictionary had been compiled by working parties throughout the country. This database was then used to select those who were given full entries. I realised that the whole database offered a more worthwhile sample than simply the *Dictionary* entries. True, its composition was drawn up by working parties, so it was not strictly a scientific sample, but if I was interested in significant cultural contributions then human selection was not an unhelpful bias. More importantly, the numbers were very much greater—15,000 individuals in the database as against 3,000 in the dictionary, and 3,688 born in the British Isles as against 1,082 born there in the dictionary. The database, unlike the dictionary entries, had not been systematically checked and included obvious errors and spelling mistakes, but for my purposes this was not a major issue. The great virtue of the database was that it was all available on the web (although just for internal use) and was searchable by field. It was a relatively simple exercise to search all those born in a particular place, and all those who were in a particular occupation or had a defined area of interest. The *DNZB* database in digital form thus opened up a much richer field of enquiry than was available through the death registers.

The first thing I noticed was that the distribution of places of origin was rather different from what we had worked out from the death registers, and indeed rather different from the census. Leaving aside Wales, which always sent very low numbers to New Zealand, and also the offshore islands, Table 1 gives the breakdown of national origins from the death registers, and Table 2 gives the percentages from the New Zealand census.[2]

---

2   Jock Phillips and Terry Hearn, *Settlers: New Zealand Immigrants from England, Ireland and Scotland 1800–1945* (Auckland: Auckland University Press, 2008), 52–53.

Table 1: National birthplaces of United Kingdom immigrants to New Zealand from Death Register sample (percentages)

Period of migration	1800–39	1840–52	1853–70	1871–90	1891–1915	1916–45
England	62.1	64.3	46.6	54.6	65.0	60.1
Scotland	20.4	20.6	30.2	21.5	22.2	28.7
Ireland	15.6	13.5	21.4	21.7	10.9	8.6

Source: Death registers, Office of Births, Deaths, and Marriages.

Table 2: National birthplaces of United Kingdom–born from New Zealand Census (percentages of all United Kingdom–born people)

	1861	1871	1891	1911	1945
England	59.3	49.7	53.5	58.5	63.3
Scotland	25.5	27.3	23.7	22.6	24.2
Ireland	14.5	22.0	21.8	17.9	5.3

Source: Census of Population and Dwellings, 1861, 1871, 1891, 1911, 1945, Statistics New Zealand.[3]

Both figures suggested that immigrants from England constituted about 55–60 per cent of all United Kingdom–born migrants; those from Scotland about 21–26 per cent; and those from Ireland about 15–20 per cent. By comparison, the breakdown of the *DNZB* database among those born in the United Kingdom was as shown in Table 3.

Table 3: National birthplaces of United Kingdom–born from *DNZB* database (percentages of all United Kingdom–born people)

England	66.2
Scotland	21.3
Ireland	10.9

Source: *DNZB* database, Ministry for Culture and Heritage.

The exact reasons for this discrepancy need not concern us greatly—perhaps it was a reflection of the biases of the working parties, more likely it reflected the fact that the English-born were very strongly represented in the founding generations of the 1840s and established their own kith and kin in positions of eminence early. What interested me was less this discrepancy than the contrast between the representation of each country

---

3 See 'Census: 1871–1916', Statistics New Zealand, accessed November 2018, www.stats.govt.nz/browse_for_stats/snapshots-of-nz/digitised-collections/census-collection.aspx.

of birth in the database as a whole, and their representation in particular fields of achievement. For this was a way of isolating the cultural contribution of each national group to New Zealand society. When I made that comparison, certain revealing trends became evident. In the database, as we have seen, those born in England were 66.2 per cent and about 60 per cent in the death registers. But among those who were included in the database because they had made a mark in public administration (that is, as politicians or civil servants) the English constituted 77.2 per cent of the United Kingdom–born among that group. In other words, they were strongly overrepresented. Less striking, but also of significance, was that among those noted for sporting accomplishment: 68.2 per cent of the United Kingdom–born were of English birth. It may not come as a surprise to discover that English migrants achieved in these two fields. The early arrival of the English and their contacts with imperial officials meant they established the main political institutions, and the preferred sporting games (golf being a striking exception) were mainly introduced by old boys of English public schools. Nevertheless, the exercise had given us good statistical evidence for the cultural contribution of the English.

Turning to the Scots, again suggestive patterns were revealed. As noted, 21.3 per cent of the United Kingdom–born in the database were born in Scotland, but among those distinguished for their role in education the figure was 23.4 per cent, while among the scientists it was 24.0 per cent, and among those noted for their contribution to the health occupations 26.8 per cent came from Scotland. The famed role of Lowland Scots in higher education and science was confirmed.[4] It helped explain why the New Zealand educational system took its model from Scotland. The most striking finding related to the Irish-born. While only 10.9 per cent of the United Kingdom–born people in the database were born in Ireland, the proportion of those who were noted for their role in the police and were born in Ireland was just over 40 per cent. Also of considerable interest was the fact that of those in the database who were distinguished for their activity in social reform movements, 57 per cent were from the Methodist, Presbyterian, or Baptist faiths, which was a significant overrepresentation. This was strong confirmation of the distinctive impact

---

4   Tom Brooking, 'Sharing Out the Haggis: The Special Scottish Contribution to New Zealand History', in *The Heather and the Fern: Scottish Migration and New Zealand Settlement*, eds Tom Brooking and Jennie Coleman (Dunedin: Otago University Press, 2003), 54; Brad Patterson, Tom Brooking, and Jim McAloon, *Unpacking the Kists: The Scots in New Zealand* (Dunedin: Otago University Press, 2013).

of those religious groups, particularly in such movements as temperance.[5] None of these findings about the cultural contributions of particular national and religious groups will surprise greatly. They accord with well-known assumptions, but the dictionary database did provide a more secure basis for claims of cultural influence than simply impressionistic claims or anecdotal references. In this way, a dictionary of national biography went beyond the study of individuals and became a tool for wider truths about the nation's cultural history.

The Integration of the *Dictionary of New Zealand Biography* and *Te Ara—The Encyclopedia of New Zealand*

My second example concerns the attempt to integrate the *Dictionary of New Zealand Biography* into a national encyclopedia. The idea for a new national encyclopedia on the web grew out of the *DNZB* project. By the late 1990s, work on the five volumes of the dictionary was winding down, because, as we have noted, there were not enough people from the 1970s and 1980s who had yet died and who might fill a next volume. We would have to wait perhaps 15 years. Further, another major national project prepared by the Historical Branch of the Department of Internal Affairs, the *New Zealand Historical Atlas*, had just been published.[6] So there were the scholarly resources and experienced people available to undertake another reference work.

A previous official national encyclopedia had been published in 1966 under the editorship of A. H. McLintock.[7] Thirty-one thousand copies of the three-volume set had been published. The whole print run was sold within three months and it was never reprinted. Since 1966 there had been major new developments in scholarship about the country. Increasingly, people came to me as the nation's chief historian—publishers, scholars, and staff at the *DNZB*—urging the Department of Internal Affairs to embark on a new encyclopedia. I was a bit reluctant, believing that primary research, rather than superficial summaries of established knowledge, was where

---

5   See John Stenhouse, 'God's Own Silence: Secular Nationalism, Christianity and the Writing of New Zealand History', *New Zealand Journal of History* 38, no. 1 (2004): 52–71; Phillips and Hearn, *Settlers*, 182–87.
6   Malcolm McKinnon, ed., *Bateman New Zealand Historical Atlas* (Auckland: Bateman, 1997).
7   A. H. McLintock, ed., *An Encyclopaedia of New Zealand* (Wellington: Government Printer, 1966).

the energy should go, but in 1998 I agreed to put in a budget bid to the government for a new official print-based encyclopedia to be produced by the department. The bid was turned down.

The next year we started the process of digitising the *DNZB* and also continued to develop the New Zealand history website. We had established the latter in 1997 originally as a shop window for our own historical publications, but increasingly it morphed into a general site about New Zealand history. We were stunned by the responses to these ventures. Very quickly nzhistory.net.nz was attracting over 50,000 visitors a month, and when the *DNZB* appeared on the web, users quickly discovered how accessible and useful it was in this form. We became convinced that the web was made for reference works, and offered exciting advantages over a print version in terms of searchability, accessibility, and the opportunity to add multimedia resources. So we prepared a new budget bid, this time for an encyclopedia of New Zealand on the web, which would be prepared in themes and published, one theme a year, over nine years. I mocked up a sample entry, gave a half-hour presentation to the minister of finance (a former historian, Michael Cullen), and briefed the prime minister, Helen Clark, who fortunately was also the minister for arts, culture, and heritage. We got the money.[8]

The question then arose as to the relationship between the *DNZB* and the new digital encyclopedia, which we soon christened—with the help of our Māori advisory committee—*Te Ara* (the pathway). Traditionally, encyclopedias have included biographies of people who are considered significant to the nation's story. The 1966 encyclopedia had contained over 550 such biographies. But there seemed little point in copying the McLintock model and commissioning new biographies, for high-quality biographies had just been completed for the *DNZB*. Since they were already in digital form, the obvious solution was to integrate those biographies into *Te Ara*. I was keen that this would not simply be a marriage of convenience. My hope was that in bringing the biographies into the encyclopedia, they could be given a wider context, and the individual lives could contribute to understanding national (and international) social and cultural processes.

---

8   On the origins of Te Ara, see 'Te Ara—A History', *Te Ara—The Encyclopedia of New Zealand*, accessed 30 June 2017, www.TeAra.govt.nz/en/te-ara-a-history.

The first theme of *Te Ara* concerned the peoples of New Zealand—about half the entries on the iwi or tribes of the country, and half on the settlement or immigrant groups.[9] As we prepared it, we decided to link relevant biographies closely to the encyclopedia content. Each *Te Ara* entry was broken down into what we called subentries of 400 to 700 words in length. This was partly to make the presentation work better on the web. The entries varied in length from that on the English which had 14 subentries, and that about Ngāi Tahu which had 10, to those on the Tokelauans and the Rangitāne tribe which each had four. We decided that each subentry would be linked to up to six *DNZB* biographies, of individuals who came from that community and were pertinent to the theme of that page. Initially, we introduced each biography with a short summarising blurb that spelled out the relevance of the person's life to the theme of that subentry. For example, in the page in the English entry about that group's contribution to sport and popular culture, we find biographies of Kathleen Nunneley, a pioneering tennis player; Henry Redwood, a racehorse breeder known as 'Father of the New Zealand turf'; and Joel Polack, who among other things established the country's first brewery.[10] After the first theme, however, we decided that this exercise of writing explanatory blurbs was just too demanding of our writers' time. Instead we simply linked the biographies to the subentry.

This was still a significant contribution. On the basis of oral comments and notes to the *Te Ara* team, we realised that users did find the linked biographies significantly added to the experience of using *Te Ara*. Hyperlinking biographies gave a human richness and a telling detail to stories which necessarily were highly generalised. Let us take another example. In the entry about mountaineering in New Zealand there is a subentry entitled 'Beginnings'. It tells us, among other things, that:

> In defiance of Māori tapu, Taranaki was climbed in 1839 by the whaler James Heberley and scientist Ernst Dieffenbach … Subsequently, climbers were active on North Island mountains mainly for recreation and instruction. There are difficult winter ice-climbing routes on Taranaki and Ruapehu. Taranaki has claimed many lives, and on 26 July 1953 six died on its slopes.[11]

---

9   'Māori New Zealanders', *Te Ara—The Encyclopedia of New Zealand*, accessed 30 June 2017, www.teara.govt.nz/en/maori-new-zealanders; 'New Zealand Peoples', *Te Ara—The Encyclopedia of New Zealand*, accessed 30 June 2017, www.teara.govt.nz/en/new-zealand-peoples.
10   Terry Hearn, 'English—Popular Culture', *Te Ara—The Encyclopedia of New Zealand*, updated 13 July 2012, accessed 30 June 2017, www.TeAra.govt.nz/en/english/page-12.
11   John Wilson, 'Mountaineering—Beginnings', *Te Ara—The Encyclopedia of New Zealand*, accessed 30 June 2017, www.TeAra.govt.nz/en/mountaineering/page-2.

That is all we learn about climbing on Taranaki, or Mt Egmont as it has also been known. But among the linked biographies we find Harry Peters, a German immigrant who bought a farm on the slopes of Mt Egmont. The biography tells us that Peters had made his first ascent of Mt Egmont in 1885 using a new route, and six years later he had a military barracks moved from Marsland Hill, the site of the British camp in the New Zealand Wars, and placed on North Egmont at the start of the new route. Peters became the custodian and official guide and led almost 90 expeditions up the mountain including a famous 18-hour ascent by the 78-year-old ex-premier Sir William Fox.[12] The biographical link provides a humanity and fascinating level of detail, which the simple encyclopedia entry cannot achieve.

So the *DNZB* enriches the national story and contributes to an understanding beyond the interest of an individual life. But what about the reverse process? If the *DNZB* entries can give detail to the encyclopedia's broad topics, those broad topics could also inform and give context to the individual life. Let us stay with the same subentry, 'Beginnings' in the 'Mountaineering' story, and, since 2016 was the centenary of his death, let us start exploring (a well-chosen word in the circumstance) the life of Charlie Douglas. On this subentry there is a link to his biography and also a picture of Douglas with his climbing mate, A. P. Harper. If we go to his biography we learn that, as his nickname 'Mr Explorer Douglas' suggests, Douglas was of some significance as an explorer of the valleys of the West Coast of the South Island. It was an area of huge rainfall, where Douglas believed the barometer 'did not appear to have much effect on the weather'. Rivers ran dangerously high, but Douglas learned that 'not being able to swim had saved his life many a time'.[13]

The biography gives us nice quotes and personal details about an eccentric man. But what was his larger significance? The biography certainly ends with the claim that he was 'one of New Zealand's greatest explorers'.[14] To get a larger perspective, however, we can go to the *Te Ara* entries where he is mentioned. The obvious place to start is the entry on 'European

---

12   Ron Lambert, 'Peters, Harry', *Dictionary of New Zealand Biography*, first published 1993. *Te Ara—the Encyclopedia of New Zealand*, accessed 30 June 2017, www.TeAra.govt.nz/en/biographies/2p12/peters-harry.
13   Graham Langton, 'Douglas, Charles Edward', *Dictionary of New Zealand Biography*, first published in 1993, updated November 2007. *Te Ara—The Encyclopedia of New Zealand*, accessed 30 June 2017, www.TeAra.govt.nz/en/biographies/2d16/douglas-charles-edward.
14   Langton, 'Douglas, Charles Edward'.

Exploration'. There are nine subentries in that story. The last one is entitled 'The End of Exploration' and two-thirds of the page is devoted to Douglas, giving some sense of his importance. The page begins:

> By the mid-1860s, Europeans had penetrated all of New Zealand's habitable land. All that remained were the least accessible valleys and mountains of the Southern Alps … More than anyone else, Charlie Douglas, one of the real characters in New Zealand exploration, was responsible for putting alpine South Westland onto the country's maps.[15]

The page also confirms his stature as an explorer by noting that he was awarded the Gill Memorial Prize by the Royal Geographical Society for his persistent explorations of Westland. On the same page, there are two revealing images. The first is his sketch of Baker's Saddle, which tells us that Douglas was of some importance as an artist, and next is a map he made of the Haast River area, where we learn that Douglas was also an outstanding map-maker whose collection of maps, one of which was five metres wide, were displayed at the International Exhibition at Christchurch in 1906 and 1907. So he is important as a cartographer. This page gives us a wider context, but it also fills out some interesting details. We find out, for example, that he had a skill in bestowing names: 'Charlie Douglas liked classical names for mountains, such as Castor and Pollux. He also coined names for creeks on the west side of the Waiatoto: Lucky Rill, Tingling Brook, Ferny Rivulet, Whizzing Water, Thrill Creek and Madcap Torrent'.[16]

Where else do we find Charlie Douglas in *Te Ara*? We get taken to the entry on 'Birdwatching', where in the page on 'New Zealand's Bird-Watching History' we discover that his diaries contained important descriptions of bird behaviour including ways to catch and cook different species.[17] This is confirmed by the section on kākāpō in the entry on 'Large Forest Birds', where Douglas's observations are the main source of evidence for their decline in the nineteenth century. We learn that:

---

15 Jock Phillips, 'European Exploration—The End of Exploration', *Te Ara—The Encyclopedia of New Zealand*, accessed 30 June 2017, www.TeAra.govt.nz/en/european-exploration/page-9.
16 Phillips, 'European Exploration—The End of Exploration'.
17 Gordon Ell, 'Birdwatching—New Zealand's Birdwatching History', *Te Ara—The Encyclopedia of New Zealand*, accessed 30 June 2017, www.TeAra.govt.nz/en/birdwatching/page-6.

In 1899, the explorer Charlie Douglas forecast that the kākāpō was 'doomed to extinction long before the Kiwi and the Roa [great spotted kiwi] are a thing of the past'. Partial to boiled kākāpō himself, Douglas noted that 'they could be caught in the moonlight, when on the low scrub, by simply shaking the tree or bush till they tumbled on the ground, something like shaking down apples.'[18]

Similarly, using the search engine to search for Charlie Douglas takes us to the entry on 'Kiwi', which tells us that Douglas was one of the few Europeans to eat kiwi: 'He thought the eggs made great fritters when fried in oil from the kākāpō bird, but was less sure about the meat … He said the best description of the taste was "a piece of pork boiled in an old coffin"'.[19] He appears in the story about 'Freshwater Fish', where his observations of the giant kōkopu or cock-a-bulla are noted,[20] and in the one on 'Glaciers', where his explorations and pioneering survey of the Fox Glacier are highlighted for allowing the documentation of changes to the glacier.[21]

Finally, there are two other intriguing mentions of Douglas. In the story about 'Scots', he is listed among a group of others of that origin who made contributions to exploring and natural history;[22] in the story about 'Pets', he is cited as the best example of the dependence of people on animals in extreme situations: 'From the late 1860s Charlie Douglas spent nearly 20 years exploring and mapping South Westland with only a dog for company (all his dogs were called Betsey Jane)'.[23] In sum, by exploring *Te Ara* alongside his biography, we can both position Charlie Douglas in his larger significance in New Zealand history, and also gain intriguing details about this unusual man. Moving both ways, from *Te Ara* subentries to biographies, and from biographies to entries, is informative, enriching

---

18   Gerard Hutching, 'Large Forest Birds—Kākāpō', *Te Ara—The Encyclopedia of New Zealand*, accessed 30 June 2017, www.TeAra.govt.nz/en/large-forest-birds/page-5.
19   Jock Phillips, 'Kiwi—Kiwi and People: Early History', *Te Ara—The Encyclopedia of New Zealand*, accessed 30 June 2017, www.TeAra.govt.nz/en/kiwi/page-4.
20   Bob McDowall, 'Freshwater Fish—More Galaxiids', *Te Ara—The Encyclopedia of New Zealand*, accessed 30 June 2017, www.TeAra.govt.nz/en/freshwater-fish/page-4.
21   Eileen McSaveney, 'Glaciers and Glaciation—Glaciers and People', *Te Ara—The Encyclopedia of New Zealand*, accessed 30 June 2017, www.TeAra.govt.nz/en/zoomify/10751/map-of-the-franz-josef-glacier.
22   John Wilson, 'Scots—Education', *Te Ara—The Encyclopedia of New Zealand*, accessed 30 June 2017, www.TeAra.govt.nz/en/scots/page-9.
23   Nancy Swarbrick, 'Pets—History of Pets in New Zealand', *Te Ara—The Encyclopedia of New Zealand*, accessed 30 June 2017, www.TeAra.govt.nz/en/pets/page-2.

understanding and context. Sadly, while I was able to establish links between the *Te Ara* entries and the *DNZB*, the reverse process—from biographies to Te Ara context—was never automated and the user has to draw on the search engine in order to accomplish it.

A New Home Page and New Biographies

There were several other ways in which we did succeed in giving the biographies a larger place in the national story while integrating the *DNZB* with *Te Ara*. One was to introduce a new home page for the biographies.[24] Here we provided two suggestive groupings. We provided a facility whereby the user could group people by occupation—carvers, criminals, inventors, nurses, and so on. The idea was to encourage users to make broader generalisations and to offer a quick entry point for people thinking about those pursuits in general. The other device was to pull together themes within photographs and paintings. One of the steps forward in digitising the *DNZB* was that it allowed us to add portraits. So this device takes elements from within those portraits and pulls them together. The theme might be musical instruments, or beards, or moko (Māori face tattoos), or hats. Contrast and comparison is encouraged.

The second development was to begin planning new biographies for people who had died since the last volume of the *DNZB* was completed in 2000. It was clearly unacceptable to have a national encyclopedia that failed to include a decent entry on such a national hero as the mountaineer Sir Edmund Hillary. But Hillary had died after the last volume was completed. We decided to add 15 new biographies of the most significant people who had died since then. They included, besides Hillary, politicians like Sir Robert Muldoon and David Lange; creative artists like Hone Tuwhare, Allen Curnow, Barry Crump, Janet Frame, and Douglas Lilburn; and sportspeople like the great athletics coach Arthur Lydiard. Here we took the opportunity to make reading the biographies more user-friendly by adding to their presentation the tricks we had developed for *Te Ara*—dividing the whole biography into shorter subentries; adding headings within the text; and greatly enriching the story with more illustrative resources, such as photographs, paintings,

---

24 'Biographies', *Te Ara—The Encyclopedia of New Zealand*, accessed 30 June 2017, www.teara.govt.nz/en/biographies.

and cartoons, but also interactive maps and videos. These again served to widen the appeal of the entries beyond the simple factual biography. In Hillary's biography, you will find a map showing the stages of the climb up Everest in 1953;[25] in Curnow's you will find two telling excerpts from a film about him, *Early Days Yet*; while in the additional sources on Curnow there is a link to the full film on the moving image website, NZonscreen (www.nzonscreen.com).[26] The focus remains biographical, but the richness of the visual and sound resources certainly broadens the understanding of the individual's life.

The Making of Modern New Zealand— A Proposal

As we developed these 15 new biographies, and then as the initial *Te Ara* build came to an end, we began to realise that so much time had elapsed there was now a sufficient number of significant people who had flourished in the period since the 1950s and had then died that a new tranche of biographies was called for. However, I was not persuaded that simply bidding for a revival of the old *DNZB* would have much political appeal. Furthermore, I was even more strongly convinced from our experience that pulling together individual biographies with contextual material on a digital platform was an exciting way to go. The biographies needed to work as a contribution to the general history of the nation.

Therefore, we developed a proposal entitled 'The Making of Modern New Zealand'. We would prepare interpretive essays about the history of New Zealand since 1960, with an underlying argument that New Zealand had undergone a massive change in culture and identity over those years. We would explore this change in various areas, such as high culture, popular culture, ethnicity and immigration, the place of Māori in society, gender roles, attitudes towards the environment, sport, religion, foreign policy, the rise of the city, industrial development, and farming. The high-level topics already covered in *Te Ara* would provide a good starting

---

25   Shaun Barnett, 'Hillary, Edmund Percival', *Dictionary of New Zealand Biography*, first published in 2010. *Te Ara—The Encyclopedia of New Zealand*, accessed 30 June 2017, www.teara.govt.nz/en/interactive/28428/final-ascent-of-everest.
26   Terry Sturm, 'Curnow, Thomas Allen Monro', *Dictionary of New Zealand Biography*, first published in 2010. *Te Ara—The Encyclopedia of New Zealand*, accessed 30 June 2017, www.teara.govt.nz/en/biographies/6c1/curnow-thomas-allen-monro/sources.

point. Alongside this exercise, we would research and write biographies of significant people who had flourished since 1960. The idea was that the specialists whom we contracted to prepare the general essays would also suggest new relevant biographies. The interpretive essays would have rich linking to the new biographies, and in turn the biographies would be written with the contextual essays in mind. Thus the user would be led almost seamlessly from an essay about, for example, the transformation of New Zealand film-making, to essays about the prominent directors and producers and actors who made it happen. And if you started with an interest in a particular film-maker, you would be encouraged to explore the contextual essays. Obviously this would have been a challenging exercise, and there might have been a danger that significant people who did not fit easily into one sphere of significant activity and change might fall by the wayside. But I find it hard to think of such a person, and in any case a contribution to an important area of New Zealand life would seem like a good place to begin choosing dictionary of national biography subjects.

The idea received quite a warm reception. Many people recognised that the past half-century had indeed seen a revolution of national identity following Britain's entry into the European Economic Community, the rise of a baby boomer generation with new ideas and politics, and the massive movement of Māori into the city and a greater number of non-British immigrants into the nation as a whole. New Zealand became a diverse, urban, and cosmopolitan society. But there had been little real research on this transformation. People could see the intellectual need, and there was a warm response to the idea of doing general work alongside individual biographies. The idea, however, never came to fruition, largely because of fiscal stringency, and a government department which had looked with envious eyes on the funding dedicated to *Te Ara* as a route out of its own insolvency. Not only did this project never get funded, but the staff and funding dedicated to *Te Ara* disappeared and we had the absurd situation of a major dictionary of biography and a national encyclopedia available on the web, but few resources or person power to keep them up to date. Finally, in 2017, it was announced that there would be 15 new biographies a year added to the *Dictionary of New Zealand Biography*. This was a welcome step forward. What remains disappointing is that the attempt to link biography and national context in the preparation of a significant national reference work never got off the ground.

When major reference works such as a dictionary of national biography or a national encyclopedia are funded through the taxpayers of the nation, it is hard to avoid the whims of our political masters. We should be grateful that at least for almost 30 years, from 1984 to 2014, the New Zealand Government gave us the money to produce the *DNZB* and *Te Ara*. What we must now hope is that the resumption of work on the dictionary also triggers a new look at ways of linking that reference work with *Te Ara*. The intellectual possibilities of such a linkage are too good an opportunity to leave undeveloped.

3

THE IRISH WORLD: HOW TO REVISE A LONG-STANDING DICTIONARY PROJECT

TURLOUGH O'RIORDAN

The gradual emergence of digital resources since the 1980s has transformed biographical research. The proliferation of digital resources—ubiquitous and searchable—generates profound questions for the integrity of biographical research. The digitisation of existing scholarly material (monographs, edited collections, journal articles) and new digital platforms (newspaper archives, online repositories), when combined with digital search techniques, facilitate the querying of vast amounts of information. The purpose of biographical reference remains unaltered. Offering accuracy and precision, national biographical dictionaries present rigorously researched factual biographies, incorporating relevant contextual analysis, based on verifiable sources.

Although perceived in analogue terms, national biographical dictionaries are expected to incorporate the outputs of the digital revolution. The increasing prevalence of digitised primary resources—newspapers and periodicals; official and public papers; specialised archives and collections—has transformed historical research practices. Digital platforms, editions, and tools deliver an ever-expanding abundance of information. However, established qualitative research methods, developed in analogue contexts, are unquestionably applied to digital material and resources.

Digital publication allows new content to be rapidly disseminated and easily searched. Scholarship assesses the veracity and authenticity of information. It must also consider how such information is (or is not) presented to us. Fluid conceptual boundaries between digital editions, archives, and online platforms[1] (all structured databases) are blurred by how keyword searching guides scholarship. Our unquestioned reliance upon these tools, whose operation is little understood, is troubling. The experience of the *Dictionary of Irish Biography* (*DIB*), facing into a world increasingly reliant upon digitally mediated research, may be instructive.

The *Dictionary of Irish Biography*

The *DIB* commenced in spring 1983. Preliminary scoping work by the Royal Irish Academy focused on trawling sources and consulting widely amongst experts. As initially conceived, external specialists would research lives from defined periods, to be collected and periodically published. Editorial planning became orientated towards developing a database to be published as a CD-ROM. James McGuire was appointed as managing editor in the early 1990s. A publishing contract with Cambridge University Press, agreed in 1997, was soon followed by significant funding from the Irish Higher Education Authority. An enlarged in-house research staff of specialist scholars had, by 2003, completed around 70 per cent of the planned *Dictionary*; it was decided that year to publish simultaneously in both hard copy and online. Completed in the spring of 2009, the *Dictionary* was published that November by Cambridge University Press and the Royal Irish Academy. Launched in Dublin by An Taoiseach (prime minister) Brian Cowen, the hard copy—over 8 million words spread across 10,000 pages and nine volumes—then mirrored exactly the online platform, having been conceived and executed as a hard-copy reference project.

---

1   Kenneth M. Price, 'Edition, Project, Database, Archive, Thematic Research Collection: What's in a Name?', *DHQ: Digital Humanities Quarterly* 3, no. 3 (2009), accessed 2 November 2016, digitalhumanities.org:8081/dhq/vol/3/3/000053/000053.html. *RIDE: A Review Journal for Digital Editions and Resources* (ride.i-d-e.de) seeks to redress the extent to which digital editions and platforms are ignored by established journals, subjecting them to rigorous scholarly peer-review.

Emphasising factual accuracy, embracing modern scholarship, and seeking to ensure accessibility to the general reader, the *DIB* is a general biographical reference work.[2] The 2009 edition comprises individuals who died before the end of 2002, either born in Ireland (with careers within or outside Ireland) or elsewhere (with careers in Ireland). The 'essential criterion of selection is presence in Ireland'.[3] The preponderance of military, ecclesiastical, judicial, and political subjects in earlier Irish biographical dictionaries saw the editors give 'primacy to achievement over position', seeking to include 'those names which seem most likely to be the objects of enquiry in the twenty-first century'.[4]

Encompassing mythical figures such as the tragic Deirdre 'of the sorrows', the legendary warrior Fionn mac Cumhaill, and Molly Malone (the figurative Dublin street hawker), all likely euhemerised, the *DIB* includes saints—such as Finbarr of Cork and of course St Patrick—and the medieval lodestar Gerald of Wales, author of the *Typographia Hibernia*. Arkle, the famous horse, could not be included, though his owner Anne, Duchess of Westminster, is given extensive treatment. Questions of Irishness are resolved by treating the island of Ireland from the earliest times to the present day.

The 9,700 lives (in 9,014 signed entries) comprising the 2009 first edition were presented identically to readers in nine volumes and online. From late 2009, the *DIB* began adding supplementary lives (biannually in June and December); individuals are considered for inclusion six years after their death. Gradually, we commenced revising existing entries and addressing corrigenda (biannually each spring and autumn). Errors of fact and interpretation are rectified, guided by our own research and external submissions. Assessing new sources and evaluating existing findings is an important, though resource-intensive, part of our work. There has been a gradual bifurcation between the static, analogue, hard-copy dictionary and the iterative online digital platform.[5]

---

2   What constitutes a 'general reader' is of course open to debate, and has been the source of some of the most enjoyable discussions with colleagues on the *DIB* over the last 18 years.
3   James McGuire and James Quinn, 'Introduction', in *Dictionary of Irish Biography*, eds James McGuire and James Quinn, vol. 1, *A–Burchill* (Cambridge: Cambridge University Press, 2009), xi.
4   McGuire and Quinn, 'Introduction', xxi.
5   The June 2018 supplemental update to the *DIB* online brings the total number of lives to 10,461. In August 2018, hard-copy volumes 10 and 11 of the *DIB*, comprising those who died between 2003 and 2010 alongside the first two batches of 'missing persons', were published by Cambridge University Press.

Editorial Considerations

Assessment of the recently dead requires sensitivity. The absence of accessible primary source material led to many such entries being written by contemporaries who knew those treated, or had notable insight into their life and times. Issues of objectivity and sensitivity also impinge upon supplementary lives added to the *DIB* since 2009, especially those dying in contentious or tragic circumstances, or who were involved in traumatic events.

Consultation amongst experts yields a viable collection of subjects for consideration. Blind spots can be rectified by the later identification and the inclusion of 'missing persons'; 82 such lives were added to the *DIB* in December 2013, 75 in December 2015, and a further 57 in December 2017. Historiographical developments guide selection, aided by newly digitised sources being fully text-searchable.

Questions of representation and coverage (reliant on subjective assessments) reflect the wider composition of society and its expectations. Newspaper obituaries, though sometimes unreliable, guide initial identification. However, those who have emigrated, or died long after their peer group, may suffer from exclusion bias in the reporting of Irish newspapers and the publications of professional and voluntary associations. Certain careers—for example, engineering, medicine, and science—are increasingly professionally introverted. The specialisation upon which professional achievement is based means notable individuals are often little known beyond their specialist fields.

The Irish World

Periods of sustained emigration from Ireland spur transnational lives, which are easily overlooked. David Orr (1922–2008), a leading United Kingdom businessman, was of some prominence in Ireland, while Arthur Gwynn (1908–2008), a medic, naturalist, and explorer in Australia, was little known in Ireland and less so in Australia.[6] Orr's public profile

---

6   Turlough O'Riordan, 'Arthur Montagu Gwynn (1908–2008)', and 'David Alexander Orr (1922–2008)', *Dictionary of Irish Biography*, June 2014, accessed 9 August 2017, dib.cambridge.org.

(a British soldier awarded the prestigious Military Cross, who became a leading captain of industry), and to a lesser extent Gwynn's, being a scion of a prominent Irish scholarly family, brought each to our attention.

Bryan Beirne (1918–1998), a world-renowned entomologist in Canada, emigrated there after a starred university career in Dublin. Jeremy Swan (1922–2005), a prominent cardiologist in the United States of America, and John Crofton (1912–2009), a tuberculosis physician and public health expert in the United Kingdom, followed similar paths.[7] Though little known in Ireland, each reached the apex of their specialist fields overseas, their emigration spurred by a dearth of postwar opportunities in Ireland. Crofton and international relations scholar Fred Halliday (1946–2009) both compiled *Who's Who* entries. Beirne and political scientist Peter Mair (1951–2011) both left published *curricula vitae*, valuable for compiling professional chronologies for those active in academia and the sciences. Halliday, born in Ireland, spent most of his life in the United Kingdom. Mair, educated in Ireland, emigrated as a postgraduate and rose to prominence in Europe.[8] Irish people with overseas careers are often harder to identify and thus less likely to be considered for inclusion. Unfortunately emigration from Ireland continues, with 480,000 people emigrating from Ireland between 2008 and 2014, just under 10 per cent of our population.[9]

It is significantly easier to identify figures coming to Ireland. Heinrich Böll (1917–1985), the German writer, spent time in Ireland during the 1950s and 1960s. His *Irisches Tagebuch* (*Irish Journal*), published in 1957 and translated into English in 1967, was influential in both countries. Ivan Beshoff, 'Russian immigrant and purveyor of fish and chips',[10] was a mutineer of the Russian battleship *Potemkin,* introduced to Lenin in London by the Irish labour leader James Larkin (1874–1947).[11] They

---

7   Turlough O'Riordan, 'Bryan Patrick Beirne (1908–1998)', 'Jeremy Swan (1922–2005)', and 'John Wenman Crofton (1912–2009)', *Dictionary of Irish Biography*, 2011–16, accessed 9 August 2017, dib.cambridge.org.
8   Turlough O'Riordan, 'Fred Haillday (1946–2009)', and 'Peter Mair (1951–2011)', *Dictionary of Irish Biography*, June and December 2016, accessed 9 August 2017, dib.cambridge.org.
9   Tom Healy, 'Emigration Has Taken Its Toll', Nevin Economic Research Institute, 3 July 2015, accessed 3 July 2017, www.nerinstitute.net/blog/2015/07/03/emigration-has-taken-its-toll/. This draws on (Irish) Central Statistics Office data, accessed 3 July 2017, www.cso.ie/en/statistics/population/archive/.
10 C. J. Woods, 'Ivan Beshoff (1882?–1987)', *Dictionary of Irish Biography*, 2009, accessed August 2017, dib.cambridge.org.
11 Emmet O'Connor, 'James Larkin (1874–1947)', *Dictionary of Irish Biography*, 2009, accessed August 2017, dib.cambridge.org.

may be contrasted with Erwin Shrödinger (1887–1961) and George Friedrich Handel (1685–1759), included due to their brief stays in Ireland.[12]

Many 'missing persons' added to the *DIB* since 2009 had previously overlooked transnational lives. Sara Blomfield (1859–1939), a Bahá'í pioneer and humanitarian in the United Kingdom; Joanna Hiffernan (c. 1843–post 1903?), an artist's model and muse of James Whistler in Paris; Tony Mullane (1859–1944), a baseball player in nineteenth-century America; William Desmond Taylor (1877–1922), a silent film director in America and celebrity murder victim; James Dalton (1834–1919), a pastoralist and merchant in Australia; and Mary Latchford Kingsmill Jones (1877–1968), a public representative in the UK, are amongst a selection added to the *DIB* since 2009.[13] Those emigrating to non-Anglophone countries are less likely to come to our attention. Jennifer Musa (1917–2008), politician and Pushtun tribal elder in Balochistan, Pakistan, and James Skinner (1923–2008), politician and lawyer in Zambia and Malawi, are amongst many fascinating supplementary transnational lives to be found in the *DIB*.[14] Musa, working as a nurse in Oxford, England, met and married the scion of a prominent Pushtun family, returning to Balochistan with him. Skinner, after training as a lawyer and facing bleak employment prospects in postwar Ireland, emigrated to the Federation of Rhodesia and Nyasaland.

---

12 Paul Collins, 'George Friedrich Handel (1685–1759)' and Patricia M. Byrne, 'Erwin Shrödinger (1881–1961)', *Dictionary of Irish Biography*, 2009, accessed August 2017, dib.cambridge.org.

13 Turlough O'Riordan, 'Sara Louise Blomfield (1859–1939)', Lawrence William White, 'Joanne Hiffernan (c.1843–p.1903?)' and 'Anthony John Mullane (1859–1944)', Patrick Maume, 'William Desmond Taylor 1872–1922)', Derek Barry, 'James Dalton (1834–1919)' and Arnold Horner, 'Mary Latchford (Kingsmill) Jones (1877–1968)', *Dictionary of Irish Biography*, 2013–15, accessed August 2017, dib.cambridge.org.

14 Turlough O'Riordan, 'Jennifer Musa (1917–2008)' and 'James John Skinner (1923–2008)', *Dictionary of Irish Biography*, June and December 2014, accessed August 2017, dib.cambridge.org.

Digital Research

Knowledge of Musa and Skinner's lives came from Anglophone sources. The cultural and linguistic affinities shared amongst postcolonial states conditioned their emigration. Are those who emigrate to non-Anglophone cultures as likely to come to our attention? Researching less prominent individuals in culturally, scientifically, or politically important though unheralded sectors (for instance, the nontraditional arts, central banking, medicine, and scientific research) benefits from digital research methods. The digitisation of material covering their lives—easily searchable and accessible—aids initial identification and subsequent research. Transnational and marginal lives are now more likely to receive due consideration and recognition. That digital resources can be easily searched undoubtedly furthers biographical research into less prominent lives.

Entry length can also be problematic, implicitly suggestive of relative importance.[15] While any subjective judgment will vary over time, national biographical dictionaries should arguably strive most to account for the lives of lesser-known individuals. Their contributions to specialist fields or less prominent sections of society,[16] likely given little coverage elsewhere, are arguably most deserving of detailed treatment. Those not treated in standard narratives due to their marginality, or given only passing mention, deserve our greatest efforts. The digital revolution greatly serves this goal: aiding the inclusion of 'missing persons' and facilitating the researching of their exploits in ways that would have been until recently unimaginable. Yet the ability to search ever more widely and deeply also generates demands for the revision or expansion of existing entries.

Beyond rectifying egregious errors and omissions, there is no obvious rubric guiding the incorporation of new information, sources, or research findings. Digital publication is provisional due to the ability to amend what is presented to readers, which subtly alters their expectations. There may even be a case for considering excluding individuals from the *DIB* as their historical worth is re-evaluated. If the practice of revision incorporates 'who to include', should it not concomitantly assess 'who to exclude'?

---

15   *DIB* entries range from circa 200 words to over 9,000 words for major figures, such as Éamon De Valera (1882–1975), St Patrick (c. 420–490?), and W. B. Yeats (1865–1935).
16   Discussion with colleagues has yet to yield a positive, non-pejorative term for such figures.

Revision

Lives from the eighteenth century onwards are most likely to undergo revision as relevant sources are digitised. A coterie of late twentieth-century figures, subject to various forms of public inquiry during and after their deaths, have necessitated revision.[17] James Gogarty (1917–2005), an engineer and building company executive, gave testimony into political and planning corruption that laid bare squalid malfeasance.

> [Gogarty] opened a Pandora's box of alleged corruption and cronyism, regarding the probity of the planning process, and monies received under questionable circumstances by elected politicians at local and national level, and by appointed officials. The planning tribunal launched on the basis of Gogarty's allegations sat for fifteen years (1997–2012), the longest tribunal of inquiry in the history of the Irish state.[18]

Subsequent complex legal proceedings resulted in the January 2015 withdrawal of many findings of fact against named individuals based on Gogarty's evidence. This in turn required the revision of *DIB* entries treating associated business and political figures. Two medics, Margaret Dunlevy (1909–2002) and Patrick Meenan (1917–2008), were variably involved in vaccine trials undertaken in Irish children's homes in the 1960s and 1970s.[19] Legal proceedings concluded in 2003, and 2015 public revelations, impacted how the historical record construes their careers. Emergent legal, or more likely historical, findings will require the future revision of relevant *DIB* entries. The key historiographical issue is what constitutes a reasonable assessment of the known facts at a given point in time.

On Shelves and Screens

Factual accuracy and robust interpretation, the core functions of biographical reference, require pertinent new sources to be reviewed. A balance must be struck between accuracy on the one hand, and

---

17 'Tribunals of enquiry' and other statutory forms of public investigation are common in addressing political, religious, and judicial scandals in Irish public life.
18 Lawrence William White, 'James Martin Gogarty (1917–2005)', *Dictionary of Irish Biography*, revised April 2015, accessed November 2016, dib.cambridge.org.
19 Turlough O'Riordan, 'Patrick Meenan (1917–2008)' and 'Margaret Dunlevy (1909–2002)', *Dictionary of Irish Biography*, June and December 2015, accessed November 2016, dib.cambridge.org.

immediacy and completeness on the other. Colin Allen, Uri Nodelman, and Edward Zalta posit how online reference works face an impossible triad: between 'authoritative', 'comprehensive', and 'up to date'; only two are possible.[20] Humanities scholarship demands the rigorous discussion and attribution of evidence. These scholarly editorial practices are what fundamentally distinguish academic reference works from Wikipedia and other crowd-sourced platforms. Yet Wikipedia, John Naughton argues, has developed 'a remarkable system of collective governance that combines transparency, a respect for neutrality and pragmatism'.[21]

Humanities scholarship interprets evidence in pursuit of rigorous discussion in contrast to the binary analyses found in the pure and applied sciences. The objective balancing of evidence against scientific theory may better suit the communal, mediated nature of Wikipedia. Inadequate when a topic demands critical appraisal (humanities and social science), useful when a topic is centred on uncontested factual information (pure and applied sciences), Wikipedia's 'increasing ubiquity as a source of information' risks engendering widespread reliance upon a single source, what Jack Lynch terms an 'information monoculture'.[22] The reinforcing nature of online search promotes open-access content: the more people search for and use a resource, the more it is returned in search results, the more it is used, and so on. Yet Wikipedia's popularity, magnified by its noble open-access model, should not be maligned. The quality and utility of many of its articles, biographical or otherwise, was praised by Roy Rosenzweig in a seminal 2006 article arguing the value of 'open-source' history could no longer be ignored by the academy.[23]

The experience of other academic reference works, with various organisational and funding models, may be instructive. The *Oxford English Dictionary* decided in 2012 to discontinue hard-copy publication

---

20   Colin Allen, Uri Nodelman, and Edward N. Zalta, 'The Stanford Encyclopedia of Philosophy: A Developed Dynamic Reference Work', *Metaphilosophy* 33, nos 1–2 (2002): 210–28. doi.org/10.1111/1467-9973.00225.
21   John Naughton, 'Jimmy Wales Goes After the Truth. Brave Man', *Guardian*, 30 April 2017, accessed 9 August 2017, www.theguardian.com/commentisfree/2017/apr/30/jimmy-wales-goes-after-truth-brave-man-wikipedia.
22   Peter Thoneman, 'The All-Conquering Wikipedia?', *Times Literary Supplement*, 25 May 2016, accessed 29 November 2016, www.the-tls.co.uk/articles/public/encyclopedic-knowledge.
23   Roy Rosenzweig, 'Can History Be Open Source? Wikipedia and the Future of the Past', *Journal of American History* 93, no. 1 (2006): 117–46. doi.org/10.2307/4486062.

and proceed solely as an iterative digital publication.[24] The online *Stanford Dictionary of Philosophy* provides 'authoritative, rigorously accurate knowledge, at no cost to readers'.[25] Alongside arxiv.org (which serves academic physics and mathematics),[26] these nonprofit projects, hosted by institutional libraries,[27] may be instructive to national biographical dictionaries, whose future lies primarily online.

The transformation of information from analogue to digital formats alters how we access and consume it. Our ability to access copious information reifies the value of considered knowledge. Herbert Simon suggests 'a wealth of information creates a poverty of attention and a need to allocate that attention efficiently among the overabundance of information sources that might consume it'.[28] The increasing volume of information amassed within the digital revolution, reinforcing the value of reference works, has been transformative for national biographical dictionaries.

Attribution and Use

The mode of access of a reader can influence how the *DIB* is considered. Revision of the *DIB* has created a divergence between the static hard-copy entries and their amended online versions. We have found examples of scholars relying on an updated online *DIB* entry, yet referencing the

---

24 Alastair Jamieson, 'Oxford English Dictionary Will Not Be Printed Again', *Daily Telegraph*, 29 August 2010, accessed 7 September 2018, www.telegraph.co.uk/culture/books/booknews/7970391/Oxford-English-Dictionary-will-not-be-printed-again.html.
25 Nikhil Sonnad, 'The Philosopher's Stone: This Free Online Encyclopedia Has Achieved What Wikipedia Can Only Dream of', 21 September 2015, accessed 21 September 2015, qz.com/480741/this-free-online-encyclopedia-has-achieved-what-wikipedia-can-only-dream-of; Allen, Nodelman, and Zalta, 'The Stanford Encyclopedia of Philosophy', 210–28; Joint Conference on Digital Libraries, July 2002, accessed November 2016, plato.stanford.edu/pubs/jcdl2.pdf.
26 'arXiv.org', Cornell University Library, arxiv.org. 'PsyArXiv', Psychology's dedicated open-access digital archive, launched on 16 December 2016, promising 'to create free, open access to psychological science, even for papers that are ultimately published in journals that are only accessible to subscribers'. David Barner, Benjamin Brown, and Alex Holcombe, 'Introducing PsyArXiv: Psychology's Dedicated Open Access Digital Archive', 8 December 2016, accessed 11 August 2017, blog.psyarxiv.com/psyarxiv/2016/12/08/psyarxiv-press-release/.
27 Stanford University Library and Cornell University Library, respectively.
28 H. A. Simon, 'Designing Organizations for an Information-Rich World', in *Computers, Communication, and the Public Interest*, ed. Martin Greenberger (Baltimore, MD: The Johns Hopkins Press, 1971), 40–41.

2009 hard-copy volumes.²⁹ The static multivolume edition, organised alphabetically by surname, contrasts with the online platform, which can be interrogated in various ways. The well-understood form of discrete ownership, implicit in the former, contrasts with what is effectively a form of rental agreement governing access to the latter.

The *DIB* was extensively drawn upon in recent works spurred by the Irish 'decade of centenaries' (1912–22). Citation form varies, with the *DIB* sometimes cited *en masse,* when it is clear a small number of specific entries have been used—easily identifiable by the presence of memes exclusive to the *DIB* being reproduced, unattributed, in the text. Neither a monograph nor an edited collection, the *DIB* endures inconsistent citation. Either the entire multivolume work (by title and editors, and perhaps volume), or the discrete *DIB* entry (by title and author alone) are given. These two forms are in turn subject to a wide variety of construction and formatting, which undermines citation and impact analysis.³⁰

Many scholarly sources can now be accessed through online platforms; for example, a printed journal article accessed as a PDF through JSTOR.³¹ Should scholars cite the analogue form of a resource when it has been accessed digitally? Online material (for example, newsletters, blog posts, or online comments) is inherently difficult to reference. The *DIB* provides as much information as possible (title, author, date, and URL). The static representation of dynamic online resources will remain problematic.³²

---

29   Evidenced by their usage of specific information only found in the revised online entry. This pattern is reinforced by Jonathan Blaney, 'The Problem of Citation in the Digital Humanities', conference presentation, 7 September 2012, accessed 9 August 2017, www.sheffield.ac.uk/polopoly_fs/1.209016!/file/JonathanBlaney.pptx. Blarney's case studies examining British History Online are available at 'British History Online', *TIDSR: Toolkit for the Impact of Digitised Scholarly Resources*, Oxford Internet Institute, University of Oxford, last modified 14 May 2011, microsites.oii.ox.ac.uk/tidsr/case-study/348/british-history-online.
30   'The footnote varies as widely in nature and content as any other complex scientific or technical practice … footnotes appear in enough forms to challenge any taxonomists ingenuity.' Anthony Grafton, *The Footnote: A Curious History* (Cambridge, MA: Harvard University Press, 1999), 11.
31   'JSTOR provides access to more than 10 million academic journal articles, books, and primary sources in 75 disciplines.' 'About JSTOR', JSTOR, accessed 14 August 2017, about.jstor.org/.
32   Uniform Resource Locator is a specific form of, and sometimes confused with, U(niform) R(esource) I(dentifier), akin to a web address. D(igital) O(bject) I(dentifiers) serve a similar function in controlled research environments, their operation governed by an ISO. For a useful discussion of persistent identifiers, see Ryan Moats, 'URN Syntax', memo, May 1997, accessed November 2018, www.rfc-editor.org/rfc/pdfrfc/rfc2141.txt.pdf; Emma Tonkin, 'Persistent Identifiers: Considering the Options', *Ariadne*, no. 56 (2008), accessed November 2018, www.ariadne.ac.uk/issue56/tonkin?lt%3B%2FA=&gt%3B=&lt%3B%2FP=.

In the United Kingdom, the Joint Information Services Committee, which supports higher education research, undertook a sequence of surveys in 2009 and 2010, assessing how 'British History Online' project resources were referenced. They found a bias towards academics encouraging students to cite hard-copy versions of sources, even when those sources have been accessed exclusively online, emphasising the absence of agreed citation standards across historical publications.[33] Lara Putnam notes that digitised material is more likely to be used and cited, and analogue material less so, referencing Tim Hitchcock's findings that, despite online access and keyword searching, ensuing bibliographic references are predominantly to hard-copy versions of texts.[34]

Despite efforts to archive selections of the internet, much online content will perish. What is captured may not be rendered at its original location or in its original form. Capturing Irish-related material is a key goal of the National Library of Ireland.[35] Such institutional efforts, alongside voluntary endeavours undertaken by the likes of the Internet Archive,[36] face significant technical difficulties and resource constraints. We can only hope that such noble efforts to capture resources integral to future biographical research are successful.

---

33   JISC, 'The Impact and Embedding of an Established Resource: British History Online as a Case Study', Jonathan Blaney and Peter Webster, Institute of Historical Research, School of Advanced Study, University of London, March 2011.
34   Putnam quotes Hitchcock saying that '[t]he vast majority of both journal articles and early modern and nineteenth-century printed sources are now accessed online and cherry-picked for relevant content via keyword searching. Yet references to these materials are still made to a hard copy on a library shelf, implying a process of immersive reading'. Lara Putnam, 'The Transnational and the Text-Searchable: Digitized Sources and the Shadows They Cast', *American Historical Review* 121, no. 2 (2016): 388. doi.org/10.1093/ahr/121.2.377.
35   Charlie Taylor, 'Ireland's Digital Content in Danger of Disappearing, Specialist Warns', *Irish Times*, 20 July 2017, accessed 25 July 2017, www.irishtimes.com/business/technology/ireland-s-digital-content-in-danger-of-disappearing-specialist-warns-1.3157792.
36   'Internet Archive is a non-profit library of millions of free books, movies, software, music, websites, and more.' Internet Archive, accessed 14 August 2017, archive.org/.

3. THE IRISH WORLD

Ireland Online

The Bureau of Military History collections and the 1901 and 1911 census of Ireland, both recently digitised, have transformed biographical research in Ireland.[37] The digital edition of the *1641 Depositions*, over 8,000 witness accounts of a rebellion that year in Ireland, serves early modern scholarship.[38] Newspapers, periodicals, and serials continue to be digitised.[39] The digitisation of Irish civil and religious records (detailing births, marriages, and deaths) has made slower progress.[40] Recent work to harmonise digital humanities best practice, centred around standardising data formats, interoperable metadata, and linked data technologies, have been spurred by the impressive Digital Repository of Ireland.[41] The impact of these projects has been enormous, especially in designating familial relationships amongst and between *DIB* subjects.[42]

Websites such as Findagrave, Archiseek, and the Commonwealth War Graves Commission sit alongside a growing range of ephemera housed at the Internet Archive.[43] The latter's 'Wayback Machine' captures versions of deleted, defunct, or otherwise lost websites.[44] The ability to interrogate such digital resources was almost unimaginable during initial preparation of the *DIB* in the 1990s. Enthusiasts and voluntary bodies collect online obscure publications, newsletters, fanzines, sporting memorabilia, and

---

37 'Bureau of Military History', Military Archives and National Archives, www.bureaufmilitary history.ie/; 'Census of Ireland 1901/1911 and Census Fragments and Substitutes, 1821–51', National Archives of Ireland, www.census.nationalarchives.ie/. For a history of Irish Digital Humanities see James O'Sullivan, Órla Murphy, and Shawn Day, 'The Emergence of the Digital Humanities in Ireland', *Breac: A Digital Journal of Irish Studies*, 7 October 2015, accessed 9 August 2017, breac.nd.edu/articles/the-emergence-of-the-digital-humanities-in-ireland/.
38 '1641 Depositions', Trinity College Dublin, 1641.tcd.ie. A collaboration between Trinity College Dublin, the University of Aberdeen, the University of Cambridge, and IBM, the project launched in 2010.
39 See the work of the 'Newspaper and Periodical History Forum of Ireland', accessed November 2018, newspapersperiodicals.org/.
40 Various resources are collected at 'Irish Genealogy.ie', accessed November 2018, www.irishgenealogy.ie/en/. A range of private sector and voluntary services aggregate abstracts of the same records.
41 'Digital Repository of Ireland', Royal Irish Academy, repository.dri.ie/; A. O'Carroll and S. Webb, *Digital Archiving in Ireland: National Survey of the Humanities and Social Sciences*, National University of Ireland Maynooth, 2012. doi.org/10.3318/DRI.2012.1. See also 'The Placenames Database of Ireland', accessed November 2018, www.logainm.ie/.
42 The *DIB* online is extensively cross-referenced, with over 60,000 cross-reference hyperlinks between over 10,000 articles.
43 'Find a Grave', secure.findagrave.com; 'Archiseek', archiseek.com; 'Commonwealth War Graves Commission', www.cwgc.org; 'Internet Archive', accessed November 2018, archive.org.
44 'Explore more than 304 billion web pages saved over time.' Wayback Machine, accessed 14 August 2017, archive.org/web/.

other ephemera. As artists, cultural figures, and 'celebrities' enter the *DIB* in greater numbers, we increasingly rely on such material to account for their lives.

Divergent methodological practices govern hard-copy and online publication. The scholarly and technical provenance of the digital resources we rely on must be considered. Veracity, explicitly addressed on the printed page through attribution and citation, collectively emerges from the content and structure of a hard-copy volume. A survey of historians' methodological approaches to digital humanities resources identified a widespread and limited understanding of the basic technical foundations of search functionality.[45]

Hard-copy access is mediated by indexes and page heads. Online access is digitally mediated, reliant on interwoven layers of hardware, software, and data. Technical implementation is as important as any scholarly methodology when presenting published or archival material online. Technical considerations subtly inflect methodological and editorial issues, cumulatively governing scholarly utility. Their interdependence is unfortunately widely ignored or misunderstood.

Scholarly Considerations

We assume that search results presented to us are neutral. They are in fact arbitrary, deliberately conditioned by algorithms. Their operation, opaque at best, influences user behaviour, tailoring the search results presented to us. It has been argued that 'we have replaced our guardians of information with algorithms that are dumb and that can be toyed with and manipulated'.[46] The perceived opportunity to search widely and deeply is illusory. The search results presented to us, lacking objectivity, are subjective abstractions.

---

45   Fred Gibbs and Trevor Owens, 'Building Better Digital Humanities Tools: Toward Broader Audiences and User-Centered Designs', *Digital Humanities Quarterly* 6, no. 2 (2012), accessed November 2018, digitalhumanities.org:8081/dhq/vol/6/2/000136/000136.html.
46   Carole Cadwalladr, 'Google "Must Review Its Search Rankings because of Rightwing Manipulation"', *Guardian*, 5 December 2016, accessed 11 August 2017, www.theguardian.com/technology/2016/dec/05/google-must-review-its-search-rankings-because-of-rightwing-manipulation.

We complacently search vast swathes of digital content without considering how digital resources are designed.[47] There is a widespread disinterest in how search functionality operates. Ethereal in nature, search functionality is construed as a technical issue to be discussed by geeks. Algorithms limit what users are presented with, determining how digital content is accessed and interrogated. The ubiquity of digital search functionality is unfortunately mirrored by widespread ignorance of its operation.

Janine Solberg notes how 'the digital tools and structures that increasingly support our research efforts have material and epistemological implications for how we discover, access and make sense of the past'.[48] Such considerations—assessing the provenance and accuracy of ensuing findings—have been internalised within traditional humanities scholarly practices. Humanities scholarship must similarly assess the work of the database creator, designer, and publisher.

Mitchell Whitelaw suggests 'search fails to match the ample abundance of our digital collections'.[49] A survey of the digital research practices of humanities scholars identified a prevalence of keyword searching, in contrast to how little used advanced search options were. The authors identify a paradoxical attitude of scholars towards searching: 'provenance and context are deemed key academic qualities, [yet] these do not appear to be common considerations in digital research practices'.[50]

D. Sculley and Bradley Pasanek urge scholars to examine and account for their own biases and assumptions. In the face of the 'superficial objectivity of computational methods', humanists must deploy and observe scholarly boundaries between computational results and their interpretation, analysis, and presentation.[51] The scholarly use of digital resources requires

---

47 Evgeny Morozov, *To Save Everything, Click Here: Technology, Solutionism, and the Urge to Fix Problems That Don't Exist* (London: Penguin UK, 2013).
48 Janine Solberg, 'Googling the Archive: Digital Tools and the Practice of History', *Advances in the History of Rhetoric* 15, no. 1 (2012): 54. doi.org/10.1080/15362426.2012.657052.
49 Mitchell Whitelaw, 'Generous Interfaces for Digital Cultural Collections', *Digital Humanities Quarterly* 9, no. 1 (2015): 3, accessed 2 November 2016, digitalhumanities.org:8081/dhq/vol/9/1/000205/000205.html#p3.
50 Max Kemman, Martijn Kleppe, and Stef Scagliola, 'Just Google It—Digital Research Practices of Humanities Scholars', *arXiv:1309.2434 [Cs]*, 10 September 2013, last revised 22 April 2014, 16, arxiv.org/abs/1309.2434.
51 D. Sculley and Bradley M. Pasanek, 'Meaning and Mining: The Impact of Implicit Assumptions in Data Mining for the Humanities', *Literary and Linguistic Computing* 23, no. 4 (2008): 409. doi.org/10.1093/llc/fqn019.

due consideration of how they are created and published. The engineering and technical considerations that govern their use must be properly assessed.

Scholarly conventions require the standardisation of dates, name forms, and other named entities. Yet such issues are documented in only the highest quality digital humanities resources and databases. Digital technology is a means to an end. We should outline the parameters it operates within, ensure our objectives are met, and reject novelty for its own sake.

Algorithms, OCR and False Negatives

Erroneous indexing and metadata, alongside subjective algorithms and personally tailored search results, have a monumental impact on how we interrogate digital resources. Digital newspaper archives use optical character recognition (OCR) to scan hard-copy text. The impact of OCR technology from the 1980s was truly revolutionary, allowing masses of material to be digitised. When automated OCR generates a transcription error, left in situ or rectified by an automated error-correcting algorithm (accepting the error, or 'correcting' it—erroneously or otherwise), a new version of a text is produced. This new algorithmically generated intermediate text is inserted between the user and the underlying source material. This has profound implications for scholarly practice. Search algorithms and OCR technology together frame much of our biographical research.

For example, in researching an individual in the *Irish Times*, identical search parameters generated 19 results in the ProQuest database, compared with 378 results in the paper's own digital archive.[52] When queried, the ProQuest IT team could not explain this massive anomaly. This example reinforces the need to try out name variants and a variety of approaches when using digital archives. Certainly, the distinct onomastics of Irish names require variable search techniques. However, unless a researcher suspects search results are anomalous (here the researcher's intuition

---

52 The search term was 'Fred O'Donovan', the date range 1 January 1938 to 31 December 2010, and the search was undertaken on 22 June 2016 at both the *Irish Times* newspaper archive (www.irishtimes.com/search) and the ProQuest portal of the same (search.proquest.com/hnpirishtimes/). I am hugely grateful to my colleague Dr Linde Lunney for bringing this example to my attention.

emanated from decades of professional biographical research experience), such a false negative is highly likely to be accepted at face value. In this case, familiarity with the area being researched led to the conscious questioning of the results presented.

Each newspaper article in a database is a rendition of the original from which metadata (to facilitate indexing, search, and retrieval) is drawn under (at best) limited human supervision. Understandably, trade-offs between cost, efficiency, and accuracy impact large-scale digitisation projects. Scanning and indexing millions of analogue items is expensive. Yet technical and editorial provenance has profound implications for scholarly users. Digital databases are not pure renditions of their analogue content; errors are inevitable. Databases must be recognised for what they are: erratic and incomplete digital abstractions. David Berry has observed how 'little understood is the way in which the digital archives being created are deeply computational in structure and content … [c]omputational techniques are not merely an instrument wielded by traditional methods, rather they have profound effects on all aspects of the disciplines' using them.[53] Thomas Hughes observes that engineered systems are not mere technical or scientific apparitions, but the result of complex social, cultural, and political processes.[54]

Our subconscious reliance upon algorithmically delivered results subtly denudes our inquisitiveness. Algorithms embody the biases of their creators, delimiting the results presented to users. The return of false positives is obvious (incorrect answers to our queries). The return of false negatives (when a negative result indicates, incorrectly, the absence of something that is in fact present) remains unseen. Any faults in a book, such as imprecise or limited indexing, will become apparent after extended use. The technical structure of a digital resource or collection, and the metadata drawn upon by the search algorithm, are hidden from a user. Furthermore, as search functionality mediates our access to digital

---

53 David M. Berry, 'The Computational Turn: Thinking About the Digital Humanities', *Culture Machine* 12 (2011): 13, accessed November 2016, www.culturemachine.net/index.php/cm/article/view/440.
54 Thomas Hughes, *Human Built World: How to Think About Technology and Culture* (Chicago and London: University of Chicago Press, 2004), quoted in James Smithies, 'A View from IT', *Digital Humanities Quarterly* 5, no. 3 (2011), accessed November 2018, digitalhumanities.org:8081/dhq/vol/5/3/000107/000107.html.

resources, it precludes the 'serendipity of browsing'.⁵⁵ Chance occurrences during casual browsing have been the spark for several transnational lives and 'missing persons' added to the *DIB* since 2009.

Our past search queries and online behaviour are tracked, to personalise the search results presented to us. This creates an echo chamber.⁵⁶ Different users, using the exact search query, may return different results, whether they are sitting next to each other or on different continents. Such technology, regarded as valuable intellectual property, is explicitly hidden from view. We are presented with results the algorithm *thinks* we want, not necessarily *all* results for a specific search term.

Some have argued for 'algorithmic accountability' to audit the 'black boxes' that govern online search. A recent review of the impact of algorithms argued for their assessment across five principles: responsibility, explainability, accuracy, auditability, and fairness. We must consider algorithms as human creations and consciously address their inputs and outputs so as to mitigate their inevitable errors and biases.⁵⁷ Sue Halpern recently concluded 'there is a tendency to assume that data is neutral, that it does not reflect inherent biases … We need to recognize that the fallibility of human beings is written into the algorithms that humans write'.⁵⁸

Putnam, discussing how full-text searching has become the new norm, elucidates how 'the new topography of information has systemic blind spots' and 'opens short cuts that enable ignorance as well as knowledge'.⁵⁹ Digital interrogation, for Putnam, subtly conditions what questions are 'efficiently answerable, and therefore worth asking'.⁶⁰ A grim circularity is sadly possible. Material that remains undigitised may be less visible to

---

55   'The serendipity of browsing … has yet to be successfully recreated in electronic form.' Steven Poole, '*You Could Look It Up* by Jack Lynch, Review—Search Engines Can't Do Everything', *Guardian*, 21 April 2016, accessed August 2016, www.theguardian.com/books/2016/apr/21/you-could-look-it-up-jack-lynch-review.
56   Carole Cadwalladr, 'Google, Democracy and the Truth About Internet Search', *Guardian*, 4 December 2016, accessed 9 August 2017, www.theguardian.com/technology/2016/dec/04/google-democracy-truth-internet-search-facebook.
57   Nicholas Diakopoulos and Sorelle Friedler, 'How to Hold Algorithms Accountable', *MIT Technology Review*, 17 November 2016, accessed 9 August 2017, www.technologyreview.com/s/602933/how-to-hold-algorithms-accountable/.
58   Sue Halpern, 'They Have, Right Now, Another You', *New York Review of Books*, 22 December 2016, accessed 9 August 2016, www.nybooks.com/articles/2016/12/22/they-have-right-now-another-you/.
59   Putnam, 'The Transnational and the Text-Searchable', 375.
60   Putnam, 'The Transnational and the Text-Searchable', 367.

scholars. Such material, as it cannot be searched digitally, may then be less likely to be consulted. Information that remains analogue is in danger of being ignored. We must consciously address the technical foundations of the digital resources we use.

Conclusion

Humanities research increasingly relies on digital technologies, mediated by the ubiquitous search box. Biographical research, into transnational lives and those at the margins of history, underserved in existing historiography, has benefited considerably. Yet our reliance on digital research, especially our dependence upon search algorithms, requires conscious consideration. Objective searching of vast digitised collections is somewhat illusory. Our trust in the search results presented to us (either positive or negative) is unwarranted.

Our scholarly inquisitiveness requires us to challenge the results presented to us by digital resources. In doing so, we must recognise how little we understand the technical and engineering principles that govern our digital research. That is not to sanctify the tangible, analogue outputs of traditional scholarship and publishing. Only by recognising deficiencies in our research practices can we address flawed assumptions that may undermine biographical scholarship. Traditional values—cautious scholarly assessment and considered editorial review—remain paramount as we face the digital future.

4

WHAT IS NATIONAL BIOGRAPHY FOR? DICTIONARIES AND DIGITAL HISTORY

PHILIP CARTER

Ask the purpose of national biography and you may be forgiven for thinking this an easier question for previous generations to answer. In June 1900 the original British *Dictionary of National Biography* (*DNB*) reached its completion with the publication of a 63rd and final volume—an event hailed as a triumph by reviewers and compilers alike. For the *Pall Mall Gazette*, this was 'the best dictionary of home biography possessed of any nation', while the *Athenaeum* championed 'our British lexicographers' who 'have had the satisfaction of administering a handsome beating to their most formidable rivals, the Germans'.[1]

The *DNB*'s editor at the time was the Elizabethan literary scholar Sidney Lee, who had driven the project on during the 1890s and infused it with an enhanced degree of scholarly rigour. Lee celebrated the *Dictionary*'s completion in similarly confident fashion, praising an 'undertaking of exceptional magnitude in the history of publishing' that was more extensive, coherent, and rapidly produced than 'cyclopaedias of national

---

1   Quoted in Keith Thomas, *Changing Conceptions of National Biography: The Oxford DNB in Historical Perspective* (Cambridge: Cambridge University Press, 2005), 27. doi.org/10.1017/CBO 9780511497582; '*Dictionary of National Biography*. Edited by Sidney Lee—Vol. LXII', *Athenaeum*, 14 July 1900, 45, quoted in Juliette Atkinson, *Victorian Biography Reconsidered: A Study of Nineteenth-Century 'Hidden' Lives* (Oxford: Oxford University Press, 2010), 231. doi.org/10.1093/acprof:oso/9780199572137.001.0001.

biography abroad', including those of Belgium, the Netherlands, Sweden, the United States of America, and again Germany. For Lee, the *Dictionary* also served as a record of incremental national progress over time, and especially the century just passed: a charting of 'the multiplication of intellectual callings' by which 'the opportunities of distinction have been of late conspicuously augmented'.[2] Lee's view echoed earlier assessments, including one from Henry Reeve, editor of the *Edinburgh Review*, for whom the *Dictionary*'s opening volumes offered 'striking proof of the advancement of civilization' that was 'honourably characteristic of the present age'.[3] Ask 'what national biography was for' in 1900 and the answer seems clear: to facilitate national and historical comparisons that revealed the British to be best, and the late Victorian British to be best of all.

Nor was this idea of national biography as national celebration and self-definition reserved for the British. Those rival dictionaries, which Lee and others considered too partial or too slow to appear, were themselves formations and expressions of new nation states. As Iain McCalman has argued:

> whereas a newly established state of the late twentieth century might seek to patent its identity by funding a national airline service; its nineteenth-century counterpart was likely to have launched a multi-volume biographical dictionary so as to display historical credentials, to define geographical, linguistic and cultural boundaries, and to instil a unified sense of national pride.[4]

McCalman's observation appears in his 'Introduction' to the proceedings of the conference, held in Canberra in February 1995, at which national biographers first gathered to discuss the relationship of 'National Biographies and National Identity', and on which contributors to this latest volume reflect and build following a second gathering two decades later.

---

2   Sidney Lee, 'A Statistical Account', *Dictionary of National Biography*, vol. 63, *Wordsworth–Zuylestein* (London: Smith, Elder and Co., 1900), i, vii–xi.
3   Henry Reeve, 'The Literature and Language of the Age', *Edinburgh Review*, 169 (August 1889), 350, quoted in Atkinson, *Victorian Biography Reconsidered*, 232.
4   Iain McCalman, 'Introduction', in *National Biographies and National Identity: A Critical Approach to Theory and Editorial Practice*, eds Iain McCalman with Jodi Parvey and Misty Cook (Canberra: Humanities Research Centre, The Australian National University, 1996), i; also Peter Burke, *A Social History of Knowledge*, vol. 2, *From the* Encyclopédie *to* Wikipedia (Cambridge: Polity Press, 2012), 192–97.

4. WHAT IS NATIONAL BIOGRAPHY FOR?

By the time of the first Canberra conference, work was underway on a completely new, and considerably extended, edition of the British *Dictionary of National Biography*, subsequently published simultaneously in print and online as the *Oxford Dictionary of National Biography* (*ODNB*) in 2004. Its founding editor, the nineteenth-century historian Colin Matthew, was present in Canberra in 1995 and used a lecture on that occasion to consider the purpose of *his* new *Dictionary*. For Matthew, a late twentieth- and early twenty-first-century national biography would be a work of historical record: a gathering and assessment of contributions by a historical profession whose origins owed much to the structures and practices developed during the making of the original *DNB*. In addition, Matthew envisaged the new *Dictionary* as serving current members of the historical and humanities professions in teaching and research: 'The modern national biography will be the first point of reference for anyone interested in the British biographical past'.[5] It would, as he presciently noted, also exist as a predominantly digital (or as it was described then an 'electronic' or 'computerised') resource. Matthew's national biography would therefore combine classic reference (being the first place to which people in search of information would go), with the potential for connections and lines of enquiry hitherto untraced. Online reference would, in turn, be the gateway to transnational integration prompted by ineluctable political and technological transition. 'As nationality in Europe gives way to the European Union', he suggested, 'so national reference works, at least in Europe, will do so also' while, thanks to their online existence, 'we will see the gradual aggregation of our various dictionaries of national biography'.[6]

Though issued nearly a century apart, these two statements of national biographical purpose—Lee's from 1900, Matthew's from 1995—are defined in their different ways by confidence in a job well done and optimism for the future. But where are we now—and 'what is national biography for'—nearly 25 years on from Colin Matthew's observations? Certainly the present and the future course of national biography may

---

5   H. C. G. Matthew, *Leslie Stephen and the* New Dictionary of National Biography (Cambridge: Cambridge University Press, 1997), 37.
6   H. C. G. Matthew, 'Dictionaries of National Biography', in McCalman with Parvey and Cook, *National Biographies and National Identity*, 16–17. Integration of national biographies was also anticipated by Robert Faber and Brian Harrison (respectively the *ODNB*'s project director and general editor) in 'The *Dictionary of National Biography*: A Publishing History', in *Lives in Print: Biography and the Book Trade from the Middle Ages to the 21st Century*, eds Robin Myers, Michael Harris, and Giles Mandelbrote (New Castle, DE: Oak Knoll Press, 2003), 189.

initially seem rather less certain. For what defines this short time span is a transformation—possible to anticipate in 1995 but impossible to predict in its extent—in information gathering, storage, retrieval, and dissemination. It is a transformation well captured in a recent history of reference publishing by the American literary scholar Jack Lynch, who describes the two decades that separate the Canberra conferences of 1995 and 2016 as the most turbulent in the long history of a traditionally stable form of scholarship and publishing. Central to this change is, of course, the rise of user-driven content and online resources such as Wikipedia, vast both in terms of scope and the speed of its revision. As Lynch argues, more has changed in the last 20 years with regards to reference publishing than in the previous 3,000. The result is an 'information monoculture', dominated by Wikipedia, which—despite its being a non-commercial venture—poses to information provision many of the dangers of a traditional monopoly.[7]

It is not hard to see why such developments may be unwelcome for national biography, not least since life writing, especially of figures in western historical and contemporary culture, has been a major area of recent growth for sites like Wikipedia. There are, moreover, further potential challenges to the genre of national biography at this time. Prominent among these is the historiographical trend for transnational and global studies that question the value of the nation state (and so perhaps the national dictionary, however broadly defined) as a meaningful category for human activity in the past. Significant too are digital histories, grounded in analysis of 'big data', that encourage longer-term periodisation and studies of human activity in aggregate, and which similarly often, and determinedly, transcend the political and cultural identities that first gave rise to national biographies.[8] And closer to home there is the ongoing debate within Britain about the stability of the United Kingdom itself—stirred by devolution in the late 1990s, the subsequent rise of political nationalisms, and now reignited following the June 2016 vote to leave the European Union—which prompts further questions about the future

---

7 Jack Lynch, *You Could Look It Up: The Reference Shelf from Ancient Babylon to Wikipedia* (London: Bloomsbury Press, 2016), 389.
8 See Jo Guldi and David Armitage, *The History Manifesto* (Cambridge: Cambridge University Press, 2014), ch. 4; and David Armitage and Jo Guldi, 'The Return of the *Longue Durée*: An Anglo-American Perspective', *Annales. Histoire, Sciences Sociales*, 70, no. 2 (2015): 219–47. doi.org/10.1017/S2398568200001126 in which biography—with its focus on 'a purportedly diachronic category of "character"'—is contrasted with the 'power of digital tools to promote *longue durée* synthesis that includes perspectives other than that of the nation-state' (227, 245).

of the British nation state. Viewed from the mid to late 2010s, therefore, the *Athenaeum*'s late Victorian equation of national biography as personification and celebration of a definable nation, or Matthew's claim to provide an increasingly transnational 'first point of reference' for a new digital age, seem less secure than they once did. The journey of national biography—now undertaken across a landscape of digitised research practices and publishing—could, in short, be one nearing its terminus.

Notwithstanding these challenges, and while not denying their significance and as yet unresolved consequences, this chapter seeks to offer a more optimistic response regarding the purposes of contemporary national biography within a research context that has seen considerable recent change. The scholars and their projects who gathered in July 2016 for the second Canberra conference are evidence that national and collective biographies remain many and varied, active and ambitious. Moreover, as the work of an earlier generation of biographers has come to fruition—through first-time publication (of, say, the *Oxford DNB*) or continuation (of the *Australian Dictionary of Biography*)—national biography has re-emerged to become an accepted staple of contemporary humanities research and scholarly literature. That individual entries within national biographies are read, and regularly cited, suggests this is a genre with credibility and reinvigorated scholarly purpose. Even so, an important question remains: how far does this sense of purpose extend beyond the individual biography, and the notion of online dictionaries as 'super accessible print',[9] to become something more dynamic, integral, and valuable to contemporary scholarship? That is, to become both a beneficiary of, and a contributor to, new forms of historical practice that serve to realise and disseminate ambitions championed by earlier, predigital editors like Lee and Matthew.

Key to this chapter is the assertion that national biography is on the cusp of significant development and opportunity, and that—broadly speaking—we should be enthusiastic about this, and about how national biography may be incorporated within and contribute to emerging forms of historical scholarship. At the heart of this more positive future for national biographies are, of course, the same digital transformations that have reshaped reference publishing in recent years, and have shaken some

---

9   Philip Carter, 'Opportunities for National Biography Online: The *Oxford Dictionary of National Biography*, 2005–2012', in *The ADB's Story*, eds Melanie Nolan and Christine Fernon (Canberra: ANU E Press, 2013), 346. doi.org/10.22459/ADBS.10.2013.11.

of the core beliefs that characterised the first Canberra gathering in 1995. To embrace digital opportunities in the mid to late 2010s does not require national biographers to compete directly with online alternatives, but rather to identify and promote ways in which their work is both distinctive (and in some ways superior) but also integral to the digital ecosystem that we inhabit when undertaking historical study. Central to this concept of national biography is the potential it now provides to undertake original academic research: the ability to use national biographies both as written collections and as data to make connections and trace patterns that could not be identified without the existence of collective biography in digital form.

'True national biography': Who Could and Who Should Be Included?

If future prospects offer promise, it is equally the case that the historical aims and ends of national biography have been rather more contested. Thus, despite the positive opinions quoted at the start of this chapter, it would be wrong to assume that former dictionary-makers necessarily shared a common purpose in their endeavours. In truth, debate and differences of opinion have characterised the making of the *Dictionary of National Biography* from its origins in the 1880s, and on occasions to a degree that would raise concern in a modern publishing house or academic department. The confident patriotism championed in June 1900 was, in large part, the verdict of the press, rather than of those directly involved in the *DNB*'s conceptualisation and composition. Principal among these less emphatic dictionary-makers was the *DNB*'s founding editor, Leslie Stephen, who served in this capacity from 1882 until 1891 when, suffering from ill health, he gave way to his deputy, Lee.

Stephen's conception of national biography was defined less by singularity and superiority than diversity and movement. For Stephen, a collective statement on national identity was required to embrace the international connections that shape any nation, and which had been an especially important theme in British history. As Matthew argued, the 'national' in Stephen's 'national biography' was 'inclusive, fluid and pragmatic, and in a sense international'.[10] In the light of this, it comes as little surprise that

---

10   Matthew, *Leslie Stephen*, 36.

in Stephen's *DNB*—a work celebrated in some quarters for its beating of continental rivals—the first entry was for Jacques Abbadie (baptised 1654?–1727), a future dean in the Church of Ireland, who hailed from Béarn, France; and the last William van Nassau van Zuylestein, who was born near Utrecht in the early 1690s.

The contested nature of Victorian national biography can also be seen in a series of striking intereditorial debates over who should, and should not, be prioritised for inclusion. In January 1896 Lee, then nearly five years into his editorship, lectured on 'National Biography' at the Royal Institution, London. Lee engaged directly with the question of inclusion and especially his understanding of national biography as a record of 'people of distinction'. Biography, he argued, was the literary format best placed to commemorate those who 'by character and exploits, have distinguished themselves from the mass of their countrymen', and whose achievements are—as he later wrote—'capable of moving the interest of posterity' and outliving the 'fashion or taste of the hour'.[11] Several months on, Stephen gave his response in a lecture, also entitled 'National Biography', and subsequently published in the *National Review*. In contrast to Lee's focus on commemorating and memorialising the distinguished, Stephen championed what he termed the 'second-rate people ... whose lives have to be reconstructed from obituary notices or from references in memoirs and collections of letters'.[12] In doing so, he echoed views from an earlier essay that it was the 'timid and third-rate lives' who would 'prove the real test of the value of the book ... the less conspicuous people about whom it is hard to get information elsewhere'.[13] They, for Stephen, were the core purpose of national biography. To modern readers, of course, it is less Stephen than his daughter, Virginia Woolf, who is most closely associated with this notion of the 'hidden' or 'little' life as equally worthy of historical record. Woolf's celebrated challenge—'Is not anyone who has lived a life, and left a record of that life, worthy of biography ... the humble as well as the illustrious?'—served for later generations as a Bloomsbury swipe at late Victorian biography and the makers of voluminous national

---

11 Sidney Lee, 'National Biography', *Cornhill Magazine*, 26 (March 1896), 258; Sidney Lee, *Principles of Biography* (Cambridge: Cambridge University Press, 1911), quoted in Atkinson, *Victorian Biography*, 224.
12 Leslie Stephen, 'National Biography', *National Review* 27 (1896), reprinted in his *Studies of a Biographer*, 4 vols (London: Duckworth and Co., 1898), 1:21–22.
13 Leslie Stephen, 'Biography', *National Review*, 22 (1893–94): 176–77, quoted in Atkinson, *Victorian Biography*, 222.

biographies.[14] But in many ways Woolf's father got there first, and was himself building on the interests of an earlier generation of biographers, as Juliette Atkinson has shown.[15] For Stephen, national biography was a unique publishing opportunity—not just to record Lee's 'emulative' or Woolf's 'illustrious', but also to reconstruct those forgotten individuals whose lives have 'to be painfully dug out of collections of manuscripts', or pieced together from 'references in memoirs and collections of letters'.[16]

If such debates show the purpose of 'national biography' to have been long contested, they also remind us that the journey taken by the *DNB*— from the late nineteenth to the early twenty-first century—is one of continuation and evolution rather than sudden transition or redefinition. The continuities that shape national biography are clearly apparent when today's editors consider the question of inclusion: who should we add, and why? Here the current purpose of the *Dictionary* resonates with both that of Stephen and Lee, notwithstanding their public disagreements on this subject. Contemporary Oxford editors define their national biography as a record of historically 'noteworthy' lives; that is, people of interest to scholars who will, it is expected, continue to be of significance for later generations—not just with regard to the person him or herself, but also as commentaries on what historians of the time thought worthy of record. To do so follows Lee's call to remember those 'capable of moving the interest of posterity', albeit without Lee's insinuation of the moral value of such distinguished lives. At the same time, they heed Stephen's injunction to reconstruct biographies of forgotten individuals whose life stories are 'dug out' from manuscripts or pieced together from references in memoirs and correspondence.

The opportunities to dig, discover, and reconstruct are today considerably enhanced by the growing availability of digitised resources. This provision and accessibility of biographical data is a further transformation that distinguishes the research environment of the mid-1990s from that of the present day. In the United Kingdom alone these digitally accessible resources include (to name just the principal primary records): census returns from 1841 to 1911; registers of births, marriages, and deaths

---

14 Virginia Woolf, 'The Art of Biography' (1939), in *Selected Essays*, ed. David Bradshaw (Oxford: Oxford University Press, 2009), 121.
15 Atkinson, *Victorian Biography*. On the proximity of Stephen and Woolf, see also Alison Booth, 'Fighting for Lives in the *ODNB*: or Taking Prosopography Personally', *Journal of Victorian Culture* 10 (2005): 270–71. doi.org/10.3366/jvc.2005.10.2.267.
16 Stephen, *Studies of a Biographer*, 1:22.

for England and Wales from 1837, and Scotland from 1854; and parish registers providing details of births, baptisms, marriages, deaths, and burials for earlier periods. Many biographers and historians now also have access to digitised electoral registers, poll books, telephone directories, passenger embarkation and disembarkation lists, criminal registers and prison records, transportation lists, trade directories, medical and nursing registers, military service and medal files, scanned copies of early modern wills held at the National Archives, and probate records from the 1860s onwards. To this can be added millions of pages of national and regional newspapers from the seventeenth to the nineteenth centuries, and selected national newspapers into the early twenty-first century. Leading this expansion of sources is Ancestry.com, which, as of 2015, had made available some 14 billion documents worldwide. In the United Kingdom, meanwhile, D. C. Thompson, creators of Find My Past, have been responsible for the digitisation of a further 1.8 billion records.[17]

In the wake of these records have come new opportunities for the construction of biographies, digitally and step by step, 'from the bottom up'. As a result, the possibilities for inclusion in a national biography have expanded markedly, even since the *Oxford DNB*'s first publication in 2004. Such first-time 'discoveries' are now numerous, among them one Henry Croft (1861–1930), founder in the late 1890s of the London tradition of pearly kings and queens who, arranged in city-wide networks modelled on the royal family, undertook charitable activities.[18] Such a figure is an obvious candidate for the *Oxford DNB* given his contribution to late Victorian voluntarism, and a legacy of charitable dynasties that continue to thrive across the London boroughs. Googling 'Henry Croft' a few years ago revealed no shortage of references to the man and his 'pearly kings'; but it was equally clear that much of this material was partial, anecdotal, and repetitious. This is online history at its least edifying, though it is more than made up for by the digitised sources that enabled his life story to be reconstructed.

---

17 David Thomas and Valerie Johnson, 'From the Library in Alexandria to the Google Campus: Has the Digital Changed the Way We Do Research?', in *Is Digital Different?*, eds Michael Moss, Barbara Endicott-Popovsky, and Marc J. Dupuis (London: Facet Publishing, 2015), 192.
18 Philip Carter, 'Croft, Henry [*called* the Original Pearly King] (1861–1930)', *Oxford Dictionary of National Biography*, Oxford University Press, May 2012; online edn, October 2012, accessed 17 April 2017. doi.org/10.1093/ref:odnb/97112.

The starting point for Croft's life story came at its end with the chance discovery of a Pathé News clip of his funeral procession, broadcast in January 1930. With an approximate death date, it was possible to search the digitised indexes of the General Register Office with a degree of precision. Croft's death certificate provided his place of death (the St Pancras workhouse, close to the modern British Library); his age at death (68 years); and his profession—for his entire working life, from 1876 to 1928, Henry worked as a road sweeper for the St Pancras Corporation. Knowing his age at death made possible a search for his birth certificate, which revealed he had been born—also at the St Pancras workhouse—on 24 May 1861. These markers enabled a trawl of the census returns for 1861 onwards to fill out details of Henry's wider family: his parents—John, a street musician who died in 1871, and his mother, Elizabeth. Henry's death certificate also provided the forename of his wife, Lily, who witnessed this record in 1930. This led to Lily Newton (1874–1940), the daughter of a Kentish Town house painter, whom Henry married at Bedford New Town Chapel, St Pancras, in February 1892. From here, again using the census returns, it was possible to piece together Henry and Lily's married life: their family (by 1911 nine children aged between 17 years and eight months) and their residences: from 1901 the Crofts lived at 15 Charles Street, off the Euston Road, in a 10-room house they shared with another family, the Wilsons and their three children. A digital edition of Charles Booth's poverty maps and police notebooks for 1898 provides further information about Croft's domestic environment ('good working-class'),[19] while digitised newspapers and periodicals led to his first known appearance as a public figure: a 1902 magazine article introducing 'Mr Croft', the 'Pearlie king of Somers Town', photographed in a handmade suit of 5,000 buttons. Subsequent newspaper articles identified Croft in various 'pearly' roles: raising money for charity, taking part in annual horse and donkey shows, and a meeting with Edward VII at Olympia in 1907.[20]

---

19 'Charles Booth's London', London School of Economics & Political Science, accessed 17 April 2017, booth.lse.ac.uk; London School of Economics, University of London, Booth MSS, B/356.

20 On the contribution of digital resources to late nineteenth- and early twentieth-century working-class biography, see also Tim Hitchcock and Robert Shoemaker, 'Making History Online', *Transactions of the Royal Historical Society* 25 (2015): 75–93. doi.org/10.1017/S0080440115000031. As Hitchcock and Shoemaker demonstrate: 'In half an hour's search we can put together a life, an experience and an emotional and empathetic contact with one of the more than three million mostly anonymous men and women who lived in London in 1871' (78).

In writing a life of Henry Croft (and many like him), the availability of digitised sources is clearly of enormous benefit. Returning to the question 'what is national biography for?', Croft's example shows the modern genre to be more than a conspectus of existing information distilled into a reference format; rather it is now in addition a home for, and generator of, first-time research. However, ready access to first-time information about ever-greater numbers of historical individuals also raises an important question: where should editors stop when it comes to adding people to a national biography? It is one first considered in 2004 by the historian Keith Thomas in a lecture to mark publication of the *Oxford DNB*. As Thomas noted, following the rise of social and cultural history, scholars were now engaging with all sections of past populations, and often doing so—in the wake of the 'biographical turn'—via the medium of individual and group lives. 'There is in principle', he continued, 'no reason why many of these hidden lives should not be recovered, and there is no technological obstacle to storing them electronically. One day perhaps we may have a database so vast that its claim to be a true national biography will be incontrovertible.'[21]

Thomas's proposal is a common reference point for each of the chapters in this volume. However, it seems of special significance when considering the potential influence of digital research practices and digital publishing. In short, is a 'true national biography', comprised of the myriad lives now traceable online, a suitable destination for current journeys in, and conceptions of, national biography? This is particularly interesting in the context of the *Oxford DNB*, which has adopted 'historical noteworthiness' as its defining criterion for inclusion—a framing principle distinct from the notion of 'representativeness' that shapes the population of, for example, the *Australian Dictionary of Biography* (*ADB*). 'Noteworthiness' is a historical judgment on who is now, and seems likely to be, considered of interest to current and future generations of scholars, as determined by the historians and editors whose judgments concerning article length also speak to an understanding of a person's relative historical significance. While equally alert to subjects' relative importance, 'representativeness' places greater emphasis on reflecting the past through a spectrum of lives that best characterise a particular period.[22]

---

21 Thomas, *Changing Conceptions of National Biography*, 56.
22 On representation as a framing principle of the *ADB*, see Paul Longley Arthur, 'Biographical Dictionaries in the Digital Era', in *Advancing Digital Humanities: Research, Methods, Theories*, eds Katherine Bode and Paul Longley Arthur (London: Palgrave, 2014), 83–94. doi.org/10.1057/ 9781137337016_6; and 'Re-imagining a Nation: The *Australian Dictionary of Biography* Online', *European Journal of Life Writing* 4 (2015): 108–24. doi.org/10.5463/ejlw.4.163.

Noteworthiness creates boundaries on who should be included, as judged by historically informed editors, and so sets limits on Thomas's idea of an ever larger database that points to a 'true national biography', defined more by scale than historical evaluation. Editors at the *Oxford DNB* regularly receive correspondence from relatives seeking the inclusion of a forebear. Some are excellent suggestions and are reviewed and added to the *Dictionary*. But others are not considered 'noteworthy' and for these are suggested alternative forms of publication—including blogs, Wikipedia, or social media—that have greatly expanded the opportunities for life writing in the decade and a half since Thomas's observation. In this context, one purpose of contemporary national biography may be to hold the line between who should be included and who could be included, based on historical assessment—irrespective of whether (or indeed precisely because) that life can now be written with access to digital sources.

National Biography and Digital History

The remainder of this chapter maintains a focus on contemporary national biography but shifts from individual lives to consider a little further its purpose as a genre, especially in the context of digital historical practices and the discipline of digital history. Three areas—extensibility and audience, engagement with user-generated content, and potential research options—will be highlighted with examples of work recently undertaken by editors at the *Oxford DNB*. With inevitable challenges come new opportunities, if—as academics and publishers—we adopt a broader conception of the scholarly purposes of historical reference. These proposals are, therefore, three reasons for cautious optimism as regards future journeys for national biography.

As digital collections national biographies are, firstly, highly adaptable and extensible, not least through external and reciprocal linking. When it was first published in 2004, the *Oxford DNB* already had in place many thousands of links to external resources that connected individual biographies to, for example, images of the subject in the National Portrait Gallery or to his or her papers listed in the National Archives. In a program begun in 2015, Oxford editors have since extended the number and scope of these curated connections. Recently added links now provide onward journeys to writers' digitised manuscripts in the British Library; to records of subjects' funeral monuments in Westminster Abbey;

4. WHAT IS NATIONAL BIOGRAPHY FOR?

to images and addresses of houses in which a person lived (via English Heritage's Blue Plaque scheme); and to historical voice recordings held by the British Library, the Poetry Society, and the British Broadcasting Corporation's (BBC) radio and film archive. Further project partnerships have established reciprocal links to the financial records of British slave-owners (drawing on records at the National Archives, and now recorded via the 'Legacies of British Slave-Ownership' website); to Art UK, which connects 2,200 British artists in the *Oxford DNB* to digitised galleries of their art works held in public collections; and to the Commonwealth War Graves Commission website, which provides additional information on service, death, and burial for the *Dictionary*'s military personnel killed in combat since 1914.[23]

These linking projects offer interesting alternative perspectives on a person's life. With them, *Dictionary* users are now able to move from a traditional biographical text to examples of manuscript works revealing an author's hand and working methods; the house and street where a person lived, and who else in the *ODNB* lived nearby; or the sound of their voice or sight of their mannerisms via sound and film footage. This ability to see a person or to hear them speak is a particularly important innovation. Like nothing else, it reminds us that a distant historical figure was a living person as well as the subject of a biographical text. Sound and vision promise to bring a new dimension to national biography, and could be extended, for example, to performance recordings for historical musicians, or archive commentaries for sporting figures. It is also worth noting that while these additions are relatively new, they have long been considered. At the first Canberra conference in 1995, the *Oxford DNB*'s founding editor, Colin Matthew, foresaw the potential of digital national biography, predicting that 'we may in time be able to have Churchill's memoir … plus a recording of him speaking, and a film of him electioneering'.[24] In 2016 a recording of the prime minister's 'Finest Hour' speech was at last made available via links from the *ODNB*'s Churchill biography to the BBC's sound and film archive.

---

23 'Legacies of British Slave-ownership', University College London, accessed 17 November 2018, www.ucl.ac.uk/lbs/; 'Art UK', artuk.org/; 'Commonwealth War Graves Commission', accessed 17 November 2018, www.cwgc.org.
24 Matthew, 'Dictionaries of National Biography', 16. See Paul Addison, 'Churchill, Sir Winston Leonard Spencer (1874–1965)', *Oxford Dictionary of National Biography*, Oxford University Press, 2004; online edn, September 2004. doi.org/10.1093/ref:odnb/32413.

Online national biography is also extensible in terms of its format, of which the *Oxford DNB*'s biography podcast—comprising more than 300 recordings—is one notable instance. With some editing, the consistent format of a national biography entry lends itself well to a scripted podcast. Episodes range from 10 minutes to narrate the life of John Simpson Kirkpatrick (1892–1915), the 'Man with the Donkey' at Gallipoli, to 40 minutes for an edited version of the life and legacy of the author and advocate of women's rights, Mary Wollstonecraft (1759–1796). Originally available free via the *ODNB* site and iTunes, recordings are now also accessible on the music and streaming platform SoundCloud.[25] With roughly 50,000 downloads per month, this variation on the biographical form is both popular and readily discoverable, making scholarly content available to many, worldwide, who would not otherwise engage with a work of historical reference. Other forms of social media, notably Twitter, have also been embraced by *ODNB* editors as channels not just for promoting content but also to observe third-party conversations—typically among digitally literate postgraduate researchers—about the project, its strengths, and its weaknesses. Social media comments identifying historical individuals not yet in the *Dictionary* have led to the commissioning of a number of new biographies, including for the linguist Claudius Hollyband (1534/5–1597) and the designer Peggy Angus (1904–1993).

Coming of age in the era of Web 2.0, modern national biographies and their editors must balance positives of this kind with potentially less welcome developments, of which user-generated reference content—and Wikipedia especially—is a prime instance. Here, as Lynch identifies, is a resource and a resulting research culture that risks threatening the meaningfulness and utility of scholarly reference and national biography as we understand it: as curated collections of content written by, and attributed to, specialist authors in processes of creation and revision, overseen by academic editors. Wikipedia—and specifically whether, and how, these academic editors engage with this resource—provides a second intersection of national biography and digital history. For its part, the *Oxford DNB* has pursued a course of pragmatic accommodation, appreciative of the fact that such resources cannot be 'beaten' on account of their scale, accessibility, and popularity. Editors have therefore worked profitably with the Wikipedia community to add and standardise

---

25 'Oxford DNB', SoundCloud, accessed 17 November 2018, soundcloud.com/odnb.

citations to the *ODNB* or to create links from a Wikipedia entry to a relevant biography on the Oxford site. Via these links it is possible for the *ODNB* to remain if not Matthew's 'first' then at least the second 'point of biographical reference' for many students—and perhaps still to retain its status within British historiography as the principal work of curated scholarly reference. Whether this engagement will go further, extending even to the uploading of national biographical content on Wikipedia, as proposed by Kent Fitch, is open for debate and will likely be determined by the funding structures adopted by individual dictionaries.[26]

While collaboration has proved productive, equally we should not overlook those qualities that continue to distinguish national biography in an age of user-generated reference. In 2006 the radical historian Roy Rosenzweig, himself a pioneer in digital history, undertook a comparative survey of biographical content in Wikipedia and the online edition of the *American National Biography* (*ANB*). Rosenzweig concluded that on the matters of factual accuracy there was little to distinguish the entries in these two sources. However, as works of history—that is, as written texts, composed and edited by subject specialists—*ANB* content was both of markedly higher quality and of a form and length that more accurately reflected scholarly evaluations of historical significance.[27] Since the editorship of Leslie Stephen, national biographies have been compiled and evaluated as historical works, not just as encyclopedias—a process that requires close attention to and an expectation of the artistry, clarity, and judgment of good historical writing. This will come as no surprise to those responsible for compiling and editing national biographies, but it is worth remembering when promoting such works to students.

As a determinedly neutral synthesis of 'what is known', Wikipedia also resists original research or informed opinion. Modern national biographies are, by contrast, increasingly rich repositories of first-time scholarship thanks to their growing appreciation of digitised resources and research practices. As noted, this potential for new biographical writing is at the same time corralled by the editorial principles—be it noteworthiness,

---

26   Kent Fitch, 'ADB v. Wikipedia', *Biography Footnotes*, no. 16 (2016): 13–17. Similar uses for Wikipedia are proposed by academic advocates of open-access publishing. See Paul Martin Eve, *Open Access and the Humanities* (Cambridge: Cambridge University Press, 2014), ch. 4. doi.org/10.1017/CBO9781316161012.
27   Roy Rosenzweig, 'Can History Be Open Source? Wikipedia and the Future of the Past', *Journal of American History* 93, no. 1 (2006): 117–46. doi.org/10.2307/4486062, reprinted in his *Clio Wired: The Future of the Past in the Digital Age* (New York: Columbia University Press, 2010).

representativeness, or some other—that underpin and frame an individual national biography. In each case editorial curation, however defined, brings with it a degree of informed selection. This, for many, is another increasingly important attribute of modern national biography given our ability to generate and suffer from 'information overload'. As Paul Arthur has recently argued—in a comment relevant to national biographers in the round—while the purpose of the *Australian Dictionary of Biography* remains 'to remedy the paucity of knowledge of Australians in history', it is increasingly the *ADB*'s capacity to 'counteract the overabundance of information [that] is now proving most valuable for many'.[28]

Overabundance is not, it is worth remembering, a perception reserved for the digital era. In his 1896 lecture, Stephen spoke with ambivalence of the 'innumerable sources of knowledge' that had recently become available and which now threatened to overwhelm the late Victorian historian. As Stephen candidly admitted, to visit the British Museum reading room and 'look at the gigantic catalogue of printed books, and remember the huge mass of printed materials' brought forth 'a kind of nightmare sensation'.[29] In seeking 'a means of cutting through the morass of information', it was to national biography that Stephen turned as one of the 'contrivances for making it accessible'. This notion of the *DNB* as an 'indispensable guide' to useful knowledge was, he concluded, 'the end that the national dictionary is intended in the first place to correspond … Every student ought, I will not say to have it in his personal library, but at least to carry it about with him (metaphorically speaking) in his pocket'.[30] Defined in this way, 'true national biography' in the twenty-first century, as in the late nineteenth, might be understood less in terms of extent than, in the context of multiplying sources of ill-defined provenance, as a historically informed and curated collection of lives that best facilitates study of the national past. Stephen's promotion of the multivolume *DNB* as a new device for consolidating and containing information is also striking, not least given the consequences of later technological advances

---

28 Arthur, 'Biographical Dictionaries in the Digital Era', 89.
29 Stephen, 'National Biography', 9.
30 Stephen, 'National Biography', 11. Earlier intersections of information abundance and reference publishing are considered in Ann M. Blair, *Too Much to Know: Managing Scholarly Information before the Modern Age* (New Haven: Yale University Press, 2010), ch. 5. Stephen also considered excess in his 1893 essay on 'Biography' in which the national dictionary served as a 'literary condensing machine' and the national biographer as bringing 'into some sort of order … the chaos of materials which is already so vast and so rapidly accumulating', in *Men, Books, and Mountains. Essays by Leslie Stephen* (London: Hogarth Press, 1956), 131–32.

for the physical scale of historical reference. Following the *DNB*'s first appearance as a 63-volume set, publishing innovations have incrementally limited its size: from the first *Concise* edition (1903) to a 22-volume second edition (1908), and the *DNB on CD-Rom* (1996) to the desktop (2004). Now, with responsive platforms, tablets, and smartphones, Stephen's pocket-sized national biography is no longer metaphorical.

National biography as a means of studying a nation's past, broadly conceived, leads to a third and final proposal: that, as digital resources, dictionaries should be better promoted as a source for original historical research—to interpret and study the past in ways impossible without the availability of a collection online. This potential for national biographies as a starting point for research, rather than as 'mere' repositories of existing knowledge first featured in perceptive early reviews of the *Oxford DNB*. Writing in 2005, the literary scholar Alison Booth noted how digital editions offered 'almost boundless possibilities for interweaving lives, the prosopographer's dream', while Stefan Collini predicted 'generations to come making use of this vast consolidation of scholarly accuracy for purposes of their own that may be barely imaginable to us now'.[31] More recently (and once again in this volume), Melanie Nolan has drawn attention to the 'research potential' of the *ADB* online 'to study the associational patterns of Australians and their place in biographical history', a projection reiterated in Paul Arthur's identification of 'unprecedented … research opportunities … for "making and re-making" aspects of the Australian story'.[32] Nor is this a wholly modern perspective; indeed, appreciations of the national biography's utility for humanities and social scientific research have a long history. Published in 1904, Havelock Ellis's *Study of British Genius* used the *DNB* to 'obtain a comprehensive view of the men and women who have chiefly built up English civilization', while studies produced over the following two decades considered occupational choices in father/son relations, educational cohorts, and the psychology of celebrity.[33]

---

31 Booth, 'Fighting for Lives', 269; Stefan Collini, 'National Lives', in his *Common Reading: Critics, Historians, Publics* (Oxford: Oxford University Press, 2008), 315.
32 Melanie Nolan, 'From Book to Digital Culture: Redesigning the *ADB*', in Nolan and Fernon, *The ADB's Story*, 392. doi.org/10.22459/ADBS.10.2013.12; Arthur, 'Re-imagining a Nation', 110.
33 Havelock Ellis, *A Study of British Genius* (London: Hurst and Blackett, 1904), 1. Other early research publications drawing on *DNB* data include Emily Perrin, 'On the Contingency Between Occupation in the Case of Fathers and Sons', *Biometrika* 3, no. 4 (1904): 467–69. doi.org/10.2307/2331733; and Joseph Schneider, 'The Cultural Situation as a Condition for the Achievement of Fame', *American Sociological Review* 2, no. 4 (1937): 480–91. doi.org/10.2307/2084767.

The contemporary research aspirations of Booth and Collini and others are welcome and have been taken up to a degree. Publication of the *Oxford DNB* in 2004 gave rise to a series of scholarly articles, divided broadly between specialist surveys of inclusion and coverage, and studies of historical themes drawing on *Dictionary* content.[34] But it remains striking that there are not more instances of scholarly research based on the *Oxford DNB*, and on other national biographies—given the scale of the available corpus and its flexibility in a richly coded online edition, and its potential for 'big data' and 'distant reading' analyses. When it has been undertaken, research to date has tended towards studies that engage online national collections as a tool for finding and grouping. By contrast, getting students and academics to appreciate the potential of online national biography—and particularly its underlying metadata—for new forms of enquiry has proved harder than might have been expected.

There are, of course, a few exceptions, of which 'Six Degrees of Francis Bacon', designed by a collaboration of literary scholars and digital humanists from the universities of Carnegie Mellon and Georgetown, is a leading example.[35] Their project is an interactive visual reconstruction of the social network of early modern Britain, comprising 13,000 historical individuals and more than 200,000 potential relationships.[36] At the heart of 'Six Degrees' are those figures active between 1500 and 1700 with entries in the *Oxford DNB*. Starting with the *Dictionary* text, and by applying named-entity recognition software, the project created structured data

---

34 Examples include Helen Foxhall Forbes, Matthias Ammon, Elizabeth Boyle, Conan T. Doyle, Peter D. Evan, Rosa Maria Fera, Paul Gazzoli, Helen Imhoff, Anna Matheson, Sophie Rixon, and Levi Roach, 'Anglo-Saxon and Related Entries in the *Oxford Dictionary of National Biography*', *Anglo-Saxon England* 37 (2008): 183–232. doi.org/10.1017/S0263675109990202; Ruth Watts, 'Collecting Women's Lives in "National" History: Opportunities and Challenges in Writing for the *ODNB*', *Women's History Review* 19, no. 1 (2010): 109–24. doi.org/10.1080/09612020903444700; Christine MacLeod and Alessandro Nuvolari, 'The Pitfalls of Prosopography: Inventors in the *Dictionary of National Biography*', *Technology and Culture* 47, no. 4 (2006): 757–76. doi.org/10.1353/tech.2006.0240; Helen O'Neill, 'The London Library and the Intelligentsia of Victorian London', *Carlyle Studies Annual* 31 (2015): 183–215.
35 'Six Degrees of Francis Bacon', accessed 21 April 2017, www.sixdegreesoffrancisbacon.com/.
36 Christopher N. Warren, Daniel Shore, Jessica Otis, Lawrence Wang, Mike Finegold, and Cosma Shalizi, 'Six Degrees of Francis Bacon: A Statistical Method for Reconstructing Large Historical Social Networks', *Digital Humanities Quarterly* 10, no. 3 (2016), digitalhumanities.org/dhq/vol/10/3/000244/000244.html. On historians' growing interest in social networks, especially within the field of digital humanities, see Joanna Innes, '"Networks" in British History', *East Asian Journal of British History* 5 (2016): 51–72; Ruth Ahnert, 'Maps Versus Networks', in *News Networks in Early Modern Europe*, eds Noah Moxham and Joad Raymond (Leiden: Brill, 2016), 130–57. doi.org/10.1163/9789004277199_006; and Dan Edelstein, Paula Findlen, Giovanna Ceserani, Caroline Winterer, and Nicole Coleman, 'Historical Research in a Digital Age: Reflections From the Mapping the Republic of Letters Project', *American Historical Review* 122, no. 2 (2017): 400–24. doi.org/10.1093/ahr/122.2.400.

initially to extract personal names (appearing on five or more occasions) and then to infer social relationships—who knew whom—based on the incidence and relation of personal names within individual *ODNB* entries. The outcomes are probabilistic and the network visualisation of early modern social relations remains suggestive—based as it is on written (and edited) *Dictionary* texts rather than proven relations. Nonetheless, the findings are of considerable interest, not least in allowing users to identify those individuals (*nodes*) who do not themselves have entries in the *Oxford DNB*, but who are rich in social contacts (*edges*). Analysis of 'high-degree nodes without ODNB entries shows an intriguingly high representation of schoolmasters and publishers'; that is, little-known figures who, being of note in early modern intellectual life, prompt further research and possible inclusion in a national biography.[37]

It seems likely that future journeys of national biography in an age of digital history will take one of several directions. A further outcome from the 'Six Degrees' project has been to identify the estimated 450,000 discrete persons mentioned across the *Oxford DNB*'s 72 million words of text. The great majority of these names will remain just that, never meriting new research let alone a freestanding entry. At the same time, as many as 250,000 historical figures are mentioned on account of their having been close family or professional relations of full *Dictionary* subjects, and for whom the *Dictionary* holds well-structured data comprising names, life dates, occupations, and places of association. There is certainly the scope here, aided by private researchers and genealogists, to add to what is known about this 'secondary family' category of lives, with the outcomes of this research perhaps sitting alongside, and linked to, the main *Dictionary*. In doing so, we might move closer to Keith Thomas's notion of a richer, more extensive national biography, without compromising the *ODNB* as a record of historically informed noteworthiness.

---

37 Warren et al., 'Six Degrees of Francis Bacon', digitalhumanities.org/dhq/vol/10/3/000244/000244. html#p44. For further research findings from this project, see series of posts by Jessica M. Otis on 'Tales from the Raw NER Data', 'Six Degrees of Francis Bacon: Reassembling the Early Modern Social Network', accessed 23 April 2017, 6dfb.tumblr.com/tagged/tales-from-the-raw-ner-data/.

There are opportunities too for digital humanists working with current and future generations of national biographers. In collaboration with the *Oxford DNB*, Christopher Warren, co-creator of 'Six Degrees of Francis Bacon', is currently engaged in a 'distant reading' of the complete *Dictionary* corpus for what it can tell us both about historical identities and networks of association, place, and kinship, and the historiographical preoccupations of its authors and editors.[38] Those editors—conscious of the complexities and mutability of personal identities, and their many variations in multiple datasets—are also mindful of the research potential of standardised and linked data. Working again with Wikipedians, the *ODNB* has mapped the unique identifiers for the majority of its 60,000 main subjects to Wikipedia metadata (Wikidata). As the providers of equivalent data do likewise, the potential to link between biographical content in discrete resources and to related content (including personal relations, creative works, or places visited)—and at a scale that exceeds those handcrafted linking projects described earlier—becomes ever greater.[39]

Given these opportunities, it is striking that more has not been done to better integrate existing national biographies. At the first Canberra conference one of the most confident predictions, born of forthcoming 'electronic' editions, was the seemingly inevitable shift to European, imperial, or world collections of biography. On that occasion it was Matthew's assertion that 'in the course of the next fifty years we will see the gradual aggregation of our various dictionaries of national biography. We will be much blamed by our users if we do not!'[40] More than 20 years into this timetable, Matthew's words seem as, if not more, relevant given twenty-first-century interest in transnational history and its discontents. That relatively little has been achieved here owes much to the pull of the national in national biography, as well as to limited resources for expansion and the challenges of sharing content between several publishers and funding models. And yet, through closer integration of national dictionaries we hold open the possibility of forms of transnational history

---

38   Franco Moretti, *Distant Reading* (London: Verso, 2013); Christopher N. Warren, 'Historiography's Two Voices: Data Infrastructure and History at Scale in the *Oxford Dictionary of National Biography* (ODNB)', *Journal of Cultural Analytics* (November 2018). doi.org/10.31235/osf.io/rbkdh.
39   Andrew Gray, 'Introducing: Six Degrees on Wikidata', in 'Six Degrees of Francis Bacon: Reassembling the Early Modern Social Network', accessed 26 June 2017, 6dfb.tumblr.com/post/161020960651/introducing-six-degrees-on-wikidata.
40   Matthew, 'Dictionaries of National Biography', 17.

shaped, informed, and humanised by historical biography. Global history, which at first sight appears to threaten the purpose of national biography, may prove a discipline to which the genre has much to contribute.[41]

This chapter began by questioning whether contemporary national biographers should speak of their work with the same confidence as earlier generations of dictionary makers, including those who attended the first Canberra conference nearly a quarter of a century ago. To an extent, this caution is justified. Transformations in digital research and publishing present competitors and challenges unforeseeable by those who gathered to propose the future of national biography in the mid-1990s. And yet, while the nature of and potential for national biography is changing fast, the genre—ever prone to debate regarding its purpose—is far from undergoing an existential crisis.

Rather, contemporary national biography serves multiple purposes: from traditional qualities—such as quick reference, background reading, and fact-checking—to newer opportunities for tracing a single life through linked online resources, and the potential for big data research into professions, networks, and places over time. Consequently, modern national biographers are thinking more carefully about the relationship between national biography and history, and the opportunities for national biography to ensure more personal and humane perspectives on 'big' digital and global histories, and to assert the genre's relevance and research potential.

The availability of online national biography and new digital historical approaches may indeed provide new opportunities for intersecting biography and history, though greater efforts are undoubtedly required from national biographers working in collaboration and with researchers. But here, again, we should be mindful how the journeys of national biography—and of the British *Dictionary of National Biography* in

---

41   On the relationship of biography and global history, see, for example, Margot Finn, 'Anglo-Indian Lives in the Later Eighteenth and Early Nineteenth Centuries', *Journal for Eighteenth-Century Studies* 33, no. 1 (2010): 49–65. doi.org/10.1111/j.1754-0208.2009.00210.x; Miles Ogborn, *Global Lives: Britain and the World, 1500–1800* (Cambridge: Cambridge University Press, 2008); Jeffrey A. Fortin and Mark Meuwerel, eds, *Atlantic Biographies: Individuals and People in the Atlantic World* (Leiden: Brill, 2014); and Francesca Trivellato, 'Is There a Future for Italian Microhistory in the Age of Global History?', *California Italian Studies* 2, no. 1 (2011), accessed 26 June 2017, escholarship.org/uc/item/0z94n9hq. Book-length studies that elide the biographical, global, and microhistorical include Linda Colley, *The Ordeal of Elizabeth Marsh* (London: Harper Press, 2007) and Natalie Zemon Davis, *Trickster Travels: The Search for Leo Africanus* (London: Faber and Faber, 2007).

particular—are evolutionary and organic. As a result, much of what we do now, and will likely do in years to come, remains a variation of a long-standing principle. Addressing his audience in January 1896, Sidney Lee set down a mark, similar to this chapter, with his challenge to the 'English historian' to embrace 'pedestrian biography' as a source, 'for he will shortly have at his command a completed register of national biography'.[42] Later that year, Leslie Stephen also considered 'what national biography was for', and provided a response of characteristic insight. As he wrote on that occasion: 'the proper office of the national biographer is to facilitate what I may call the proper reaction between biography and history; to make each throw all possible light on the other'.[43] Though in markedly different, and now rapidly evolving, contexts, it is an end on which national biographers—past, present, and future—share common purpose.

---

42 Lee, 'National Biography', 264.
43 Stephen, 'National Biography', 15.

5
USING LIVES: THE *AUSTRALIAN DICTIONARY OF BIOGRAPHY* AND ITS RELATED CORPORA

MELANIE NOLAN

The *Australian Dictionary of Biography* (*ADB*) is one of many biographical dictionary projects developing advanced biographical functions. The *ADB* is the largest and longest-running project of national collaboration of social scientists in Australia, having started in the late 1950s. Over 4,500 authors have contributed to its 13,500 entries. In 2006 the *ADB* made the cultural journey from a printed book to an online digital research resource. Since then staff have created companion biographical websites: Obituaries Australia, which reproduces published obituaries; and People Australia, which features other biographical material such as records from *Who's Who* and out-of-copyright compendiums of biography. People Australia also acts as a Biographical Register. These companion websites now give us the technical capacity to register all deceased Australians in our websites. Since 2011 we have also begun to comprehensively index all entries, which, in turn, allows us to automatically generate visualisation tools, such as family trees.

In my history of the *ADB*, I argued that three main activities have laid at the heart of the *ADB* project since 1957: publishing books of concise entries, the Biographical Register, and indexes of entries. The *ADB*'s core activities remain well-researched concise articles, a Biographical Register, and being able to navigate around both.¹ A fundamental transformation of the project, however, has been concomitant with the digital redesign. We are now able to identify and add whole groups of 'missing persons', create bigger data and manipulate it—lump and split groups of articles for research purposes and link them to other digital resources. Prosaic matters constrain our ambitions: navigating new research infrastructure; trying to innovate while at the same time addressing our existing flaws; and honouring our national mission. In this chapter I discuss the extent to which our methodologies have been redesigned too. While we have an expanding set of digital activities, and are developing tools to generate advanced biographical research, we are still concerned with a couple of basic problems; namely, balancing representativeness and significance, and dealing with the tension between the few and the many. I will begin by discussing the practical problems: our resources, the need to observe the discipline of a dictionary, and, in light of both these matters, setting priorities.

New Research Infrastructures to Meet Research and Funding Challenges

Unlike a number of other biographical dictionary projects, the *ADB* has a requirement to use the data we have developed, especially the indexing or fielding capacity, to develop biographical practice, to answer research questions, and to disseminate our material both freely and widely. This is a relatively new imperative but it builds on earlier practice. From the outset, the *ADB* has been hosted in a university, The Australian National University (ANU). During this time it has been subject to a series of reviews.² Most recently in 2007 Professor Bob Gregory chaired a working party to investigate the *ADB*'s priorities and future directions. As a result of the Gregory Report, the *ADB* was subsumed into a newly developed National Centre of Biography (NCB) in 2008. This restructuring was premised on the view that the *ADB* should

---

1 Melanie Nolan, 'From Book to Digital Culture: Redesigning the *ADB*', in *The* ADB*'s Story*, eds Melanie Nolan and Christine Fernon (Canberra: ANU E Press, 2013), 373–93. doi.org/10.22459/ADBS.10.2013.12.
2 Melanie Nolan, '"Insufficiently Engineered": A Dictionary Designed to Stand the Test of Time?', in Nolan and Fernon, *The* ADB*'s Story*, 5–33. doi.org/10.22459/ADBS.10.2013.01.

act as a focus for, and to develop proficiency in, the study and writing of biography in Australia; to coordinate the activities of biographers throughout the ANU; to conduct public lectures, seminars, symposia and other forms of academic and scholarly exchange in the field; to attract outstanding scholars on visiting scholarships and short-term appointments; to train the next generation of biographers through postgraduate and summer school programs; to produce new volumes of the ADB up to Volume 20; to continue to develop the ADB online; and to work more closely with, and conduct joint research and exhibitions with, the national cultural institutions.[3]

The *ADB* was integrated into the School of History in 2010 to help realise these objectives. So, after half a century, the *ADB* was tasked with a broader research program of connecting its research within wider biographical practice. Since 2008 the *ADB* has progressively included a group of academic, as well as professional, staff, and it has been charged with developing a broader agenda appropriate to a biographical research centre which hosts a dictionary project.

At the same time, the *ADB* is not a commercial endeavour but has imperatives to make its work freely accessible. This derives from its being a national collaboration that ANU brings together. The *ADB* is made up of autonomous working parties in the states and territories. There are also some thematic working parties. Its design is organic and federal. Chairs and representatives of working parties are brought together in an editorial board, which advises the unit, or 'headquarters', at ANU. Membership of the editorial board has always been deliberately inclusive of a range of colleagues from across Australia. ANU has managed to construct a work of such complexity only by being a national collaboration. Remarkably, for over 50 years the editorial board—as well as working party members and contributors—have given their time freely to the project without payment.

Of course it has behoved ANU to host the *ADB* on these terms. ANU was established in 1946 with a nation-building charter charging it to encourage and provide facilities for research and postgraduate study,

---

3   Darryl Bennet, 'The Di Langmore Era, and Going Online, 2002–2008', in Nolan and Fernon, *The ADB's Story*, 190–91. doi.org/10.22459/ADBS.10.2013.06, summarising R. G. Gregory, Tom Griffiths, Ann Curthoys, Linda Boterill, and Daniel Stoljar, 'Australian Dictionary of Biography Working Party Report to the Director', Research School of Social Sciences Review (2007), NCB/ADB files, 1, ANU Archives, Canberra.

especially in relation to subjects of national importance to Australia.[4] Professor Keith Hancock took up the dictionary project in 1957 as part of his professorial leadership and to provide a rationale in terms of the history profession for ANU leadership.[5] The *ADB* has been funded under the national institutes 'block grant', now known as the National Institutes Grant. This is provided to ANU and three other higher education providers in recognition of the role they play in facilitating key activities that are of national significance.[6] Furthermore, the *ADB* was the recipient of Australian Research Council (ARC) funding, which, together with some endowment funds, underwrote its going online.[7] It received the funding to extend the *ADB*'s capacity and to render it a

> key agent in the development of a national open-information network for research in the humanities and social sciences [in Australia]. In association with national cultural institutions, the project … [was designed to] create sustainable links between information systems and … pioneer ground-breaking research capabilities. Setting new standards for accessibility and usability, it … [was expected to] be a major driver in the development of a comprehensive network of digitised resources.[8]

As a consequence of its being a national collaboration funded by university-generated resources, the *ADB* has been required to be accessible and usable. ANU is committed to disseminating the *ADB*'s enriched data and tools as widely as possible and 'free to air'. As a consequence of its being free to air, the *Dictionary*'s 9 million words, and increasingly enhanced research tools, attract over 60 million hits a year.

The *ADB*, moreover, is being enmeshed in a range of national digital infrastructures, which have been developed with public funds and, in turn, are also provided free to air: Trove and Humanities Networked

---

4   Hon. John Johnstone Dedman, MP, Minister for Post-War Reconstruction, 'Second Reading Speech—Australian National University Bill 1946', *Hansard*, 19 June 1946.
5   Melanie Nolan, 'Country and Kin Calling? Keith Hancock, the National Dictionary Collaboration, and the Promotion of Life Writing in Australia', in *Clio's Lives: Biographies and Autobiographies of Historians*, eds Doug Munro and John G. Reid (Canberra: ANU Press, 2017), 247–72. doi.org/10.22459/CL.10.2017.11.
6   The Australian National University, the Australian Maritime College (AMC), Batchelor Institute of Indigenous Tertiary Education (BIITE), and the Victorian College of the Arts at the University of Melbourne all receive funding under the National Institutes Program.
7   The *ADB* used $300,000 of its endowment together with three Australian Research Council, Linkage Infrastructure, Equipment & Facilities (LIEF) Grants to go online in 2004–06: LE0452798 in 2004; LE0560774 in 2005; and LE0668026 in 2006.
8   ARC Final Report—Linkage-Infrastructure—LE0668026, B1, 2007.

Infrastructure (HuNI). In 2009, the National Library of Australia created Trove, a free online database of Australian library resources, with a powerful search engine, which built on earlier catalogues.[9] Included in that treasure trove of resources are digitised newspapers starting from the very first to have been published in Australia. Some of the newspapers go as far as the 1990s, though most stop at 1954. More than 1,000 Australian newspapers have so far been digitised.[10] They include the major dailies, regional papers, religious newspapers, and trade papers. The *ADB* and the NLA have signed a memorandum of agreement to share resources.[11] As part of that agreement Trove is promoting *ADB* and Obituaries Australia entries on its site. Trove is the Commonwealth's fourth most heavily used website with more than 55,000 visitors a day.[12] In 2016 Trove was the recipient of funding from the Public Service Modernisation Fund to digitise material and upgrade its system.

Trove has been a fundamental part of the online development of the *ADB*. Its digitised newspapers contain hundreds of thousands of obituaries for us to mine for Obituaries Australia. So far the *ADB* has selectively added 7,500 to Obituaries Australia. We are also enriching *ADB* and Obituaries Australia entries by linking to references of the subjects in digitised newspapers. And the NCB's Digitisation Facility, which operated from 2010 to 2014, digitised over 250 out-of-copyright compendiums of biography, which will eventually be available to the public through the National Library's Trove search facility.[13]

The *ADB* is part of another national consortium, HuNI, a project aimed at 'unlocking and uniting Australia's Cultural Data'. HuNI was federally funded through the National eResearch Collaboration Tools and

---

9   Catriona Bryce, 'Trove—A Brief History', National Library of Australia, 5 November 2014, accessed 12 August 2017, www.nla.gov.au/blogs/trove/2014/11/06/trove-a-brief-history.
10 The modestly funded Australian Newspapers Digitisation Program at the National Library of Australia estimates that a total of 7,700 newspaper titles have been published in Australia: 'Australian Newspaper Digitisation Program', accessed 30 July 2018, www.nla.gov.au/content/newspaper-digitisation-program.
11 Memorandum of Understanding (MoU), contribution of data for Trove, signed by Debbie Campbell, Director, Collaborative Services, NLA (2 October 2012) and Melanie Nolan, Director, National Centre of Biography, and General Editor, Australian Dictionary of Biography, Research School of Social Sciences (26 September 2012), NCB/ADB Archives.
12 The most heavily used Australian websites are, in order: the Bureau of Meteorology, Centrelink, the Department of Human Services, and then Trove, the latter with more than 55,000 visitors a day. Australian Library and Information Association, submission in response to the Productivity Commission Data Availability and Use Issues Paper, 29 July 2016, accessed 30 July 2018, www.pc.gov.au/inquiries/completed/data-access/submissions.
13 *Biography Footnotes*, no. 14 (June 2015): 4.

Resources (NeCTAR). The project involved building a virtual laboratory or network of digitised resources, providing a single 'federated' source for information on any significant Australian, with searches in turn being directed to linked resources in Australian and overseas collections.[14] The government's investment in National Research Infrastructure for Australia has been made on the basis that it enhances the use of data, 'such as open access policies and provisions … to encourage a collaborative, sustainable approach to research data and research data infrastructure in Australia'.[15]

Both the Trove and HuNI collaborations have been developed on the basis that the *ADB* is freely accessible online in aid of national objectives. The *ADB*'s research strategy and its accessibility is overdetermined then by its foundational culture which has been reinforced by the new research infrastructure it finds itself embedded in since it went online in 2006.

Balancing Significance and Representation

Although the *ADB* has the ability to register all Australians in our websites, if it wanted to, it maintains the discipline of the dictionary to balance significance and representation. As Bill Oliver, the inaugural *Dictionary of New Zealand Biography* (*DNZB*) general editor, noted, a balance was needed between the 'unavoidable weight' of 'major figures' and 'a sizeable representation of those who were not in their lifetimes imposing presences, but who might, given the nurture of research and writing, become memorable historical presences'.[16] National biographical dictionaries are uniquely positioned to play a critical role in larger historiographical conversations, in large part because of the sheer breadth and scope of their contents, but which are short of being all-inclusive.

---

14   NeCTAR, HuNI, CI Prof Melanie Nolan and Dr Paul Arthur Deakin Humanities Networked Infrastructure (NeCTAR) Fund No. S4430304 Aries ID 17825, CIs Paul Arthur and Melanie Nolan.
15   National Research Infrastructure for Australia, *The Australian Research Data Infrastructure Strategy. The Data Revolution: Seizing the Opportunity*, 2016. See the earlier National Collaborative Research Infrastructure Strategy (NCRIS), *2011 Strategic Roadmap for Australian Research Infrastructure*.
16   W. H. Oliver, 'Introduction', in *Dictionary of New Zealand Biography*, ed. W. H. Oliver, vol. 1, *1769–1869* (Auckland: Auckland University Press, 1990), vii. This is similar to Sidney Lee's criteria: 'the probability that his (or her) career would be the subject of intelligent enquiry on the part of an appreciable number of people a generation or more hence'. Gillian Fenwick, *Women and the Dictionary of National Biography: A Guide to DNB Volumes 1885–1985 and Missing Persons* (Aldershot: Scolar Press, 1994), 21.

In this regard, the *ADB* might have an advantage over many other biographical dictionary projects. The criteria for inclusion in the *Oxford Dictionary of National Biography* from 1885 to now is 'people who have left their mark on an aspect of national life, worldwide, from the Romans to the early 21st century'.[17] Similarly, the inaugural editor of the *Dictionary of American Biography* in 1928, Allen Johnson, while noting that the word 'American' was fraught with ambiguities, followed the *Dictionary of National Biography* principle that 'only those who had made some significant contribution to American life' should be included.[18] The *ADB*, however, has always been more inclusive. In April 1960, the national committee, the predecessor of the editorial board, agreed that the *ADB* should reflect the federal and national character in its presentation, and 'give a representative picture of all strands of Australian life, observing the varying interests from state to state'.[19] The *ADB* has prided itself on the inclusion of representative as well as significant people: since 1966, prefaces to volumes have noted that 'Many of the names were obviously significant and worthy of inclusion. Others, less notable, were chosen simply as samples of the Australian experience'.[20] Douglas Pike, the inaugural general editor, noted about volume one that representatives 'of ethnic and social minorities and of a wider range of occupations, or as innovators, notorieties or eccentrics' had been included.[21] Currently, the *ADB* defines its scope as a 'blend of elitism and egalitarianism. As well as selecting individuals who have made a prominent contribution to the Australian nation for inclusion in the ADB' an attempt is made 'to reflect the rich variety of Australian life by including representatives of every social group and sphere of endeavour'.[22] Such a flexible, pragmatic, and

---

17 'Frequently Asked Questions', *Oxford Dictionary of National Biography*, accessed 8 January 2017, global.oup.com/oxforddnb/info/faqs/.
18 Allen Johnson, 'Introduction', *Dictionary of American Biography*, ed. Allen Johnson, vol. 1, *Abbe–Barrymore* (New York, Scribner, 1928), cited by Kristine J. Anderson, 'Dictionary of American Biography', in *Encyclopedia of Life Writing: Autobiographical and Biographical Forms*, ed. Margaretta Jolly, vol. 1, *A–K* (Chicago: Fitzroy Dearborn Publishers, 2001), 271–72.
19 A. Mozley, 'The Australian Dictionary of Biography', *Historical Studies: Australia and New Zealand* 9, no. 35 (1960): 313–14.
20 Douglas Pike, 'Preface', *Australian Dictionary of Biography*, ed. Douglas Pike, vol. 1, *1788–1850, A–H* (Carlton, Vic.: Melbourne University Press, 1966), v. See also Gerald Walsh, 'Recording "the Australian Experience": Hancock and the Australian Dictionary of Biography', in *Keith Hancock: The Legacies of an Historian*, ed. D. A. Low (Melbourne: Melbourne University Press, 2001), 249–68.
21 Pike, 'Preface', v.
22 'Frequently Asked Questions: Who Determines Which Subjects Merit an Entry in the ADB?' *Australian Dictionary of Biography*, accessed 8 January 2017, adb.anu.edu.au/frequently-asked-questions #determines.

wide-ranging principle means that the *ADB* can easily adapt to including groups previously underrepresented on class, race, gender, or sexuality grounds.

The *DNZB* followed the *ADB* in seeking representativeness as well as significance.[23] The former project began in 1983, with five volumes produced between 1990 and 2000. Compared to previous dictionaries, it was designed to 'provide a balance of individuals from across New Zealand society', especially to include women, Māori (non-Europeans), and other minority groups.[24] The *DNZB* had the advantage of being designed and developed later than other projects. As Lawrence Jones noted, 'democratic in its inclusion and in its method of selection determinedly bicultural and non-sexist … the project is very much the expression of the cultural aspirations of New Zealand of the 1980s and 1990s'.[25] However, as Jock Phillips discusses in his chapter in this volume, the *Dictionary* was in abeyance and its revival is minimalist.

I argue that the digital challenge presents the *ADB* with little soul-searching or need for new principles or mission in terms of conceiving new groups of people to include in the *ADB* over time. What we consider important social categories have changed over time.[26] Challenging though the new digital environment is, we can fairly easily adapt to it because of ongoing concern with both significant and representative subjects. Accumulating bigger databases and developing longitudinal processing methods to use lives is compatible with our long-standing mission and concerns with the relationship between the few and many, biography and history. The dilemma for the *ADB* is both more prosaic and democratic: the institutional and funding constraints to our ability to carry out our mission. The trick is to avoid replicating our current shortcomings in the process of developing data and allowing free public digital access to the new developments in a challenging financial environment.

---

23 Melanie Nolan, 'The Politics of Dictionaries of Biography in New Zealand', in *After the Treaty: The Settler State, Race Relations and the Exercise of Power in Colonial New Zealand*, eds Brad Patterson, Richard S. Hill, and Kathryn Patterson (Wellington: Steele Roberts Aotearoa, 2016), 40–61.
24 'How Are People Selected for Inclusion?', *Dictionary of New Zealand Biography*, accessed 30 July 2018, teara.govt.nz/en/dnzb. Contrast with 'Frequently Asked Questions: What Are the Criteria for Inclusion in the Oxford DNB?', accessed 8 January 2017, global.oup.com/oxforddnb/info/faqs/.
25 Lawrence Jones, 'Dictionary of New Zealand Biography', in *Encyclopedia of Life Writing: Autobiographical and Biographical Forms*, ed. Margaretta Jolly, vol. 1, *A–K* (Chicago: Fitzroy Dearborn Publishers, 2001), 274–75.
26 See Miles Fairburn, 'The Problem of Absent Social Categories', in Miles Fairburn, *Social History: Problems, Strategies and Methods* (Basingstoke, Hampshire: Macmillan Press, 1999), 13–38. doi.org/10.1007/978-1-349-27517-5.

The principles and process of selection may not have changed but the people making the selections have adapted and these are related. The *ADB*'s advisory groups, the editorial board and the working parties, have altered over time. There has been a periodic refreshing of its aims and, with it, membership. For instance, in 1977 it was decided that there needed to be a female member of the editorial board. Heather Radi was the first woman appointed. In 1985 the board was 'revamped', as Geoff Serle, then general editor, made clear, with some 'younger members, more women members, and people with twentieth-century interests': historians Ann Curthoys and Jill Roe together with Don Aitkin, a political scientist, were appointed.[27]

A new dynamic is implicit in recent years: the *ADB* is beginning to revise its entries, especially its range of representation, as well as highlight the research potential of the *ADB* and its companion sites; a changing editorial board membership is both facilitating and reflecting these developments. The First Three Fleets project with family tree constructions is showcasing the *ADB*'s research potential, which I deal with in the next section. In terms of revisions, the *ADB* would like to rewrite at least the earliest volumes, which were published 50 years ago when the study of Australian history was in its infancy. But where is the money to come from? We have not been able to find it so far. In the meantime, we have embarked on a program to at least ensure that all birth, death, and marriage details are correct in our earliest volumes (volumes one and two published in 1966 and 1967 respectively). This modest aim is proving to be a considerable undertaking by two former deputy general editors, Darryl Bennet and Chris Cunneen, who both joined the editorial board in 2011. As deputy general editors, they knew that most corrigenda related to the first two volumes. Two other revision projects have also been initiated by new editorial board members: an ARC-funded Indigenous Australian Dictionary of Biography project, which Shino Konishi discusses in another chapter in this collection, and a colonial women's project.

In 2015 the ANU vice chancellor, Professor Ian Young, appointed the first Indigenous members to the board, welcoming Konishi and Stephen Kinnane, as part of the ANU's commitment to its Reconciliation Action

---

27 Jill Roe, 'National Collaboration: The ADB Editorial Board and the Working Parties', in Nolan and Fernon, *The* ADB's *Story*, 278. doi.org/10.22459/ADBS.10.2013.09.

Plan.[28] In addition to Konishi and Kinnane, Odette Best, who has recently been appointed chair of the *ADB*'s all-Indigenous working party, joined the editorial board at the beginning of 2017, as did Katerina Teaiwa, the chair of the *ADB*'s new Oceania working party.[29] The new 24-member editorial board is now virtually gender-balanced. Ten years ago, women comprised less than a third of the 17-member board, but the addition of Konishi, Best, Joy Damousi, Bridget Griffen-Foley, Catherine Kevin, Lenore Layman, Carolyn Rasmussen, and Teaiwa has transformed its advisory groups. They have initiated or supported projects on convicts, colonial women, and Indigenous Australians.

We are also widening our temporal span. A number of other historians are attempting to shift the historical focus from discovery and colonisation in 1788.[30] The first two volumes of the *ADB* covered the period 1788 to 1850. The *ADB* has recently commissioned articles on Mungo Man and Mungo Woman, the cremated remains of a family who lived 42,000 years ago around the shores of Lake Mungo in what is now south-west New South Wales. The articles will not be biographical in the usual sense. They will be ground-breaking entries for the *ADB*, the first to use sources such as bones.[31] Furthermore we are able to manage these projects because we have *ADB* academic staff who specialise in Aboriginal, women's, and family history, complementing editorial board members.

For instance, Konishi (University of Western Australia), Malcolm Allbrook (ANU), and Tom Griffiths (ANU), working closely with Kinnane (University of Notre Dame of Australia and ANU), successfully applied for an ARC Discovery (Indigenous) grant of $732,704 over four years. They are all members of the *ADB* editorial board with Griffiths being its chair and Allbrook the *ADB*'s managing editor. The project will work closely with the *ADB*'s Indigenous working party, which consists of over a dozen Indigenous scholars from around Australia.

---

28   The delegation to approve the appointment of editorial board members lies with the vice chancellor of ANU. The protocol for appointing members is for the *ADB*'s general editor, in consultation with the chair of the editorial board, to come to an informal agreement over membership, and then for the general editor to formally recommend members to the vice chancellor who then extends the invitation in writing to a person to become a board member.
29   A previous Indigenous working party operated briefly from 2006 to 2009.
30   For example, Nick Brodie, *1787: The Lost Chapters of Australia's Beginning* (Melbourne: Hardie Grant, 2016).
31   Malcolm Allbrook, 'Inscribed in Stone and Bone: Writing Ancient Australian Lives', unpublished paper to the 2015 Australian Historical Association Conference, 'Foundational Histories', Sydney, 6–9 July 2015.

Similarly, membership changes in the Victorian working party (VWP) relate to the colonial women's project. There are 10 women to 565 men in volume one, and 11 women to 596 men in volume two in the *ADB* covering the period 1788–1850. Even after the missing persons volume in 2005, the number of women subjects in the *ADB* who 'flourished' before 1901 is just 161, compared to 3,895 men (and of those women subjects, 28 had shared entries or were minor entries). By contrast, nearly a quarter of those in the period currently being commissioned (those who died between 1991 and 2000) are women. The proportion of colonial women is woeful by any measure. VWP members Damousi, Rasmussen, and Patricia Grimshaw, are working with the general editor to add a further 1,500 entries about women to the pre-1900 period.

We now have the capacity to register many people and to tell their stories. There are limits nonetheless. Online users expect online information to be up to date. But we simply do not have the resources to keep updating entries when new information is discovered. We do make exceptions for prominent individuals, however. When Mary Mackillop was made the first Australian saint, an extra paragraph was added to her entry to include that information. We are addressing recent work on frontier violence and will need to consider sexual abusers and those who were abused in light of enquiries such as the recent royal commission into institutional child abuse.[32] It is difficult to come up with a 'true' national biography, more difficult than one might imagine. While big data is a catch-cry today, a dictionary is not a complete who's who, a database of Australian elites, or an expanded telephone book. The discipline of a dictionary is constrained by the evidence, selections, and the need to be concise. The *ADB* has always held that a true national biography needs to capture both significant and representative Australians' lives. It needs to provide a gallery of all the possibilities of being Australian, past and present—as far as our funding allows. The difficulty lies in the fact, however, that what is considered significant or representative changes over time, so national biographies have to be sustained, dynamic, and never-ending tasks and, at some point, revised.

One other way we are developing the relationship between significant and representative individuals is by way of families. Families do not simply favour success. To the contrary, family history includes failures and dead-

---

32 See, for instance, the ARC-funded 'Colonial Frontier Massacres in Eastern Australia 1788–', University of Newcastle, accessed 6 July 2017, c21ch.newcastle.edu.au/colonialmassacres/; Royal Commission into Institutional Responses to Child Sexual Abuse, 2013–17.

ends. Family history over time can be used to interrogate typicality and representativeness, in a way that a biography or single case sometimes does not. It allows biographers 'to deal with ordinary life'.[33] The usefulness of family histories is the ability to show relation and range. As Alison Light suggests in her recent book *Common People*, '[t]racking all the members of a family over time unsettles assumptions'.[34] The *ADB*—and its companion websites—offers us the opportunity of creating 'big data' for families and mediating systematically between individuals, families, and broader developments. All of the biographical records gathered and visualisations or family trees developed are being made freely available to the public via the NCB's websites.

Dealing with the Few and the Many

As well as being concerned with revision and changing conceptions of representativeness, then, the *ADB* is focused on adding value, by developing research tools, and ensuring that these are accessible. The innovation has the potential for making a vast array of links between people. As Philip Carter has noted:

> with projects, such as Obituaries Australia, editors … are creating opportunities to establish hitherto unknown connections from, in effect, the 'bottom up.' These, moreover, are connections that go well beyond what is possible via the existing metadata of the *ADB* or the *ODNB*—for example, by bringing people together with reference to places of shared activity other than educational institution or residence, or by tracing sets of interrelated people as they move through different stages of life, from school to university to army service, and so on.[35]

The Biographical Information Management System (BIMS), developed by the NCB, and used in all its websites, is a world first among national biographical dictionaries and gives us the ability to more fully describe and visualise the relationships between individuals, and between individuals and general 'things' such as places, properties, families,

---

33 Eric Homberger and John Charmley, 'Introduction', in *The Troubled Face of Biography*, eds Eric Homberger and John Charmley (Houndmills, Basingstoke, Hampshire: Macmillan, 1988), ix.
34 Alison Light, *Common People: The History of an English Family* (Fig Tree: London, 2014), 34.
35 Philip Carter, 'Opportunities for National Biography Online: The *Oxford Dictionary of National Biography*, 2005–2012', in Nolan and Fernon, *The ADB's Story*, 354. doi.org/10.22459/ADBS.10.2013.11.

awards, and military service.[36] One recent relational project is about place. As a pilot project, we created an online map of Ludwig Leichhardt's journey of exploration from Moreton Bay to Port Essington. Users can read his digitised journal while tracing his trip via Google maps.[37] Most importantly, indexing allows us to consider the associational lives of Australians. We are creating a comprehensive database or authority file of names of organisations, including workplaces, schools, and clubs, that will be freely available to the public and can be used by other website creators to facilitate linking between sites. Families, of course, represent another kind of associational life.

A recent project which involves indexing, family history, and associational lives is based on the first three fleets to arrive in Australia. We deliberately chose this project because one of the *ADB*'s aims is to revise its early volumes, as discussed above. Adding new records to our database relating to this period will help us when the time comes to choose new entries and because many of these people are the parents, siblings, or children of people in the *ADB*. What we are doing is adding records in Obituaries Australia and People Australia for all the people—be they convict, crew, marine, or governor—who set off from England in the first three fleets to New South Wales between 1787 and 1791. As well as mapping the fortunes of the 'fleeters', we are adding records for their children and grandchildren who were born or settled in the colonies. The purpose of the study is to understand more about family life during the colonial period of New South Wales. What kind of society was transported to the colony? What impact did convictism have on a family's long-term prospects? What led to some families succeeding over the generations while others failed? We are also interested in investigating contact history. We have already registered a few marriages and partnerings between the Indigenous and settler populations. We will be naming any Indigenous massacres and skirmishes as events and indexing people known to have participated in them. We are also listing people's participation in other events, and their alliances to various causes and people. William Bligh, for

---

36   Leonore Davidoff and Catherine Hall, *Family Fortunes: Men and Women of the English Middle Class 1780–1850* (Chicago: University of Chicago Press, 1987); Andrew Gritt, *Family History in Lancashire: Issues and Approaches* (Cambridge: Cambridge Scholars Press, 2009).
37   'Leichhardt Expedition from Moreton Bay to Port Essington, 1844–1845', *Australian Dictionary of Biography*, accessed November 2018, adb.anu.edu.au/entity/8843. See Christine Fernon, 'Exploring Australia', *Biography Footnotes*, no. 13 (July 2014): 12.

example, was a very controversial figure in early Australian history.[38] *ADB* entries and obituaries about people of his time often state whether the person was for or against Bligh, so we are now recording people's stance towards him in the related entities field.

We confined our project to the first three fleets because we had to set some parameters to make the study achievable within our resource constraints and on the advice of historical demographers, who are working with us on the project. There has also been a great deal of biographical research on the first three fleets, in particular Mollie Gillen's *The Founders of Australia: A Biographical Dictionary of the First Fleet* and Michael Flynn's *The Second Fleet: Britain's Grim Convict Armada of 1790*.[39] Begun in 1982 by Keith Johnson and Malcolm Sainty as the Australian Biographical and Genealogical Record (ABGR)—with John Wilson joining as honorary treasurer—volunteer genealogists, historians, and contractors have been transcribing, indexing, and linking archival and biographical records of Australia's penal colonies and immigration schemes in a not-for-profit project, which is now known as the Biographical Database of Australia (BDA). We estimate that we will be adding 100,000 new biographical records to our databases as a result of this project. It will be a significant national resource. As well we are creating visualisation tools, all of which are being made publicly available through our websites to analyse the data that is being collected.

Given that the *ADB* is a national project, the nation's foundational culture is an obvious subject to research. What is our method here? It is national, digital, and new, but the issues the tools are addressing are long-standing in dictionary practice. Our techniques and practices are informed by British historian Lewis Namier, whose reputation rests on his innovative use of collective biography, what is known as prosopography, in the study of the eighteenth-century parliamentary system. Namier was against the view that there was continuing and inevitable victory of progress over reaction—that is, his was an anti-Whig interpretation of history. Here we need to distinguish between Namierism, Namier's historical method, and Namier's techniques.

---

38 A. G. L. Shaw, 'Bligh, William (1754–1817)', *Australian Dictionary of Biography*, National Centre of Biography, The Australian National University, adb.anu.edu.au/biography/bligh-william-1797/text2037, published first in hardcopy 1966, accessed online 14 January 2017.

39 Mollie Gillen with appendices by Yvonne Browning, Michael Flynn, and Mollie Gillen, *The Founders of Australia: A Biographical Dictionary of the First Fleet* (Sydney: Library of Australian History, 1989); Michael Flynn, *The Second Fleet: Britain's Grim Convict Armada of 1790* (Sydney: Library of Australian History, 1993).

Namier's particular interpretations on the sociopolitical structure of England in the eighteenth century have been the subject of debate but do not need to concern us here.[40] Herbert Butterfield and others were highly critical more generally of Namier's historical method. Butterfield argued that Namier's method 'atomized everything'. In other words, it broke down complex historical events to simple social categories. Namier offered structural explanations ignoring, Butterfield argued, the fact that the structure itself is the result of human choices and could be altered by human choices. Secondly, Butterfield argued that human action was inherently more complex than Namier's view suggested. Namier did not take into account the significance and diversity of history, and the role of an individual's professed ideas, beliefs, and principles.[41] His critics accused Namier of 'taking the mind of out of history', owing to his dislike of abstract political theory and his belief that much of human behaviour is 'senseless and irrational'.[42]

Be that as it may, Namier's techniques are more enduring and applicable here. Namier's was

> a fabulously microscopic examination of the composition of the successive Houses of Commons under George III: where did the M.P.'s [Members of Parliament] come from, what was their family background, into what families did they marry, what and how much did they own, what was their education, what schools had they attended, who were their friends, what prompted one or the other to take up politics and stand for Parliament, in what ways did each one get elected?[43]

---

40   L. B. Namier, *The Structure of Politics at the Accession of George III* (London: Macmillan, 1929). See, for instance, reviews by Richard Lodge, *History* 14 (1929–1930): 269–70; D. A. Winstanley, *English Historical Review* 44, no. 176 (1929): 657–60. doi.org/10.1093/ehr/XLIV.CLXXVI.657; A. L. Cross, *Journal of Modern History* 1, no. 3 (1929): 473–77; and *Times Literary Supplement*, 31 January 1929, 69–70.
41   Herbert Butterfield, *George III and the Historians* (London: Collins, 1957), 299. See discussion, Kenneth B. McIntyre, *Herbert Butterfield: History, Providence, and Skeptical Politics* (Wilmington, DE: Intercollegiate Studies Institute, 2014).
42   John Brooke, 'Namier and Namierism', *History and Theory* 3, no. 3 (1964): 331–47. doi.org/10.2307/2504236. See also John Brooke, 'Namier, Lewis Bernstein, Sir, 1888–1960', in *Makers of Modern Culture*, ed. Justin Wintle (London and New York: Routledge, 2002), 380; and Lucy S. Sutherland, 'Sir Lewis Namier, 1888–1960', *Proceedings of the British Academy, 1961* (London: British Academy, 1963): 371–85.
43   J. L. Talmon, 'The Ordeal of Sir Lewis Namier: The Man, the Historian, the Jew', *Commentary*, 1 March 1962, 237–46, accessed 30 July 2018, www.commentarymagazine.com/articles/the-ordeal-of-sir-lewis-namier-the-man-the-historian-the-jew/.

His method was based on the study of biographies of members of parliament and their constituencies and the way they worked together, and was illuminated by careful research and psychological insight. He believed in a psychoanalytical interpretation of character, upbringing, temperament, and interests. He even went so far as to consult graphologists about the handwriting of an obscure eighteenth-century squire, and he would discuss the utterances, the lapses, and the style of a Hanoverian politician with a psychoanalyst.[44] His focus was to ask questions about families, associational lives, and motivation. It proves applicable to other periods of history.

Namier's technique, like that of Ronald Syme and other prosopographers, was to study individual lives in minute detail before attempting any wider synthesis.[45] His method was prosopography, or the use of biography to explore the connections and minutiae of networks systematically, for he 'believed that in order to understand an institution or a society "it must be broken up into its component parts, and these studied in isolation and then in relation to the whole"'.[46] There were thus two parts to his technique.[47] As Linda Colley makes clear in her 1989 biography of Namier, he was committed both to the 'intensely detailed' but also to 'penetrating analysis'.[48] She goes further and suggests he really did not do as much as he meant to on the latter. He spent the last decade of his life producing three volumes of the *History of Parliament: The House of Commons 1754–1790*, which was made up of 2,000 biographies that he wrote himself by working nine hours a day in the basement of London's Institute of Historical Research, with three full-time assistants, which

---

44   Lewis Namier, 'History—Its Subject-Matter and Tasks', *History Today* 2, issue 3 (March 1952): 157–62.
45   K. S. B. Keats-Rohan, ed., *Prosopography Approaches and Applications: A Handbook* (Oxford: P & G, 2007); Lawrence Stone, 'Prosopography', *Daedalus* 100, no. 1 (1971): 46–79; Paul Magdalino, 'Prosopography and Byzantine Identity', in *Fifty Years of Prosopography: The Later Roman Empire, Byzantium and Beyond*, ed. A. Cameron (Oxford and New York: Oxford University Press, 2003): 41–56. doi.org/10.5871/bacad/9780197262924.003.0004; Jean-Michel Carrié, 'The Contribution of Papyri to the Prosopography of the Ancient World: Evaluation and Prospects', in *Fifty Years of Prosopography: The Later Roman Empire, Byzantium and Beyond*, ed. A. Cameron (Oxford and New York, 2003), 92. doi.org/10.5871/bacad/9780197262924.003.0006.
46   W. N. Medlicott, 'Contemporary History in Biography', *Journal of Contemporary History* 7, no. 1–2 (January–April 1972): 91. doi.org/10.1177/002200947200700105, quoting E. T. Williams and Helen Palmer, eds, *Dictionary of National Biography*, supplement, *1951–1960* (Oxford: Oxford University Press, 1971).
47   See E. A. Smith, 'Sir Lewis Namier and British Eighteenth Century History', *Parliamentary Affairs* 17, no. 4 (May 1964): 465–69.
48   Linda Colley, *Lewis Namier* (London: Weidenfeld and Nicolson, 1989).

the History of Parliament Trust funded, as well as volunteers.[49] By July 1960 all but 70 of the biographies were complete, and he began to plan a magisterial survey of his investigations in which he would set down his final version of eighteenth-century Britain.[50] When he died just one month later, not a word had been written.[51]

Namier saw the possibilities of considering political motivations in terms of the schools, clubs, religious, and business and trade union affiliations of members of as well as their occupations, nationality, marriages, and kinship. In theory he was not excessively preoccupied by the individual at the expense of social collectivities and context. His thorough, indeed massive, research techniques called for cooperative work on a bigger scale than Namier managed. This is clearly core dictionary business.

For the *ADB* is also only a potential piece of social research. Like Namier, we have been concentrating on accumulation, but we have had one eye on how we use the data to write political and social history. We made a start on the analysis with elite history.[52] The biographical registers of members of the various Australian parliaments were an offshoot of the original *ADB* biographical register.[53] The series of alphabetically arranged biographies, with collective biographical introductions, relating to the

---

49 David Cannadine, 'The History of Parliament: Past, Present—and Future?', *Parliamentary History* 26, no. 3 (2007): 366–86. doi.org/10.1353/pah.2007.0052.
50 The three volumes of the *History of Parliament: The House of Commons 1754–1790* were published posthumously in 1964.
51 Colley, *Lewis Namier*, 72.
52 Richard Harrison argues that, despite being selective, the *ADB*'s coverage of elites is quite high: 58 per cent of members of the Commonwealth Parliament; 42 per cent of members of the Victorian Parliament; 29 per cent of members of the Western Australian Parliament; 55 per cent of judges of superior and intermediate courts; 83 per cent of professors at the University of Melbourne; and 55 per cent of brigadiers (and equivalent) and higher ranks in the defence force. Harrison is currently compiling a broad-based register that will include members of all Australian parliaments and the judiciary in a single source. See Richard Harrison, 'Database of Australian Elites', *Biography Footnotes*, no. 10 (2010): 8–9.
53 A. W. Martin and P. Wardle, *Members of the Legislative Assembly of New South Wales, 1856–1901*, Social Science Monograph no. 16 (Canberra: The Australian National University, 1959); G. C. Bolton and Ann Mozley, *The Western Australian Legislature, 1870–1930* (Canberra: Australian National University Press, 1961); D. B. Waterson, *A Biographical Register of the Queensland Parliament: 1860–1929* (Canberra: Australian National University Press, 1972); Kathleen Thomson and Geoffrey Serle, *A Biographical Register of the Victorian Legislature 1859–1900* (Canberra: Australian National University Press, 1972); Joan Rydon, *A Biographical Register of the Commonwealth Parliament, 1901–1972* (Canberra: Australian National University Press, 1975); Heather Radi, Peter Spearritt, and Elizabeth Hinton, *Biographical Register of the NSW Parliament, 1901–1970* (Canberra: Australian National University Press, 1979); Scott Bennett and Barbara Bennett, *Biographical Register of the Tasmanian Parliament 1851–1960* (Canberra: Australian National University Press, 1980); D. B. Waterson and John Arnold, *Biographical Register of the Queensland Parliament 1930–1980 with an Outline Atlas of Queensland Electorates 1859–1980* (Canberra: Australian National University Press, 1982).

members of the Australian legislatures became, at the time, 'essential for research in Australian political history'.[54] Allan Martin and Patience Wardle published the first, a register of members of the New South Wales Legislative Assembly, in 1959. By 1961 it had been decided to produce a continuing series of registers for each state and for the federal legislatures, entitled 'Australian Parliaments: Biographical Notes'.[55]

There has been a trickle of other collective accounts of *ADB* articles. Bernard Smith and others at the Power Institute undertook a *Biographical Dictionary of Artists and Architects* with which the *ADB* was involved although it was light on analysis.[56] More directly related to *ADB* work, *The Makers of Australian Sporting Traditions* (1993, edited by Michael McKernan) and *The Diggers* (1993, edited by Chris Coulthard-Clark [now Clark]) were special editions of selected entries from the *ADB*.[57] They were envisaged as the first of a 'proposed series of illustrated compilations from the *A.D.B.* on specialist subject areas designed to reach new readers and expose the *A.D.B.* to a wider audience', but the series never eventuated.[58] One of the most systematic analyses was R. S. Neale's attempt to measure whether social mobility in the colonies was responsible for taking some of the 'sting out of the nineteenth-century radical movement' by analysing the social origins and characteristics of executive and administrative leaders in Australia from 1788 to 1856 who had entries in the first three volumes of the *ADB*.[59]

---

54   C. N. Connolly, *Biographical Register, NSW Parliament 1850–1901* (Canberra: Australian National University Press, 1983).

55   Connolly, *Biographical Register*, ix. See also C. N. Connolly, *Biographical Register, NSW Parliament 1850–1901* (Canberra: Australian National University Press, 1983); C. N. Connolly, 'Politics, Ideology and the New South Wales Legislative Council, 1856–72' (PhD thesis, The Australian National University, 1975).

56   Nolan and Fernon, *The ADB's Story*, 31. Later development under Joan Kerr's leadership was taken further with the *Dictionary of Australian Artists Online* (*DAAO*) from 2004 and the *Design & Art Australia Online* (*DAAO*) from 2010. 'History', *Design & Art Australia Online*, accessed 30 July 2018, www.daao.org.au/history/.

57   Chris Coulthard-Clark, sel. and ed., *The Diggers: Makers of the Australian Military Tradition—Lives from the Australian Dictionary of Biography* (Carlton, Vic.: Melbourne University Press, 1993); Michael McKernan, sel. and ed., *The Makers of Australia's Sporting Traditions: Lives from the Australian Dictionary of Biography* (Carlton, Vic.: Melbourne University Press, 1993). A third, 'Colonial Australians', edited by Deirdre Morris and Geoff Browne, did not appear. Later and separately came G. P. Gilbert, ed., *Australian Naval Personalities: Lives from the Australian Dictionary of Biography* (Canberra: Sea Power Centre—Australia, 2006).

58   Research School of Social Sciences, *Annual Report* (1993), 68, box 137, Q31, Australian Dictionary of Biography Archives, The Australian National University Archives.

59   R. S. Neale, 'The Colonies and Social Mobility: Governors and Executive Councillors in Australia, 1788–1856', in *Class and Ideology in the Nineteenth Century*, ed. R. S. Neale (London: Routledge and Kegan Paul, 1972), 97–120.

Now that we are developing bigger data, we require a '[p]rolonged collaborative effort and funding on a large scale' to use the data to ask and answer significant social history questions.[60] We are not concerned merely with elites.[61] In many ways, we are merely updating our methods of relating the few and the many, rather than the basic historical inclination to do so. 'Bricks are important' pronounced historian E. H. Carr in critical comments he made about Namier's work on the biographies of eighteenth-century members of the House of Commons, 'but a pile of bricks is not a house. And should the master-builder spend his time in a brick field?', seemingly unaware that Namier always intended to do both.[62] So did the *ADB*.

Conclusion: Something Old, Something Borrowed, Something New

The wider biographical turn in history is propitious but the *ADB* needs no new principles and policies to adapt to the digital age.[63] Cost, national funding, intellectual property, and ethics are obvious major issues involved in producing innovative national biographical dictionaries in the digital age. More fundamental and less obvious are the issues of ensuring the 'shortcomings' of the existing *ADB* are not magnified as we set out to employ bigger data and use lives as well as compile them. The *ADB*'s advantages lie in its existing principles and policies. It is a national collaborative project, which is freely available online. Its selection criteria emphasises both significant and representative subjects. The greatest challenge is old-fashioned: practising what it has always preached. We are enthusiastically embracing the digital environment, as far as our resources allow, for it is facilitating our 'old-fashioned' mission.

---

60 Colley, *Lewis Namier*, 75.
61 Colley argues that Namier was 'fascinated by the sociology of elites, and by the intrigues and conflict that took place between men in high office'. He was not even much interested in how such men used the power they achieved. But he himself 'deliberately chose to concentrate on biographies of MPs who were second- or even third-rate, or who were eccentric, or rogues, or in some cases insane'. She concludes that Namier, a conservative historian, was committed in the parliamentary biographies to an 'almost Marxian analysis of society and to the delineation of change'. Colley, *Lewis Namier*, 82.
62 E. H. Carr, 'English History's Towering Outsider', *Times Literary Supplement*, 21 May 1957, 577–78.
63 Prue Chamberlayne, Joanna Bornat, and Tom Wengrab, eds, *The Turn to Biographical Method in Social Science* (London: Routledge, 2000).

PART II: THE REPRESENTATIONAL CHALLENGE

6

WHY GENDER MATTERS: FOSTERING DIVERSITY IN THE *AMERICAN NATIONAL BIOGRAPHY* WITH LESSONS LEARNED FROM *NOTABLE AMERICAN WOMEN*

SUSAN WARE

When I applied for the position of general editor of the *American National Biography* (*ANB*) in 2012, one of things I did in preparation for my interview was to investigate the coverage of women in the biographical dictionary. I asked the reference librarians at the Arthur and Elizabeth Schlesinger Library on the History of Women in America at Harvard University's Radcliffe Institute for Advanced Study what they thought the percentage would be, and their guess was somewhere between one-quarter and one-third, which was about what I expected to find in a reference work that had been published in 1999. Imagine my surprise (and dismay) when I realised that fewer than 18 per cent of the entries were of women. What was worse, I later discovered women were dramatically discriminated against in terms of the length of essays: only five women (suffragist Elizabeth Cady Stanton, modern dancer

Martha Graham, writer Eudora Welty, anthropologist Margaret Mead, and reformer Florence Kelley) rated longer essays than the Three Stooges.[1] As a feminist biographer I had my work cut out for me.

It is not just the *ANB* that shows we are still far from anything approaching gender parity when it comes to biography. One only needs to look at Wikipedia, which is notorious for its underrepresentation of women (both as subjects and contributors), for confirmation of this point.[2] Similarly, women (both as authors and subjects) struggle to get attention in the *New York Times Book Review*.[3] Examples like these confirm that any notions that women will be seamlessly integrated into the larger biographical project are patently false.

Why are we still having this conversation in the second decade of the twenty-first century when the historical profession itself has become much more diverse and its embrace of subjects much broader? There is no grand conspiracy at work, just something more prosaic and closer to home. If editors and gatekeepers do not pay close attention when choosing subjects, the situation defaults back to privileging dead white males. Worthy women are out there; they just take a little more effort and research to track down. This insight applies to any nondominant social group. If American women's contributions have been missed or undervalued, it is likely that so have those of African-Americans, Latinos, gay people, and those not living on the east coast of the United States of America, to say nothing of new categories like Trans* individuals who were not even on the biographical radar until recently.

Making biographical reference works truly representative of the nations they purport to describe therefore takes a strong commitment to moving beyond 'rounding up the usual subjects' (to quote a favourite line from the 1940s movie *Casablanca*). But it is not enough just to add women: gender must be deployed intersectionally in ways that embrace other

---

1   As of November 2016, Elizabeth Cady Stanton at 3,725 words is the longest essay on a woman, and the 82nd longest overall; Martha Graham at 3,683 words is 87th; and Eudora Welty at 3,507 words is 110th. By comparison, Ralph Waldo Emerson rates 5,002 words; William James, 5,605; Oliver Wendell Holmes, 5,779; Richard Nixon, 6,205; Andrew Carnegie, 7,135; and George Washington, 7,849. The two longest entries, each clocking in at 9,900 words, cover Franklin Delano Roosevelt and Ronald Reagan.

2   Emma Paling, 'Wikipedia's Hostility to Women', *Atlantic*, 21 October 2015, accessed 21 October 2018, www.theatlantic.com/technology/archive/2015/10/how-wikipedia-is-hostile-to-women/411619/.

3   See Andrew Kahn and Rebecca Onion, 'Is History Written About Men, by Men?', *Slate*, 6 January 2016, accessed 21 October 2018, www.slate.com/articles/news_and_politics/history/2016/01/popular_history_why_are_so_many_history_books_about_men_by_men.html.

factors and characteristics such as race, class, religion, sexual identity, age, geographical location, and occupation.[4] And this approach must reckon with the realisation that the category of 'women' is often too broad to generalise about; in fact, differences between women can be just as salient as shared experiences. The treatment of women in biographical dictionaries, therefore, is often the canary in the mineshaft of how well the reference world is dealing with broader questions of diversity.

Biographical Dictionaries and Women's History

By training I am a women's historian and feminist biographer, and that background has profoundly influenced how I approach my duties as a general editor of the *American National Biography*. And nothing gave me better preparation for taking over the *ANB* than my long association with a now-defunct biographical dictionary called *Notable American Women* (*NAW*).[5] In the fall of 1971, as I was contemplating a senior thesis on the Seneca Falls convention of 1848, my Wellesley College advisor encouraged me to go to the Schlesinger Library at Radcliffe to consult a new biographical dictionary that had just been published by Harvard University Press. Her field was not women's history (nobody's field was women's history back then), but she had contributed several entries to the volume. So one afternoon I went into Cambridge and visited the library. I can still remember holding the blue-bound volumes as I sat in the reading room taking notes. Since my thesis surveyed a network of women reformers who had been involved in early women's rights activism, such handy access to biographical information about all of my subjects was an enormous boon to my research. Little did I know then how central biography, and by extension *Notable American Women*, would be to my professional career.

The idea for a biographical dictionary specifically devoted to women dated to the mid-1950s when Harvard professor Arthur Schlesinger Sr, noting the general absence of women from standard biographical reference works

---

4   On the concept of intersectionality, see Kimberle W. Crenshaw, 'Mapping the Margins: Intersectionality, Identity Politics, and Violence against Women of Color', *Stanford Law Review* 43, no. 6 (July 1991): 1241–99. doi.org/10.2307/1229039.
5   The archival records of each instalment of *Notable American Women* are held at the Arthur and Elizabeth Schlesinger Library on the History of Women in America, Radcliffe Institute for Advanced Study, Harvard University. Unless otherwise noted, the material in this section is based on those records.

and indeed women's near invisibility in the field of history, broached the idea. Case in point: the reigning biographical reference work at the time, the *Dictionary of American Biography* (*DAB*), contained more than 15,000 essays, but a mere 709 covered women. In November 1956 the advisory board of what was then called the Radcliffe Women's Archives endorsed the idea, and the following year the governing board of Radcliffe College agreed to sponsor the project. In June 1957 the job of editor was offered to Edward T. James, who had long been associated with the *Dictionary of American Biography*, and by 1958 the distinctive name of *Notable American Women* had been chosen. In January 1959 the project was formally announced. The initial expectation was that it would take five years. In the end, it took 11.[6]

Starting any biographical reference work from scratch is a huge undertaking, and *Notable* faced several major challenges. In its initial years its staff was extremely limited: Janet Wilson James joined her husband as assistant (later associate) editor in 1961, and Paul Boyer signed on as assistant editor in 1964. With the help of various local graduate students, many of whom went on to distinguished historical careers,[7] the editors combed obituaries, monographs, archives, and a range of sources to compile a database of possible subjects, of whom 1,359 were eventually selected. Each subject then had to be paired with an author, who was often tasked with creating an essay entirely out of original sources, precisely because there was so little secondary work on women as historical subjects at the time. (The job got easier in later volumes as the field of women's history exploded.) Those essays were then edited and fact-checked, a time-consuming process.

Given that the project was conceived in the 1950s, not a period generally seen as sympathetic to feminism or women's rights, and carried out in the 1960s before the American women's movement really took off, one might expect that *Notable* could have been greeted as something of a joke (along the lines of Abigail Adams's teasing reminder to her husband John in a 1776 letter to 'Remember the Ladies' when writing the code of laws

---

6   The preface by Edward T. James and Janet Wilson James to the original three volumes, *Notable American Women: A Biographical Dictionary, 1607–1950* (Cambridge, MA: Harvard University Press, 1971), covers the history of the project.
7   For example, Helen Lefkowitz Horowitz, Robert Sklar, Pauline R. Maier, Joan Burstyn, Marc L. Pachter, and Peter Stanley all worked on the project—for a pittance, Horowitz later recalled. 'Preface', xiv.

for the new country because 'all men would be tyrants if they could')[8] or certainly not serious history. But the project garnered a surprising (at least to me, when I reviewed the files) amount of support from the leading male historians of the day, many of them associated with Harvard, not then (or for many years after) exactly a bastion of support for women or women's history.[9] What explains this? Two factors stand out. Arthur M. Schlesinger Sr's enormous stature in the field and his long-time advocacy of women as a neglected topic for historical enquiry were certainly key. The selection of Ed James as editor also was crucial. Because he was so closely associated with the *Dictionary of American Biography*, which was the leading reference work at the time and greatly revered for its scholarship and standards, the imprimatur of the *DAB* enveloped *Notable* as well.

One result was that a surprising number of senior scholars and leaders in their fields wrote for the first three volumes of *Notable*. Leon Edel wrote on writers Willa Cather and Alice James; Louis Auchincloss did novelist Edith Wharton; and Lyman Butterfield did Abigail Adams. Warner Berthoff did transcendental feminist Margaret Fuller and Donald Fleming wrote on anthropologist Ruth Benedict. Oscar Handlin provided one of the first scholarly assessments of politician Belle Moskowitz, who had figured in his biography of New York governor Al Smith. One of the longest essays (close to 7,000 words) was by noted religious historian Sydney Allstrom on Mary Baker Eddy, the founder of Christian Science. The preponderance of men's names as authors reflects the general make-up of the field of history at the time, but nevertheless there were also many women scholars and writers who contributed essays. Among them were Eleanor Flexner, Barbara Miller Solomon, Jill Ker Conway, Anne Firor Scott, Alice Felt Tyler, Ishbel Ross, Alma Lutz, and Annette Baxter. Anne Firor Scott would later earn the distinction of being the only scholar to contribute essays to all three instalments.

---

8   Abigail Adams to John Adams, 31 March 1776, 'Adams Papers Digital Edition', Massachusetts Historical Society, accessed January 2019, www.masshist.org/publications/adams-papers/index.php/view/ADMS-04-01-02-0241#sn=0.
9   Henry Steele Commager wrote, 'I am delighted that you—and Radcliffe—are going to do a biographical dictionary of American women. The *DAB* did not do very well with women' (Commager to Edward James, 3 August 1960). Carl Degler said, 'I think the Dictionary a fine idea and I want to see it prosper' (Degler to Edward James, 26 November 1960). Allan Nevins offered this endorsement: 'It is pleasant to know that work on the new biographical dictionary of American women, which is much needed, is now underway' (Nevins to Edward James, 22 August 1959). A slightly more facetious but still positive response came in from Civil War historian William Hesseltine: 'I will be happy to serve as a judge in your Miss America contest—or should I say Miss Civil War' (Hesseltine to Edward James, 4 April 1960). NAW papers, Schlesinger Library.

Fifteen years in the making, the publication of the first three volumes of *Notable American Women* in 1971 was a significant achievement. Eleanor Flexner, whose 1959 *Century of Struggle* was a pioneering survey of the suffrage movement and who served on the editorial board, later said, 'I am prouder of having had my little finger in it than of anything else I have ever worked in'.[10] Extremely well timed to capture popular interest in the burgeoning women's movement of the late 1960s and early 1970s, the 1,359 entries demonstrated a range of activities by women over the course of American history from 1607 to 1950. That starting date, of course, is something that would be done differently today: we would not start with the arrival of white people on the North American continent but would seek out indigenous peoples in the century or two before, as is consistent with current standard editorial practice on other national biographical projects. The volumes received generally respectful reviews in mainstream publications like the *New York Times Book Review* and the *Times Literary Supplement*.[11] Put simply, that so many women had contributed so much to American history was big news.

Meanwhile, the field of American women's history was springing to life. Various factors came together in the 1960s and 1970s to fuel its growth: the waves of social protest set in motion by the civil rights movement in the 1950s; the revival of feminism as a national issue, sparked in part by Betty Friedan's *The Feminine Mystique* (1963); the emergence of women's liberation separate from the New Left; and demographic changes in women's lives, including higher workforce participation and widening access to education.

An especially critical intellectual factor was the rise of social history, which looked at the lives of ordinary Americans. With its emphasis on history from the bottom up, social history upended the traditional focus on wars, presidents, and great (white) men that had prevailed up to that point. Social history also presented an opportunity to regard women's lives as no less historically important than men's. This in turn shook up the larger field of biography by introducing a different type of person as worthy of biographical treatment, a widening of scope with significant implications for the future of biographical dictionaries.

---

10 Eleanor Flexner to Edward James, 29 January 1973, NAW papers, Schlesinger Library.
11 Helen Vendler, 'Given Adversity, Women Can Do Anything', *New York Times Book Review*, 17 September 1972, 1, 18; 'First and Other Ladies', *Times Literary Supplement*, 7 July 1972, 767.

The new attention to women as biographical subjects also had the effect of focusing more attention on the interplay between public and private lives, primarily because it was impossible to understand women's public contributions without interrogating the personal choices they had made in their pursuit of professional goals. Why limit this insight to women? Since gender is a key category for understanding men's lives as well as women's, biographical writing increasingly paid attention to men's personal lives alongside their public careers, a focus that most biographical dictionaries now embrace. Feminist biography does not deserve all the credit for this shift, but it played an important role.[12]

The original volumes ended with subjects who had died by 1950, which meant that the twentieth century was barely represented (only five subjects born in that century, all of whom died young—like Amelia Earhart and Hollywood actress Carole Lombard—were included). So in 1975 Radcliffe College again rose to the challenge and announced that it would sponsor an additional volume to cover women who died between 1950 and 1975. By that point, I was in graduate school at Harvard and was quite amused later to discover in the *Notable American Women* archives that my thesis advisor, Frank Freidel, had recommended me as a promising women's history scholar who might be suitable for the post of assistant editor.[13] But I was not far enough along in my doctoral program, and I did not apply. By the time the volume appeared, I had finished my PhD and my very first two publications were entries in *Notable American Women: The Modern Period*: essays on journalist Bess Furman and diplomat Florence Jaffray Harriman.

Like the original volumes in 1971, the publication of volume four in 1980 garnered quite a lot of media attention.[14] Women's history was still a new and growing field, and many of the names included in this volume were women who had made a significant mark on twentieth-century life, with Eleanor Roosevelt being the leading example. Again, like the original volumes, this one, edited by Barbara Sicherman and Carol Hurd Green, also introduced into the historical record the lives

---

12   Susan Ware, 'Writing Women's Lives: One Historian's Perspective', *Journal of Interdisciplinary History* 40, no. 3 (2010): 413–35. doi.org/10.1162/jinh.2010.40.3.413.
13   Material on the assistant editor search is found in folder 75, *Notable American Women: The Modern Period* papers, Schlesinger Library.
14   Garry Wills, 'Women Who Defied Fate', was the lead review in the *New York Times Book Review*, 21 December 1980, BR 1. See also Jean Strouse, 'A Book of Wonder Women', *Newsweek* 96, 15 December 1980, 94.

of women whose contributions were not as well known. In this way, a biographical dictionary can serve to spark further research, an extremely valuable contribution. In fact, the explosion of interest in biographies of women, both scholarly and popular, and the publication of the various volumes of *Notable American Women*, reinforced each other in ways that were highly beneficial to the broader stories of both feminist biography and women's history.

When Barbara Sicherman finished her tenure as editor of volume four, she did not anticipate that there would be future volumes or that the project would be ongoing, but I always held out hope that the project would continue. Maybe I regretted that I had just missed the chance to edit volume four and wanted a shot at it myself. Or maybe I had been influenced by a Cambridge biography group I was asked to join in the early 1980s that included the editors of all eventual three instalments of *Notable*—Janet James, Barbara Sicherman, and myself, plus Joyce Antler and Ann Lane. In any case, I took the lead just as I left my tenured position in the history department at New York University. Once again we had the support of Radcliffe College, although with the expectation that we would have to win significant outside funding to restart the project. It took us four tries, but in 2000 we finally won a grant from the National Endowment for the Humanities (NEH) that allowed us to begin the project; a second grant two years later covered it through its completion. *Notable American Women: Completing the Twentieth Century*, which covered 483 women who died between 1 January 1976 and 31 December 1999, appeared in 2004.

The publication of the final instalment of *Notable* occurred at several interesting crossroads. The clearest in retrospect is that the project started up again just before the tipping point to digital and online resources. If we had begun just three or four years later, we would have included a provision for an online equivalent or supplement, or perhaps dispensed with print altogether and gone straight to electronic publishing. As it were, we predicted that the volumes would eventually find their way online, which they eventually did.¹⁵ Who knew how quickly things would change? At the same time, I stand by the point I made in our application to the NEH: it does not matter whether the final format is print or online; the most important thing is the meticulous scholarship that informs the project.

Few people sit down to read individual volumes straight through, but there is a very important way in which the aggregation of collective biographies allows some larger generalisations and spotting of trends. In other words, the volumes are more—much more—than just the sum of their individual parts. The editor's introductions to each of the three incarnations tried to step back and provide a synthesis of the larger trends and themes that were common to women's lives across time and at specific moments.¹⁶ This, too, reinforced the importance of biography as an important tool in the construction of women's history.

There is something else—the sheer serendipity of stumbling on a life and getting sucked into the story. As Lyman Butterfield observed about the original volumes of *Notable*, 'Reading those sketches is as seductive as eating salted peanuts: You always take a few more'.¹⁷ In the print volumes, this process happened the old-fashioned way: you opened a book to an entry, and then maybe you looked at the one before it, and maybe the

---

15   Initially the text appeared only behind a pay wall on the Women and Social Movements website run by Tom Dublin and Kitty Sklar (alexanderstreet.com/products/women-and-social-movements-United-States-1600-2000). As of 2018, the Schlesinger Library website and the Harvard University Library online catalogue offer open access to the resource. See Edward T. James, Janet Wilson James, and Paul S. Boyer, eds, *Notable American Women, 1607–1950: A Biographical Dictionary*, 3 vols (Cambridge, MA: Harvard University Press, 1971), accessed 12 December 2018, id.lib.harvard.edu/alma/990008397060203941/catalog; Barbara Sicherman and Carol Hurd Green, eds, *Notable American Women, The Modern Period: A Biographical Dictionary* (Cambridge, MA: Harvard University Press, 1980), accessed 12 December 2018, id.lib.harvard.edu/alma/990008574290203941/catalog; Susan Ware and Stacy Braukman, eds, *Notable American Women: A Biographical Dictionary, Completing the Twentieth Century* (Cambridge, MA: Harvard University Press, 2004), accessed 12 December 2018, id.lib.harvard.edu/alma/990094395030203941/catalog.
16   Janet Wilson James's introduction to the original volumes provides a historical survey of 'American women in the world of affairs' from colonial times to around 1920 that is one of the earliest attempts at synthesis for American women's history. James, James, and Boyer, *Notable American Women: 1607–1950*, xvii. Barbara Sicherman and Carol Hurd Green's introduction to volume four situates individual lives against the context of 'women's changing historical situation … and the growing specialization of modern life', singling out 'the importance of women in the New Deal' as the most interesting political story to emerge. Sicherman and Green, *Notable American Women: The Modern Period*, xviii, xxi. My introduction to the final volume contrasts the strong thread of gender consciousness with the even stronger theme of individualism that runs through the entries. Ware and Braukman, *Notable American Women: Completing the Twentieth Century*, xv.
17   Quoted in Kay Marsh, 'Speaking of …', 27 April 1972, clipping found in NAW papers, Box 19, Schlesinger Library.

one after it, or you followed the cross-references. Either way you were hooked. The same thing happens online though hyperlinks. Of course we all use Wikipedia, but nothing compares with a well-crafted essay by an individual author providing both biographical facts and an assessment of the subject's career. The genre of the short biographical format is a difficult one to master, but when it is done well, the result sings.

Unlike the attention that the publications of the first four volumes received, the publication of the fifth volume in 2004 was greeted with a giant yawn.[18] To be sure the profession continued to value the volumes, as evidenced by the wide range of scholars who wrote letters in support of our NEH applications and then contributed essays. But by 2004 the idea of a biographical dictionary on women no longer represented the radical intervention in the field it had been in 1971 or 1980. Scholars and researchers were glad to have the additional essays, but using the resource no longer caused quite the same rush of excitement and discovery that had been the stuff of the early years of women's history.

So does that mean that specialised biographical dictionaries like *NAW* are no longer necessary? In a recent survey of the field of biography, Hermione Lee declared that the recovery stage of women's biography was indeed over: 'The phase of disinterring obscure lives and of claiming new status and significance for women's stories—a process of consciousness-raising that has been described as "critical to the feminist project of transforming the public sphere"—can now be spoken about in the past tense'.[19] If women's history and women's contributions were truly integrated into the wider world of scholarship—and this holds true for other overlooked or disadvantaged groups as well—then perhaps the need for specialised volumes has become redundant. But plenty of evidence points in the other direction, as my experience taking over the *ANB* shows. A chain of links from the *Dictionary of American Biography* to *Notable American Women* to the *American National Biography* brings the story full circle.

By the 1980s the volumes of the *DAB*, which were originally published between 1926 and 1937 and whose shabby treatment of women had spurred the original *Notable* project, were perceived as out of date and not in keeping with current trends in scholarship. So under the leadership of

---

18   One exception: Bob Thompson, 'Lives That Speak Volumes: Update Series Immortalizes the Work of a Growing Group of Unforgettable Women', *Washington Post*, 21 May 2004, C 01.
19   Hermione Lee, *Biography: A Very Short Introduction* (New York: Oxford University Press, 2009), 127. doi.org/10.1093/actrade/9780199533541.001.0001.

Stanley Katz and the American Council of Learned Societies, in 1986 a new project began the painstaking process of starting over under the direction of professor John Garraty of Columbia University: recommissioning essays on subjects that were being kept, dropping some entries (colonial-era New England clergy were definitely overrepresented), and determining which new entries needed to be added. The British *Dictionary of National Biography* underwent a similar process in the early 2000s, re-emerging as the *Oxford Dictionary of National Biography* in 2004.[20] In fact, it is probably incumbent on all editors of national biographical dictionaries to admit that at some point their beloved projects will need to undergo total overhauls. Where the institutional and financial support will come from for these massive revisions remains to be seen; it is already a challenge to find the funding to keep the projects operating just on a day-to-day basis.

There is no question that the *American National Biography* represented a significant step forward from the old *DAB*. As the editors concluded, 'virtually all aspects of the past are now seen from a different perspective'.[21] The scope of the volumes significantly expanded, in part because of a conscious decision to broaden the criteria for inclusion:

> An 'American' is loosely defined as someone whose significant actions occurred during his or her residence within what is now the United States or whose life or career directly influenced the course of American history. 'Significance' includes achievement (superior accomplishment as judged by contemporaries), fame (celebrity or notoriety), or influence (effect on one's own time despite lack of public notice).[22]

Even some 'ordinary' people were included if they had left noteworthy autobiographies, diaries, or other artefacts. Unlike Wikipedia, one hard and fast rule for inclusion remained: all subjects must be safely dead.

The end result was the print publication of 24 volumes in 1999 covering more than 17,000 individuals, followed by two print supplements and then online updates ever since. The total now stands at more than 19,000

---

20 Keith Thomas, *Changing Conceptions of National Biography: The Oxford DNB in Historical Perspective* (Cambridge: Cambridge University Press, 2005). doi.org/10.1017/CBO9780511497582.
21 John Arthur Garraty and Mark C. Carnes, 'Preface', in *American National Biography*, eds John Arthur Garraty and Mark C. Carnes, vol. 1, *Aarons–Baird* (New York: Oxford University Press, 1999), xvi.
22 Garraty and Carnes, 'Preface', xvii.

articles, with hundreds of new entries being added each year. In 2012 Mark C. Carnes, who had worked alongside John Garraty for the duration of the project, stepped down as general editor and I assumed the post.

Biographical Dictionaries and the Challenge of Diversity

It is probably too strong a statement to say, 'Everything I know about editing I learned at *Notable*', but as my research editor Rob Heinrich would attest, I do preface many a sentence with the phrase, 'At *Notable* we did it this way …'. And most of the lessons I learned centred around the challenge of diversifying the content.

The first lesson was that diversity is hard work. It takes time and involves constant juggling, always making sure that the final product does not have too many individuals from one field or region at the expense of others. Since *Notable* was only composed of women, the gender balance question was already settled, although if we were still doing it, I suppose we would have some interesting discussions about how exactly to define a woman. Our main diversity struggle was over race, and I am proud that in the volume I edited one-quarter of the biographies were devoted to the lives and contributions of non-white women. Regional diversity was our second biggest challenge, since American sources tend to skew towards the eastern seaboard. Luckily we had some vocal western historians on our advisory board who made sure we took that region seriously.

Now that I have served as general editor of the *ANB* for several years, I have a better understanding of how women still have a tendency to be overlooked in modern biographical projects. If editors are not paying explicit attention to gender and other markers of diversity, the tendency is to revert to Dead White Men. They are the most obvious candidates for inclusion: they still dominate the *New York Times* obituaries by a dramatic margin; they have often received the popular recognition in their fields; they win the prizes and honours that make them visible and prominent; and they are generally easier to find authors for. Women who achieve have often had a harder route to cover (or should I say, minefield to traverse): they are often overlooked or underrepresented in the fields in which they work; they have not won the public recognition of their male peers; and they still face discrimination and prejudice that limit their options and opportunities. There is no question that there are plenty of deserving women candidates. One just has to look harder and deeper for them, and that takes time, energy, and endless networking in a wide variety of fields and professions. Editors have not always had the time or the inclination to make that extra effort. So the struggle continues.

A second lesson, to paraphrase the character Blanche DuBois in Tennessee Williams's *A Streetcar Named Desire*, was to depend on the kindness of strangers. I continue to be amazed at the professional generosity of so many of the individuals we reached out to for advice or suggestions: not just scholars, but also librarians, archivists, members of professional groups, and even fan clubs. These people knew their fields inside and out, and could help us rank a list of candidates practically off the top of their heads, whereas it might have taken our small staff days to research and rank. Very often these experts had a certain vested interest in increasing professional recognition of their field and they were willing to go the extra mile to help if the end result was in their professional interest as well. But just as often, they helped simply because we asked.

Third, we learnt to cultivate a smaller core of consultants and advisory editors for individual fields. We chose to let them have the final say on where to draw the line between who to include and who not to include, which is actually a surprisingly tricky call and one where it is crucial to be consistent across all fields. For example, a second-tier actress who does not make the cut should be roughly equal to a second-tier engineer or playwright who is left out.

Lesson four was that it is necessary to secure your funding and make sure your project has a strong institutional base that guarantees its long-term viability. In this respect, I failed with *Notable*. Radcliffe was home to the project for all three of its instalments, but it was never a close fit, especially after the college morphed into the Radcliffe Institute for Advanced Study in 1999. Nor was the Schlesinger Library, busy with its own archival collections and readers' services, able to provide an independent institutional home. And the Harvard University Press never envisioned a role in the scholarly reference world akin to the one Oxford University Press has sustained over the years. Lacking an ongoing institutional base meant that each volume of *Notable* basically started over from scratch, whereas a far better model would have been an ongoing operation, with consistency of staff and procedures and updating done on a regular basis.

Staying current is in fact the most salient lesson: if you do not have the ability to continually update and expand your coverage, any biographical reference work will gradually lose its usefulness. There are only so many times users are willing to reach for the volumes or type a name in the search engine, only to realise that the person did not die in time to make the cut-off and that there are no plans to add entries in the future. Lacking that comprehensiveness, which just compounds over time, *Notable* is gradually becoming a relic, albeit a meticulously edited and much loved one. Frankly, one of the main reasons I agreed to take the position as general editor of the *ANB* was so that I could make sure 'my' women (which is how I think of them) who had died since our cut-off date in 2000 would actually be included in a major national biographical project.

Many of these lessons are directly transferable to the task of increasing the diversity of the *ANB*, especially the importance of cultivating consultants and advisory editors who can give us strong advice in our various fields, both about candidates who have died recently and those who were missed in the original print edition. Another priority, but somewhat lower, is seeking advice about which essays need to be revised in light of new research or information.

But there are also some major differences between *Notable* and the *ANB*, starting with the strong financial and institutional support the *ANB* receives from the American Council of Learned Societies and Oxford University Press. This support allows us not only to do our day-to-day business of commissioning and editing entries, but also to engage in the kinds of research and outreach that can work towards increasing the diversity of the entries in the long term.

The biggest difference, however, is that of scale. Adding up all three volumes of *Notable American Women*, the entries total 2,284; the final volume I edited contained 483 entries. That small scale gave us the ability to literally keep a map of the entire volume on a bulletin board in our office (which now resides on the third floor of my house, the gold stars we affixed when entries were submitted slowly peeling off). And harking back to what I said about our being on the cusp between print and online publishing, we knew that we were limited to no more than 500 entries if they were all to fit in one bound volume. Even if we had wanted to expand to a second volume, our budget was already so stretched that this was never an option.

As I have found out, the *ANB* is a completely different ballgame. There is no way I could have a mental or physical map of 19,000 subjects in my head—the breadth of coverage literally boggles the mind. While there were certainly physical constraints surrounding the print publication of the original 24 volumes in 1999, especially concerning length, those constraints lessened when the publication moved online. One of the greatest advantages of online publishing is that one does not have to be quite so strict about word counts (although we are pretty strict, encouraging conciseness on the part of our authors despite their tendency to submit longer essays than we commission). More to the point, one can add more entries at any time. Unlike *Notable*, which was truly a zero-sum game (if we added an extra social worker, we probably had to take out an actress or writer), we can be more capacious in our commissioning—as long as we do not commission so many entries that they overwhelm our editorial office or our ability to pay the honoraria from our royalties. This new publishing landscape should in theory make it much easier to deal with questions of diversity: if we find somebody good from an underrepresented group, we can just pop the person in. But unfortunately it is often even easier to add an entry about some second-tier male politician who got a prominent obituary in the *New York Times*.

The question of scale also means that it is very difficult to change the overall numbers in terms of diversity in categories such as race or gender. We could add only entries on women for the next 10 or 15 years and we would barely make a dent in the overall percentage. And even I admit that if we went back and started from scratch to cover all of American history, the gender balance would still skew white and male, precisely because privileged white men for most of that time were far more prominent in the public sphere than women and other underrepresented groups. But that does not mean we cannot try to redress the imbalance to the best of our ability.

Admitting that gender matters in the selection of biographical subjects is just part of a large range of other considerations that should always be front and centre when shepherding such a large project as the *ANB*. And the items on that agenda will continue to shift and grow. For example, new research is certainly going to turn up Trans* individuals who should be considered for inclusion in the historical record. We are also paying increasing attention to transnational considerations: in our increasingly globalised world, where economic, social, political, or cultural interactions rarely stop at national boundaries, it is time to be thinking about an even broader, more expansive vision which places American citizens, male and female, in the larger global context wherever appropriate.

Looking Forward, Looking Back

As a feminist biographer I always try to tell the lives of my subjects in a way that merges the personal and the professional into an integrated whole. As I contemplated the larger cultural journey of dictionaries of national biography, I found that it was necessary to tell the story of my own association with the two dictionaries of national biography that I have been privileged to serve. Now I would like to step back and reflect more broadly on the role of national biographical dictionaries in our twenty-first-century world.

To my mind, the most important contribution of such reference works is as serious works of scholarship. The entries are chosen according to professional protocols, assigned to experts in the field, and edited to high standards of factual accuracy and interpretation in order to provide researchers and general readers with a concise, informed interpretation of a subject's life. Such a meticulously created product makes an invaluable contribution to the creation and dissemination of knowledge and the general level of public discourse. Maintaining such high standards gives our products a credibility and durability that stands out in an age where superficial information and 'fake news' increasingly dominate the digital universe.

I am generally optimistic about the future of dictionaries of national biography. The transition from print to online publication has been on the whole a fortuitous change. It allows us to add new subjects, update entries, and generally be in conversation with whatever trends or developments are happening within the historical profession, to say nothing of our fast-changing world. Of course, keeping up with this rapidly evolving landscape can also be an editor's nightmare. The challenge is especially acute when resources for humanities scholarship are not the highest priority and we struggle to maintain the viability of our undertakings with small staff and limited funding. But we persevere because we believe strongly that the work we do makes an important contribution to scholarly life and civic discussion. The subjects in our dictionaries may be dead, but their lives are in constant dialogue with the world around us.

The masthead of the *American National Biography* proudly proclaims, 'the life of a nation is told by the lives of its people',[23] and I take that responsibility very seriously. As general editor, it is up to me to provide the intellectual leadership to make sure that our entries do in fact mirror the face of an ever-changing American nation, male, female, and in all its rainbow of diversity. But no single general editor can do that alone. We are part of a larger collaborative enterprise that builds on past scholarship while boldly looking to the future. I see no need for a major rebooting of our goals and methods. We know how to do our work. There will always be new challenges on the horizon, but we never start from scratch. We draw on the proud traditions that infuse individual national biographical projects and link us all in a broader global conversation.

In that spirit, I would like to close with a letter that I received from the noted writer Julia Alvarez when I was editor of *Notable American Women*. She reminded me of the Native American legend in which an old woman touches the sky, which causes Father Sky to ask, 'How did you get to be so tall?' And the old woman replies, 'I'm standing on lots of shoulders'. Then Alvarez said to me, 'You're compiling shoulders'.[24] Her profound and poetic description perfectly captures the cultural journeys of dictionaries of national biography, past, present, and future.

---

23 Susan Ware, 'Editor's Introduction', *American National Biography Online*, accessed 20 December 2018, www.anb.org/page/editors-introduction.
24 Julia Alvarez to Susan Ware, 4 April 2001, in the possession of the author.

7

WOMEN AND THE BIOGRAPHIES OF NATIONS: *THE BIOGRAPHICAL DICTIONARY OF SCOTTISH WOMEN*

ELIZABETH EWAN

While national biographical dictionaries aim to present a nation's past, they are also very much creations of that nation's present. *The Biographical Dictionary of Scottish Women* (*The BDSW*), published in 2006, is no exception.[1] The first edition was conceived at a time (2001) when Scotland had just recently reconvened its own parliament after a hiatus of nearly 300 years, gaining new powers of self-governance. In the wake of rising self-confidence in the country's future, the writing of new national histories, as well as handbooks and companions, flourished. A revised and expanded volume, *The New Biographical Dictionary of Scottish Women* (*The New BDSW*), was commissioned in late 2015, on the heels of the 2014 independence referendum. Moreover, it was compiled in the midst of the repercussions of the 2016 Brexit vote which may yet lead to the breakup of the United Kingdom, given that a majority in Scotland voted

---

1   Elizabeth Ewan, Sue Innes, Siân Reynolds, and Rose Pipes, eds, *The Biographical Dictionary of Scottish Women: From the Earliest Times to 2004* (Edinburgh: Edinburgh University Press, 2006). A paperback edition, with corrections, was published in 2007. For more detailed discussion on the work on the first edition of the dictionary, see Sue Innes, 'Reputations and Remembering: Work on the First Biographical Dictionary of Scottish Women', *Études Écossaises* 9 (2003–4): 11–26.

to remain in the European Union. On a more positive note, the new volume has also taken shape in a country where, until recently, the leaders of all three main political parties, including the first minister, were women.

This chapter looks at the roles biographical dictionaries of women can play in biographies of nations, taking Scotland as its example. It examines the context in which *The Biographical Dictionary of Scottish Women* was developed, the influence it has had to date on Scotland's approach to its history, and the lessons learned and new issues arising during work on *The New BDSW*. At the conference on which this volume is based, it became clear that there are issues in common faced by all editors of national biographical dictionaries, but also that there are contributions that can be made to the debates by those involved in what might be considered more specialist versions of such dictionaries.[2]

In the later twentieth and early twenty-first centuries, new biographical dictionaries of women have been published in several countries, alongside national biographical dictionary projects. Among these are *The New Zealand Book of Women/Ko Kui Ma Te Kaupapa* (1991), *Women of Ireland: A Biographic Dictionary* (1996), and *Notable American Women* (1971–2004).[3] The situation in Scotland has been somewhat different. Because it has not been an independent country since the Union of the Parliaments in 1707, its most recent 'biography of the nation' has been compiled as part of the larger British work, the *Oxford Dictionary of National Biography* (*ODNB*). As a result, the work of professional historians has been directed to the *ODNB* rather than to a separate Scottish biographical dictionary. As a distinct group, Scottish women have tended to be subsumed under the larger category 'British', appearing with English, Irish, and Welsh women in *The Europa Biographical Dictionary of British Women* (1983) and its revised edition *A Historical Dictionary of British Women* (2003).[4]

---

2   See also the chapters by Ware and Konishi in this volume.
3   Charlotte Macdonald, Merimeri Penfold, and Bridget Williams, eds, *The New Zealand Book of Women/Ko Kui Ma Te Kaupapa* (Wellington: Bridget Williams Books, 1991). doi.org/10.7810/9780908912049; Kit Ó Céirín and Cyril Ó Céirín, *Women of Ireland: A Biographic Dictionary* (Kinvara: Tír Eolas, 1996); Edward T. James, Janet Wilson James, and Paul S. Boyer, eds, *Notable American Women, 1607–1950: A Biographical Dictionary*, 3 vols (Cambridge, MA: Harvard University Press, 1971); Barbara Sicherman and Carol Hurd Green, eds, *Notable American Women, The Modern Period: A Biographical Dictionary* (Cambridge, MA: Harvard University Press, 1980); Susan Ware and Stacy Braukman, eds, *Notable American Women: A Biographical Dictionary, Completing the Twentieth Century* (Cambridge, MA: Harvard University Press, 2004).
4   Anne Crawford, ed., *The Europa Biographical Dictionary of British Women* (London: Europa Publications, 1983); Cathy Hartley, ed., *A Historical Dictionary of British Women* (London and New York: Europa Publications Ltd, 2003).

The Biographical Dictionary of Scottish Women, then, is the only multi-authored twenty-first-century biographical dictionary which focuses on the lives of Scottish people over two millennia and the entire country.

No biographical dictionary is truly a neutral work of reference. By its very nature it cannot be so, as principles of selection and the areas which are emphasised in individual entries shape its perspective. Nineteenth-century national biographical dictionaries tended to develop out of nationalism, with patriotic intent, celebrating the deeds of the eminent men (and occasionally women) of the nation.[5] The British *Dictionary of National Biography*, begun in the late nineteenth century, had a wider mandate, including those who made their names abroad such as 'the early settlers of America ... [and those] of less widely acknowledged importance'.[6] Many of the dictionaries compiled in the second half of the twentieth century and the early twenty-first century, especially with the rise of social history and women's history, broadened their principles of inclusion still further to include those previously neglected or marginalised in national histories. For example, the editors of the *Dictionary of Irish Biography* (2009) commented, 'The dramatic growth in research and publication in women's history has substantially changed the agenda for a work such as this'.[7] The *Dictionary of New Zealand Biography*, first published in 1990, acknowledged the importance of including traditionally underrepresented groups, including Māori people and women.[8] Who is included as being part of the 'nation' has tended to broaden as well, with some subjects being entered in dictionaries who never set foot in the country but who are deemed to have had a connection with or influence on it.[9] The issue of 'representative' entries has also come to the fore, as some subjects have

---

5   Keith Thomas, *Changing Conceptions of National Biography: The Oxford DNB in Historical Perspective* (Cambridge: Cambridge University Press, 2005), 9–17. doi.org/10.1017/CBO9780511497582.
6   Sidney Lee, 'The *Dictionary of National Biography*. A Statistical Account', in *Dictionary of National Biography*, eds Leslie Stephen and Sidney Lee (London: Smith, Elders & Co, 1908), vol. 1, x.
7   James McGuire and James Quinn, 'Introduction', in *Dictionary of Irish Biography*, eds James McGuire and James Quinn, vol. 1, *A–Burchill* (Cambridge: Cambridge University Press, 2009), xxi.
8   W. H. Oliver 'Introduction', in *Dictionary of New Zealand Biography*, ed. W. H. Oliver, vol. 1, *1769–1869* (Wellington: Allen and Unwin, 1990), viii–ix.
9   Thomas, *Changing Conceptions of National Biography*, provides a detailed examination of these developments.

been chosen not so much for what they had done but for how they were representative examples of a particular group in society.[10] All of these issues have influenced the character of *The BDSW*.

One aspect which has distinguished biographical dictionaries of women from larger national ones has been the primary purpose of their originators. Many, if not most, early national dictionaries celebrated the achievements of the great figures in a nation's history, often drawing on a wealth of previous research. In general, women's biographical dictionaries have been motivated more by the goals of discovery and recovery, seeking out those who have been neglected in the nation's story in the past or bringing back to attention those who were well-known at earlier periods but who have disappeared from popular consciousness. For a few subjects, dictionaries have been able to draw on early research from the nineteenth and early twentieth centuries on 'women worthies', and in some countries such as the United States of America, increasing numbers of biographies of individual women, but for many if not the majority of subjects, the entry in the biographical dictionary is the first public recognition of a woman's historical standing. Nineteenth-century national biographical dictionaries often had a moral purpose as well, to inspire the citizens by examples of the great and virtuous deeds of national heroes. Women's biographical dictionaries, the product of a rather different historical age, have rarely focused on such a goal, aiming instead to demonstrate the great variety of women's lives and experiences and not shying away from illustrating the bad as well as the good. For women's and gender historians, there is also a pressing need to shatter the essentialism which is expressed in the use of 'woman' as a category.[11]

---

10 Oliver, 'Introduction', vii; Melanie Nolan, '"Insufficiently Engineered": A Dictionary to Stand the Test of Time', in *The ADB's Story*, eds Melanie Nolan and Christine Fernon (Canberra: ANU E Press, 2013), 22–23. doi.org/10.22459/ADBS.10.2013.01. Some other dictionaries, while greatly broadening their scope beyond the elite, have explicitly chosen not to include 'relatively obscure persons as representatives of "ordinary" lives"', McGuire and Quinn, 'Introduction', xxi.
11 Elizabeth Ewan, Sue Innes, Siân Reynolds, and Rose Pipes, 'Introduction', in *The Biographical Dictionary of Scottish Women: From the Earliest Times to 2004*, eds Elizabeth Ewan, Sue Innes, Siân Reynolds, and Rose Pipes (Edinburgh: Edinburgh University Press, 2006), xxvii.

7. WOMEN AND THE BIOGRAPHIES OF NATIONS

Compiling a Biographical Dictionary of Women in Scotland

Why was *The BDSW* created? As mentioned above, the creation of the Scottish Parliament in 1999 encouraged new efforts to examine the country's past as a whole, including the commissioning of a number of multivolume national histories. In what may have been serendipity or perhaps as a natural result of this new enthusiasm for the nation's history, the Scottish Women's History Network (since 2005, Women's History Scotland) held a meeting in 2001 to discuss ways forward for women's history in Scotland in the new millennium. There was a general recognition that the history of women had made very little headway in being incorporated into mainstream Scottish history, particularly the latest political history of the sort that was being encouraged by the recent political events.[12] In the 1990s the Scottish historical profession began to take stock of the state of the field, with a conference on 'The State of Scottish History' held in 1993 and a special issue of the *Scottish Historical Review* devoted to the question in 1997. In neither of these did women's history have much of a presence.[13] There were a number of reasons for this, but among them were a general lack of awareness of what research had been done and a belief that the sources for such a study were lacking.[14]

One reason why Scottish women's history had not made much impact on the historical field at large as of 2001 is that women's history and gender history had a late start in Scotland compared to many other countries. They really only developed any strength in the 1990s, although early works and calls for more began to appear in the 1980s.[15] Most works in the field of gender history postdate 2000. Moreover, to some extent Scottish women have been doubly marginalised, largely ignored in Scottish history because of their sex, and in British history because of

---

12   Esther Breitenbach, '"Curiously Rare": Scottish Women in History', *Scottish Affairs* 18 (1997): 81–94. doi.org/10.3366/scot.1997.0010.
13   For discussion of these historiographical reviews, see Jane McDermid, 'No Longer Curiously Rare, But Just Within Bounds', *Women's History Review* 20, no. 3 (2010): 389–402. doi.org/10.1080/09612025.2010.509152.
14   Ian Johnston, 'Writing Women Back into History Books', *Scotsman*, 19 January 2005, 36.
15   See discussion in Lynn Abrams, 'Introduction: Gendering the Agenda', in *Gender in Scottish History Since 1700*, eds Lynn Abrams, Eleanor Gordon, Deborah Simonton, and Eileen Janes Yeo (Edinburgh: Edinburgh University Press, 2006), 1–16. doi.org/10.3366/edinburgh/9780748617609.003.0001. For work on women's history in Scotland, see the online bibliography at WISH (Women in Scottish History): 'Bibliography of Women in Scottish History', accessed 10 December 2016, womeninscottishhistory.org/wish-database/?page=bibliography.

their nationality.[16] Scottish women, like Welsh and Irish women, have been included in the larger undifferentiated category of British women, including in works such as *A Historical Dictionary of British Women*, and are not explicitly identified as Scottish, as this is not central to the books' purposes.[17] The majority of works on British history, although not all, deal primarily with English history with only a little, if any, attention paid to Scotland, Wales, and/or Ireland. This is starting to change, however, and certainly the *Oxford Dictionary of National Biography* has led by example, giving strong coverage to Scotland, although naturally this is interwoven with the much greater number of entries on figures who lived south of the border.

Out of the 2001 meeting came a proposal for a biographical dictionary of Scottish women. Several members were at the time contributing to the *ODNB* and had already undertaken some biographical research on individual women. One of the major goals of *The BDSW* project was to demonstrate the great potential for future research by illustrating the richness of the existing sources. Even more importantly, the project sought to demonstrate how women cannot be left out of a nation's history if a true biography of a nation is to be produced. Accompanying the dictionary project was a separate volume, *Gender in Scottish History since 1700*, which examined the role that gender played in Scottish history, although due to the expertise of the contributors the book focused on the last three centuries, while the *Dictionary* itself extended back two millennia.[18]

Edinburgh University Press, which was actively encouraging and publishing the new Scottish histories emerging in the post-1999 period, was very open to the proposal and commissioned *The BDSW* in 2002. A board of four—Sue Innes, Siân Reynolds, and Elizabeth Ewan as academic editors and Rose Pipes as managing editor—was created and began work, applying for funding, establishing a board of advisors from various fields to help identify potential subjects and contributors, and

---

16 Breitenbach, 'Curiously Rare', 88–89.
17 For example, Helen Archdale or Lady Isobel Barnett in Hartley, *A Historical Dictionary of British Women*, 17, 34.
18 Lynn Abrams, Eleanor Gordon, Deborah Simonton, and Eileen Janes Yeo, eds, *Gender in Scottish History Since 1700* (Edinburgh: Edinburgh University Press, 2006). doi.org/10.3366/edinburgh/9780748617609.001.0001.

commissioning entries.[19] The press had envisioned a book of about 100 entries of roughly 1,000 words each, with about 10 to 20 authors. However, early on, as more and more suggestions for women to include were received, the decision was taken to privilege broad coverage over long entries. The final book has about 850 individual entries and includes material on about 1,000 women as there are co-subjects in a number of entries, as well as some group entries. The dictionary involved the work of 270 contributors, and ranged from the earliest times to 2004. The entries vary in length from 150 to 800 words, and each has a short bibliography of sources intended to encourage further research on the subject.

Although there was no current Scottish national project underway, there were some models from the past. As in England, Scottish biographical dictionaries can be traced back to the seventeenth century with Thomas Dempster's 1627 Latin *Historia ecclesiastica gentis Scotorum*, which included everyone identified as *Scoti* (Scots).[20] Since Scoti also meant Irish in the Middle Ages, many of the entries in Dempster's work would later find a place in the *Dictionary of Irish Biography*. Further collective biographies in the English language followed in the eighteenth century, including George Mackenzie's *The Lives and Characters of the Most Eminent Writers of the Scots Nation* (1708–22). The first national biographical dictionary, Thomas Stark's *Biographica Scotica*, appeared in 1805. The nineteenth century was dominated by the work of Robert Chambers, who published the first of many editions of *A Biographical Dictionary of Eminent Scotsmen* in 1835.[21] The most recent biographical dictionary for Scotland was produced by Rosemary Goring in 1992, with about 2,300 entries, although over 20 per cent of the subjects, including almost 40 per cent of the women, were still alive at the time of publication.[22]

---

19 Sadly, Sue Innes, the *Dictionary*'s most indefatigable and enthusiastic proponent, died in 2005 before *The BDSW* was published. Her work has been carried on by Jane Rendall who is now one of the editors of the second edition.
20 (Bologna, 1627). As can be seen by the use of the term 'ecclesiastical history', Dempster was mainly concerned with demonstrating the Scottish contributions to the Catholic Church. For the tradition in England, see Thomas, *Changing Conceptions of National Biography*, 2–11.
21 Robert Chambers, *A Biographical Dictionary of Eminent Scotsmen* (Glasgow: Blackie and Son, 1835). For more detail on the history of biographical dictionaries in Scotland, see Tristram Clarke, 'Paper Monuments: Collecting the Lives of Scots', in *The Scottish Nation: Identity and History: Essays in Honour of William Ferguson*, ed. Alexander Murdoch (Edinburgh: John Donald, 2007), 18–38.
22 Rosemary Goring, ed., *Chambers Scottish Biographical Dictionary* (London: Chambers, 1992).

Women featured only sporadically in most of these works. The 1875 revised edition of Chambers's *Biographical Dictionary of Eminent Scotsmen* was described as having 'biographies and engraved portraits of Scotsmen and *some* women' (my emphasis).[23] There were 14 women (although this was an improvement on the first edition which had nine). Recent more popular biographical projects have not done much better. In 2002 a newspaper listing of the 'Top 100 Scots' included three women.[24] A popular book, Bill Fletcher's *Book of Famous Scots* (1995), had no women at all. The author was at least aware of the issue but explained that 'there are no women in our lists' because Scottish schooling had been 'entirely concentrated on the education of male children'.[25] Women's historians may have appreciated the unintended irony of such a statement as the first conference of the Scottish Women's History Network, held the year before the book's publication, focused on the history of women's education.[26]

As in other countries, there was in Scotland a tradition of collective biographies, and these included some that focused on women. James Anderson's *The Ladies of the Covenant: Memoirs of Distinguished Female Characters, Embracing the Period of the Covenant and the Persecution* (1880) was, as its title emphasised, a celebration of female religious heroines of the seventeenth century.[27] Harry Graham covered a wider range of women in his *A Group of Scottish Women* (1908), while Eunice Murray (herself a subject in *The BDSW*) produced three collective biographies which concentrated mainly or entirely on women.[28] This tradition has continued, with a collective biography of 10 nineteenth- and twentieth-century Scottish women being published in the same year as *The BDSW* itself.[29]

---

23 Robert Chambers, *A Biographical Dictionary of Eminent Scotsmen* (London: Blackie and Son, 1875).
24 '100 Greatest Scots', *Sunday Mail* (Glasgow), 2 April 2002, 3–15.
25 Bill Fletcher, *Baxter's Book of Famous Scots Who Changed the World* (Dalkeith: Lang Syne, 1995), 15.
26 McDermid, 'No Longer Curiously Rare', 390.
27 James Anderson, *The Ladies of the Covenant: Memoirs of Distinguished Female Characters, Embracing the Period of the Covenant and the Persecution* (New York: A. C. Armstrong, 1880).
28 H. J. C. Graham, *A Group of Scottish Women* (London: Methuen, 1908); Eunice Murray, *Scottish Women of Bygone Days* (Glasgow: Gowans and Gray, 1930); *A Gallery of Scottish Women* (London and Glasgow: Gowans and Gray, 1935); *Scottish Homespun* (London: Blackie and Son, 1947). She was also the first Scottish woman to stand for parliament.
29 William W. J. Knox, *Lives of Scottish Women: Women and Scottish Society, 1800–1980* (Edinburgh: Edinburgh University Press, 2006). doi.org/10.3366/edinburgh/9780748624096.001.0001.

Most of the Scottish precursors to *The BDSW* were single-authored or privately financed. The new project with its many collaborators and ambitious reach required some funding from outside sources. A small amount came from the Scottish Government's Equality Unit, but most came from a private trust, The Strathmartine Trust, which funds projects in Scottish history. With the help of a number of other small grants as well as some initial funding from the press itself, we produced the dictionary with about £25,000 of funding (about AU$50,000). This allowed us to employ a database person and a research assistant, include 60 images, and make extremely modest payments to those contributors who were unwaged, primarily postgraduate students and independent researchers. Mostly, however, *The BDSW* was funded by the unpaid time volunteered by the many contributors, advisors, and editors. As we were working on this project between 2002 and 2005, we sometimes cast envious eyes at the *ODNB* with its multimillion pound budget.[30] As became obvious during the conference on which this volume is based, however, the *ODNB* financial situation is the exception rather than the rule for national biographical dictionaries.

While the funding situation created and continues to create obvious challenges, there are some advantages. Tom Griffiths has noted the 'foundation vision of collaborative scholarship', which underlay the beginnings of the *Australian Dictionary of Biography* (*ADB*).[31] One of the most rewarding aspects of editing *The BDSW*, and one which is undoubtedly shared with editors of other biographical dictionaries, was the joy of working in a genuinely collaborative enterprise in which every participant was thoroughly committed to the goals of the project. In one respect, this commitment was especially important on the part of our academic contributors, as the world of the Research Assessment Exercise (now the REF—Research Excellence Framework) that dominates university research in the United Kingdom is not conducive to such activities. Fortunately, three of the editors also worked outside the United Kingdom university system and were not affected by this, while the

---

30 As editors, we wish to acknowledge the generous cooperation of the *ODNB* in agreeing that some of their contributors who had written on Scottish women should be free to also contribute a shorter biography to *The BDSW*. About 400 women appear in both, although in many cases the two articles on an individual woman are written by different authors.
31 Tom Griffiths, 'Foreword', in *The ADB's Story*, eds Melanie Nolan and Christine Fernon (Canberra: ANU E Press, 2013), xi.

fourth would shortly retire. Some national biographical dictionaries have had a university home; *The BDSW* has not, being housed on computer databases and in the editors' homes.

The BDSW was published in 2006, along with its companion volume *Gender in Scottish History since 1700*, which demonstrated how considering gender could revise standard interpretations of Scottish history. It was well received and reviewed, enjoyed considerable media coverage in Scotland, was mentioned in the Scottish Parliament, and even made the top of the Blackwell/*Scotland on Sunday* List of Scottish Non-Fiction in July 2007 when the paperback edition came out.[32] It has been one of Edinburgh University Press's top-selling reference books, selling well enough that the press was interested in commissioning a revised and expanded volume. *The New Biographical Dictionary of Scottish Women* was published in autumn 2018, marking the centenary of the first grant of suffrage to women in the United Kingdom. The last decade has demonstrated some of the impact that a wide-ranging women's biographical dictionary can have in helping to shape approaches to a nation's history at various levels.

While *The BDSW* has become a useful tool for academic research, much of its influence has been at a more grassroots level and on Scotland's younger citizens. One particularly rewarding and enduring result has been the Memorials of Women project, which was initially carried out with the Girl Guides in Scotland. This involved finding memorials to women in the local community and contributing this information to a website, which is still ongoing.[33] Most memorials appear as plaques or in other forms rather than as statues—in Edinburgh there are at present more statues of animals than there are of women.[34] Of particular importance to future generations has been the interest of the Scottish education authorities. Scottish history and culture were largely neglected in primary and secondary schools for much of the twentieth century. In the last few years there has been an increasing effort to expose elementary and secondary

---

32   'The Buzz', *Scotland on Sunday*, 1 July 2007, accessed 1 August 2017, www.scotsman.com/lifestyle/culture/books/the-buzz-1-1420570.
33   'Mapping Memorials to Women in Scotland', Glasgow Women's Library and Women's History Scotland with support from Girlguiding Scotland, 2010, accessed 12 December 2016, womenofscotland.org.uk.
34   Dani Garivalli, 'Where Are the Statues of Scots Women?', *Scotsman*, 23 January 2016, accessed 1 August 2017, www.scotsman.com/news/where-are-the-statues-of-scots-women-1-4009631; Fiona Pringle, 'Campaign Launched to Salute Edinburgh's Greatest Women', *Edinburgh Evening News*, 10 April 2017, accessed 1 August 2017, www.edinburghnews.scotsman.com/our-region/edinburgh/campaign-launched-to-salute-edinburgh-s-greatest-women-1-4415842.

students to the history, languages, and literatures of their own country. Learning and Teaching Scotland commissioned a project to increase the coverage of women in its schoolteaching resources; as a result it is hoped that the history of Scottish women will be seen as a natural part of the nation's history.[35]

In other initiatives, there have been a number of Women's History walks established, and some books which have provided more detailed entries on women from a particular region.[36] *The BDSW* has also been used as a primary source of information for several public exhibitions on Scottish women, including artists and suffragists.[37] It is increasingly being used for websites, including the much-debated Wikipedia, and on sites which focus on Scottish history or women, or women in history.[38] Moreover, several of the contributors have gone on to write more extensive studies of their subjects, contributing to the expansion of women's and gender history in Scotland in the last decade. Other women have been the subjects of more extensive treatments by other writers.[39] The last stocktaking of the state of the Scottish historical field at a conference in 2010 included a paper specifically on gender.[40] The published version provided a synthesis of the last two decades of research, and highlighted 'the increasing scope and sophistication of the body of work accumulating in Scottish gender history, distinctive by its application of emergent and established theoretical approaches, notably poststructuralism, oral history, spatial history, the history of everyday life and micro-history', but also pointed out that there is still much work to be done.[41]

---

[35] The resource, Scotland's History, became less accessible when Learning and Teaching Scotland became Education Scotland in 2010, but can be found at www.sath.org.uk/edscot/www.educationscotland.gov.uk/higherscottishhistory/index-2.html, accessed 5 August 2017.

[36] Susan Bennett, Mary Byatt, Jenny Main, Anne Oliver, and Jenny Trythall, eds, *Women of Moray* (Edinburgh: Luath Press, 2014); Mary Henderson, *Dundee Women's Trail* (Dundee: Dundee Women's Trail, 2008), available at www.dundeewomenstrail.org.uk.

[37] Edinburgh, Scottish National Portrait Gallery, 'Out of the Shadows: Women of Nineteenth-Century Scotland' from 2011; Edinburgh, Scottish National Gallery of Modern Art, 'Modern Scottish Women: Painters and Sculptors 1885–1965', 2015–16.

[38] For example, 'Undiscovered Scotland', accessed 4 August 2017, www.undiscoveredscotland.co.uk/usbiography/index.html.

[39] For example, Christian Fletcher in Jimmy Powdrell Campbell, *The Scottish Crown Jewels and the Minister's Wife* (Stroud: Tempus, 2007); and Jennifer Morag Henderson, *A Life: Josephine Tey* (Dingwall: Sandstone Press, 2015).

[40] Revised versions of the papers were published in *Scottish Historical Review* 92 (Supplement) (2013) and included Katie Barclay, Tanya Cheadle, and Eleanor Gordon, 'The State of Scottish History: Gender', 83–107. doi.org/10.3366/shr.2013.0169.

[41] Barclay, Cheadle and Gordon, 'State of Scottish History: Gender', 106–7.

Towards *The New BDSW*: Issues Arising

So where are we in 2019? For the first edition, we had proposed the possibility of an online version, but the publisher was not keen on the idea. Indeed, we lost out on some potential funding sources because funding agencies thought it should be online. However, when the press decided to commission *The New BDSW* in 2015, it was for a print version only. There are a number of reasons for this, especially as funding sources get tighter for national dictionary projects. University presses are under pressure to produce profits and an open-access online dictionary will not do that in and of itself. Many English-language national biographical dictionaries, such as the *ODNB*, and the ones for the United States and for Ireland are available on a subscription basis, although those of Australia, New Zealand, Canada, and Wales are freely available. Unfortunately, the cessation of funding left the New Zealand dictionary for some years without sufficient resources to be kept up to date (the project is now being revived),[42] while the Welsh one is only minimally searchable, presumably due to funding constraints. There are expectations that an online dictionary will be updated on a regular basis, and there are costs associated with that. In our case, we have the additional potential funding issue that our dictionary is not truly national in the traditional sense, as it only covers half the population—this is discussed further below.

What does the second edition look like? The press allowed us an extra 65,000 words with which to correct errors, update original articles where more work had been done on the subject since 2004, and add new women, including those who died in the years 2004–16. The initial funding was £3,000 (AU$6,000), meaning that we were even more reliant than last time on voluntary labour, although another £1,500 (AU$3,000) was secured from other sources, including the Strathmartine Trust. As we began work, we found ourselves revisiting some of the main issues which came up in the past, and which will resonate with editors of other biographical dictionaries, as well as historians in general. Because of being restricted at this time to a print publication, however, we had to make some hard decisions which might not face those whose dictionaries are now online.

---

42   See the chapter by Phillips in this collection.

One of the most important aspects of biographical dictionaries is deciding on the principles of selection of subjects. Probably the first question which occurs to readers when looking at a dictionary of Scottish women is what defines 'Scottishness'—this issue of identity is of course addressed by all editors of biographical dictionaries, and is of central importance to nations themselves. There is a certain irony that none of the present editors was born in Scotland and only two live there, although on the other hand it does reflect an international interest in the topic.

How have the editors made decisions on who is Scottish? Many biographical dictionaries, facing less severe length restrictions, have been very inclusive. The *ADB*, for example, felt that its criteria should evolve organically.[43] Because *The BDSW* consisted in its entirety of one print volume, firm decisions about inclusion had to be made at the very beginning of the project. For example, should women of Scottish descent living elsewhere be included? Many such people would self-identify as 'Scottish'. The *ODNB* has included many diaspora figures, such as Nellie McClung, a leader of the suffrage movement in Canada, who had an Irish father and a Scottish mother, but was born and spent her whole life in Canada. What of those who have no close connection to the country? The *ADB*, for example, includes those who have never been to Australia but have had some impact on the country. The Welsh *Dictionary* has some similar entries.

To be included in *The BDSW*, a woman had to have been born in Scotland, lived in Scotland for an appreciable period, or, if only there for a short time, to have influenced some aspect of Scottish national life. Being born to Scottish parents abroad was not enough by itself. It is noticeable that in *The New BDSW* because of the pressure of new entries and the continued constraints and limits of a print edition, we have been stricter about the time in Scotland aspect—if a potential subject was born in Scotland but spent most of her life somewhere else, she was less likely to be included than was the case in the earlier edition. In the first edition we attempted to provide at least some representation of Scottish-born women in the diaspora. We have been unable to continue this in the second edition, which is a matter for regret. Possibly if *The New BDSW* eventually goes online, it could collaborate with national biographical dictionaries of other countries to link to such women or to supplement entries with more material on the Scottish part of their lives.

---

43 Nolan, "'Insufficiently Engineered'", 21–22.

Two characteristics of the first edition have not been repeated in the entries which make up the additional material in *The New BDSW*. The first edition considered it crucial to give space to 'representative' women, 'women who were not remotely famous, but whose story in some way represented areas of Scottish life or economy, where women were generally present but rarely individually recorded'.[44] This is an approach taken by many biographical dictionaries in recent years.[45] The issue of representative people can be controversial—to what extent is any one individual ever representative? Due to lack of space, we have relied on the coverage provided by entries from the first edition for representative women. We also included some mythical women in *The BDSW*, either because they were central to ideas about Scottish identity, or because they had become so well known in popular culture and history as to be considered real. All of our new subjects did actually exist.

The additional space has afforded us 181 new entries, with another 99 women as 'co-subjects' who appear within entries on other women. One of the constraints of remaining as a print edition is that final decisions had to be made about who to include before publication as others cannot be added online later. This pressure has been increased by the decision to keep all the subjects from the original volume. Some inclusion decisions reflect the publisher's concerns to make the enterprise profitable, and indeed for us to make the book attractive to potential readers, as it needs to sell. This has led to the inclusion of women who have died very recently such as the novelist Muriel Spark, author of *The Prime of Miss Jean Brodie*, or Hollywood star Deborah Kerr, as including women well known in the last 20 years helps increase the attractiveness of the dictionary to the potential buying public. This means that we have included women who have died in 2016. The *ODNB* seems to have a four-year cut-off, while the *ADB* is now working on people who died in the 1990s, although the related Obituaries Australia site provides more recent biographies.[46] The Irish and Welsh dictionaries do include people who have died in the last few years. Lack of historical perspective, though, can raise issues about how they are to be represented in a biographical dictionary, and it is likely that these entries would be considerably revised in future editions.

---

44   'Introduction', *The BDSW*, xxxi.
45   Thomas, *Changing Conceptions*, 44–45. See, for example, Macdonald, Penfold, and Williams, *The Book of New Zealand Women/Ko Kui Ma Te Kaupapa*, viii.
46   'Obituaries Australia', National Centre of Biography, The Australian National University, oa.anu.edu.au/.

Which women have been selected this time? There is no longer the urgency to make the case that women in Scotland do have a history, as the first edition contributed to this (at least we hope it has), so this has led to some changes in how decisions were made about who to include. With an additional decade of research on women in Scottish history, *The New BDSW* is focusing on enhancing a body of established work, rather than creating it from scratch.

One issue which arose from the 2006 book is that of coverage, both of regions and of certain thematic categories. It was, perhaps not surprisingly given the state of research at the time, dominated by women connected with Edinburgh, Aberdeen, and Glasgow. We were particularly sensitive to the overrepresentation of women from the capital and for this reason requested that the press not entitle the volume *The Edinburgh Biographical Dictionary of Scottish Women*. This concentration is characteristic of *The New BDSW* as well, due to population distribution and other factors, but we have made a concerted effort to bring more coverage to other geographical areas. So, for example, a Shetland poet from the Northern Isles is more likely to be included than an Edinburgh poet of similar status. Writers also tended to be overrepresented in *The BDSW*, a not uncommon problem in national biographical dictionaries, and we have been more restrictive about including them among our new entries. Efforts have been made to compensate for categories that were underrepresented previously; there is a higher proportion of sportswomen and scientists. Partly as a result of the pressure to include women who have died recently, the heavy concentration on the last two centuries has increased, as only a few earlier women have been added.

One aspect of the first edition which we felt was very important was the identification of networks of women. When a woman mentioned in one entry was the subject of another entry, an asterisk indicated this. But this has its limitations. For example, if one entry mentions a woman who is the subject of another entry, that second entry may not mention the first woman, so the connection is only indicated in one place. The number of links between women in the bodies of the entries has now been expanded considerably. But somewhat ironically, our project to bring to attention women hidden from history managed to hide still other women from readers, as co-subjects could only be found in entries on other women, not in alphabetical order. *The New BDSW* makes such women and the connections between them and other women much more visible. There is now an alphabetical list of co-subjects so that readers can see at a glance who is included among them. We have also increased the number of thematic categories in the index, breaking down a number of broad categories into more specific ones (for example, adding theology as a separate category instead of including it under the broader category of religion) so that readers can see at a glance the women in a variety of fields.

Women's Biographical Dictionaries and Biographies of Nations

Biographical dictionaries of women can raise questions which are of wider interest to nations, and historians and biographers. For example, what happens to one's sense of national identity when moving to a place if it is not necessarily one's personal choice to move there? Many of the women included in *The BDSW*, especially those from earlier periods, either moved to or moved from Scotland because of marriage, rather than due to any real desire to change their place of residence. Despite this, many of them made a success of their lives in the new culture in which they found themselves, an example that is becoming increasingly important in an ever more cosmopolitan society. In a post-Brexit United Kingdom, national biographical dictionaries can play an important role in demonstrating how nations are built up not only by those whose families have lived there for generations but also by those who have arrived more recently. The present Scottish Government, in response to the majority of Scots having voted to remain in the European Union, has been making a point of defining the country increasingly as 'European' in contrast to its southern neighbours—the stories of many of its historic women could be called upon in support of this imagining of the country.

There are also issues of personal identity, raised by the fact that married women for most of history became subsumed into the legal identity and status of their husbands. One interesting aspect of Scottish life is that until the later eighteenth century most married women retained their natal family name on marriage. The change in practice has led to some practical problems with nomenclature with which other editors will be familiar. Under what name should a woman be entered: her birth name, her married name, her second married name? It can be an awkward issue when the natural reaction of modern editors is to identify women for who they are themselves, rather than as spouses. However, that is imposing modern standards on them. The choice in the case of *The BDSW* has been to use the surname by which the woman was most commonly known, but to indicate the other names immediately afterwards. Other biographical dictionaries follow a range of practices. The *Dictionary of Canadian Biography/Dictionnaire biographique du Canada* (*DCB/DBC*), for example, uses the birth names of some women who also appear in *The BDSW* under their married ones—this is another argument for making links between different dictionaries to address such issues.

The New BDSW with its more modern focus reflects the increasing practice of women to retain their birth surnames, to the great relief of biographical dictionary editors. The question of how to treat Gaelic names with their patronymics is something that is shared with the *Dictionary of Irish Biography*.[47] Our choice to follow Gaelic practice in *The BDSW* and enter women by their forenames rather than by patronymics resulted in one reviewer criticising the first edition for not including Gaelic women, as he had not realised how they had been entered.[48] Greater cross-referencing in *The New BDSW* should address this, but, as this example indicates, nomenclature is more than a technical issue; it raises issues of historical visibility as well. Linguistic factors also raise issues of visibility and identity. Scotland is a multilingual society: should Gaelic women at the least have Gaelic-language entries, as well as or instead of English-language ones, or would such a practice obscure them further?

Women's biographical dictionaries raise the issue of what it has meant to be a woman in a society in the past and how that has changed over time. All biographical dictionaries reflect changes in society over time, of course, but the rapidly changing and still altering position of women perhaps makes such changes even more visible. With recent changes in sexual mores such as the increasing legal and cultural acceptance of gay marriage and LGBTQI* rights, old categories are being broken down. For example, one of the people included in *The New BDSW* was identified at birth as a girl, but had the birth certificate altered later in life to indicate the sex as male. Such examples raise questions about gender binaries and how to deal with those who do not fit neatly into either female or male categories, as well as the language which is used to describe them.

---

47   See chapter by O'Riordan in this volume.
48   Murray Pittock, review of *The BDSW*, *Scottish Studies Review* 7, no. 2 (Autumn 2006): 109.

From the very beginning of the project, one guiding principle was that entries should be about lives, not careers. Practitioners of feminist biography have made clear 'the complex interplay between the elements in women's lives, where the common distinction between "life" and "work" rarely fits'.[49] Moreover, women's 'careers' rarely followed a straightforward trajectory. This became especially clear to the editors when it was decided to create a thematic index for *The BDSW*. How does one categorise a subject such as Clementina Stirling Graham, impersonator, author, translator, and beekeeper, or women such as Margaret Oliphant, who turned from writing for pleasure to writing as a necessity in order to support her family? The realities of many subjects' lives break down any artificial barriers between private and public spheres, as well as expanding the definition of the political. These insights, common to feminist biography and history, can inform all entries in biographical dictionaries, not just entries on women.[50]

Finally, in terms of creating new 'biographies of nations', Scotland is in a somewhat unusual position, partly due to its constitutional position within the United Kingdom (at least at present). There has been no government or university-sponsored initiative to produce a Scottish dictionary of national biography in recent times. This is probably because the *ODNB* has done such good work in including the latest in Scottish biographical research. But if biographical dictionaries really are biographies of nations, it could be argued that Scotland should also have a more recent separate one, as does Wales. Indeed, depending on the long-term effects of Brexit, it is even possible that Scotland might become an independent nation once more.

What is the role of a women's biographical dictionary when there is no national 'biography of the nation'? Brian Harrison, the editor of the *ODNB* in its later stages, commented on how 'Serendipity and practicalities ... inevitably influenced the final selection—a point which needs to be remembered by anyone embarking upon a quantitative survey of the Dictionary's contents'.[51] However, such surveys can give a rough

---

49 Williams, Macdonald, and Penfold, *The Book of New Zealand Women/Ko Kui Ma Te Kaupapa*, vii.
50 Susan Ware, 'Writing Women's Lives: One Historian's Perspective', *Journal of Interdisciplinary History* 40, no. 3 (Winter 2010): 417, 420–22. doi.org/10.1162/jinh.2010.40.3.413; Robert Rotberg, 'Biography and Historiography: Mutual Evidentiary and Interdisciplinary Considerations', *Journal of Interdisciplinary History* 40, no. 3 (Winter 2010): 322. doi.org/10.1162/jinh.2010.40.3.305.
51 Brian Harrison, 'Introduction', in *Oxford Dictionary of National Biography*, eds H. C. G. Matthew and Brian Harrison, vol. 1, *Aaron–Amory* (Oxford: Oxford University Press, 2004), ix.

impression. National biographical dictionaries elsewhere are working hard to increase the coverage of women—at present, entries on women make up about 10 per cent of the *ODNB*, 12 per cent of the *ADB*, and 6 per cent of the *DCB/DBC*.[52] This raises an interesting possibility. With proportions such as these for one-half of the population in other national biographical dictionaries, since *The New BDSW* has about 1,000 entries covering the female half of the nation's population, to make it a truly national biographical dictionary should only require the addition of about 110 men.

---

52 The first series of the *DNB* along with the three 1901 supplements had 998 entries on women out of a total of 28,201 subjects. Gillian Fenwick, *Women and the* Dictionary of National Biography*: A Guide to* DNB *Volumes 1885–1985 and* Missing Persons (Aldershot: Scolar Press, 1994), 6. In the *ODNB* as published in 2004, there were 5,627 women among the 54,922 lives, raising the percentage of women from 3.5 per cent to 10 per cent. Harrison, 'Introduction', xvii. In the *ADB* women's entries number 1,589 out of 12,899 (12 per cent). *Australian Dictionary of Biography*, faceted browse, accessed 1 August 2017, adb.anu.edu.au/facets/. In the *DCB/DBC*, 539 out of 8,663 biographies are of women. DCB search page, accessed 1 August 2017, www.biographi.ca/en/search.php. The percentage has risen from 6 per cent in the earliest volume to 15 per cent in the volume covering 1921–30. 'Women in the Dictionary of Canadian Biography/Dictionnaire biographique du Canada (DCB/DBC)', accessed 1 August 2017, www.biographi.ca/en/theme_women.html.

8
AN INDIGENOUS AUSTRALIAN DICTIONARY OF BIOGRAPHY[1]

SHINO KONISHI

An Indigenous Australian Dictionary of Biography (IADB) is a new Australian Research Council–funded research project I am leading with Malcolm Allbrook and Tom Griffiths, which seeks to redress the long-standing underrepresentation of Aboriginal and Torres Strait Islander people within the *Australian Dictionary of Biography* (*ADB*) by doubling the number of Indigenous biographies within the online *ADB*, and producing a stand-alone published volume of Indigenous short biographies. Yet, rather than just producing 190 new entries, our aim is also to rethink how Indigenous biographies can be conceptualised, being attentive to how and why Indigenous biography is distinctive, and how Indigenous people, who have long been marginalised and excluded from the national imaginary, can now be better accommodated with the *ADB*, and hence be better incorporated within the national story.

---

1   This research was supported by the Australian Government through the Australian Research Council's Discovery Projects funding scheme (project IN170100012). The views expressed herein are those of the author and are not necessarily those of the Australian Government or Australian Research Council. An earlier version of this paper was presented as the 2017 ANU Archives Annual Lecture, and I would like to thank the Friends of the Noel Butlin Archives Centre for their generous support. I also thank Malcolm Allbrook, Odette Best, Ann Curthoys, Tom Griffiths, Natalie Harkin, Barry Judd, Steve Kinnane, Melanie Nolan, and Jaky Troy for their advice and input on earlier drafts, and Karen Fox for her thoughtful editorial guidance.

In this chapter I will trace the history of the *ADB*, highlighting how it originated during the 'great Australian silence', and the various efforts made since that time to improve its representation of Aboriginal and Torres Strait Islander lives. I will analyse the way in which Indigenous people are already portrayed in the *ADB*, in order to shed light on how such biographies have been approached in the past, and assess the net effects of the *ADB*'s cooperative structure, which involves myriad authors, guided by autonomous working parties, and overseen by an evolving editorial board. Finally, this chapter will draw inspiration from other national dictionaries of biography, suggesting a range of different directions for the IADB as we embark on this new project.

The *ADB* and the Great Australian Silence

In 1957, at an Australian history conference at The Australian National University, the idea for a national biographical dictionary project was officially endorsed.[2] This project had been driven by historian Keith Hancock, who, recognising that it did not have the financial support of other national dictionaries of biography, envisaged that the *ADB* would be a voluntary and cooperative venture. Each of the states and territories would have autonomous working parties to decide on subjects and authors, and ANU would provide the staff to edit the entries, and Melbourne University Press would publish the hardcopy volumes. In 1962 the ADB's editorial board appointed the University of Tasmania historian Douglas Pike as the first general editor.[3] By 1966, the first volume was ready for publication, comprising 575 short biographies of noteworthy figures, almost exclusively European and Anglo-Australian men, who passed away between 1788 and 1850. The next year, the second volume of 607 biographies also covering 1788 to 1850 was published. Of these original

---

2   Melanie Nolan, '"Insufficiently Engineered": A Dictionary Designed to Stand the Test of Time?', in *The ADB's Story*, eds Melanie Nolan and Christine Fernon (Canberra: ANU E Press, 2013), 5. doi.org/10.22459/ADBS.10.2013.01.

3   Nolan, '"Insufficiently Engineered"', 5–21; and Bede Nairn, 'Pike, Douglas Henry (Doug) (1908–1974)', *Australian Dictionary of Biography*, National Centre of Biography, The Australian National University, adb.anu.edu.au/biography/pike-douglas-henry-doug-818/text20359, published first in hardcopy 2002, accessed online 15 August 2017.

1,182 entries only nine were on Aboriginal individuals.[4] This degree of exclusion, which seems unthinkable today, was commonplace at the time, and typified what the esteemed anthropologist William Stanner described as the 'great Australian silence'.

In his 1968 Boyer lectures entitled *After the Dreaming*, Stanner discussed his 'deep uneasiness about the past, present, and future place of Aborigines in Australian society'.[5] For his second lecture, Stanner consulted a wide array of books on Australia's history and current affairs, the 'sort of books that probably expressed well enough, and may even have helped to form, the outlook of socially conscious people between say, 1939 and 1955'. Disappointed by the disregard shown Aboriginal people and issues, he turned to later works and found that 'the lack of interest ran on even into the 1960s'. From this study, Stanner concluded that:

> A partial survey is enough to let me make the point that inattention on such a scale cannot possibly be explained by absent-mindedness. It is a structural matter, a view from a window which has been carefully placed to exclude a whole quadrant of the landscape. What may well have begun as a simple forgetting of other possible views turned into habit and over time into something like a cult of forgetfulness practised on a national scale. We have been able for so long to disremember the Aborigines that we are now hard put to keep them in mind even when we most want to do so.[6]

Thus, the colonial myth, stemming from the early nineteenth century, that Aboriginal people would simply 'melt away' and play no role in Australia's future, had ensured that they were excised from the narrative of the nation's past. Stanner deeply lamented this 'great Australian silence', and proposed the kinds of histories which he thought could break the silence:

> The history I would like to see written would bring into the main flow of its narrative the life and times of men like David Unaipon, Albert Namatjira, Robert Tudawali, Durmagam, Douglas Nichols,

---

4   See 'Table 1.2 Representation of Women and Aboriginal Subjects in the ADB', in Nolan, '"Insufficiently Engineered"', 26. Note that there were actually five Aboriginal people in volume one, not four as they list.
5   Jeremy Beckett and Melinda Hinkson, '"Going More than Half Way to Meet Them": On the Life and Legacy of WEH Stanner', in *An Appreciation of Difference: WEH Stanner and Aboriginal Australia*, eds Jeremy Beckett and Melinda Hinkson (Canberra: Aboriginal Studies Press, 2008), 2.
6   W. E. H. Stanner, *The Dreaming and Other Essays* (Melbourne: Schwartz Publishing, 2011) (Ebook), accessed 14 March 2017.

Daniel Dexter and many others. Not to scrape up significance for them but because they typify so vividly the other side of a story over which the great Australian silence reigns.[7]

Significantly, these histories were all biographical in nature, suggesting that for Stanner, it was through the lives of individuals that Indigenous history could be brought to life. He concluded his second lecture predicting that this 'silence' would not 'survive the research that is now in course', as 'our universities and research institutions are full of young people who are working actively to end it'.[8] He was right, as the 1970s saw the emergence of Aboriginal history as a distinct field, led by anthropologists, archaeologists, and historians such as Diane Barwick, Jeremy Beckett, Charles Rowley, Sylvia Hallam, John Mulvaney, Peter Corris, Peter Read, Bob Reece, Henry Reynolds, and Lyndall Ryan, as well as the members of Aboriginal History Inc., who established the eponymous journal in 1977, nine years after Stanner's Boyer lectures.[9]

Yet, despite this flourishing scholarship on Aboriginal history, the great Australian silence that Stanner observed from the 1930s through to the 1960s continued to resound within the *ADB* throughout the 1970s and 1980s. Bede Nairn and Geoff Serle were the general editors during this period, and during their tenure implemented some changes to the *ADB*'s processes—most significantly, Serle appointed more editorial staff which allowed an increase in the scale of the volumes and in 1975 he contacted the Refractory Girl feminist collective for advice on how to improve the representation of women in the *ADB*.[10] Yet they did not seem to explicitly

---

7   Stanner, *The Dreaming and Other Essays*. Note that most of these individuals were eventually included in the *ADB* except for Durmagam and Daniel Dexter: Unaipon in 1990, Namatjira in 2000, Tudawali in 2002, and Nicholls in 2012. See Philip Jones, 'Unaipon, David (1872–1967)', *Australian Dictionary of Biography*, National Centre of Biography, The Australian National University, adb.anu.edu.au/biography/unaipon-david-8898/text15631, published first in hardcopy 1990, accessed online 18 July 2017; Sylvia Kleinert, 'Namatjira, Albert (Elea) (1902–1959)', *Australian Dictionary of Biography*, National Centre of Biography, The Australian National University, adb.anu.edu.au/biography/namatjira-albert-elea-11217/text19999, published first in hardcopy 2000, accessed online 18 July 2017; Peter Forrest, 'Tudawali, Robert (1929–1967)', *Australian Dictionary of Biography*, National Centre of Biography, The Australian National University, adb.anu.edu.au/biography/tudawali-robert-11889/text21293, published first in hardcopy 2002, accessed online 18 July 2017; and Richard Broome, 'Nicholls, Sir Douglas Ralph (Doug) (1906–1988)', *Australian Dictionary of Biography*, National Centre of Biography, The Australian National University, adb.anu.edu.au/biography/nicholls-sir-douglas-ralph-doug-14920/text26109, published first in hardcopy 2012, accessed online 18 July 2017.
8   Stanner, *The Dreaming and Other Essays*.
9   See Bain Attwood, 'The Founding of *Aboriginal History* and the Forming of Aboriginal History', *Aboriginal History* 36 (2012): 119–71. doi.org/10.22459/AH.36.2013.06.
10 Nolan, '"Insufficiently Engineered"', 25.

engage with the new Aboriginal historiography. This was perhaps partly due to the fact that, as Chris Cuneen observed, both Nairn and Serle were traditional 'blokey' men who were both 'criticised by the "New Left" historians of the 1970s',[11] and also due to the fact that Aboriginal history was largely seen as a separate field from Australian history at this time. The 10 volumes (numbers 3–12) published between 1969 and 1990, each containing at least 526 entries, had at most five biographies of Aboriginal people per volume. In fact, the 12 volumes marking the lives of 7,851 significant Australian individuals who passed away between 1788 and 1940 contained a mere 32 Aboriginal and Torres Strait Islander people in total (0.4 per cent). It was not until 1996 that the first *ADB* volume which approached parity with the present-day Aboriginal and Torres Strait Islander proportion of the population was published (2.6 per cent).[12]

Finally, in the mid-1990s and early 2000s, the *ADB* achieved a more representative 2.35 per cent of entries on Indigenous people for volumes 13 to 16, covering individuals who had passed away between 1940 and 1980. This improvement was not just a consequence of the *ADB* catching up to the historiographical shift that began in the 1970s, and was then fuelled by the political assertion, in the lead up to the Bicentenary celebrations of 1988, that 'White Australia has a Black history'. As Aboriginal history became more mainstream, as evident from its incorporation into school and university curricula, the editorial board also recognised that the *ADB* needed to undergo political changes, and acknowledge that many Australian groups were underrepresented in the *ADB*, primarily women, and people from working class and non-Anglo backgrounds. As Melanie Nolan outlines in her history of the *Dictionary*, the 1980s saw critics from within the *ADB* echo reviewers' complaints about its lack of representation: editorial board members Ann Curthoys and Heather Radi respectively complained about the overrepresentation of military personnel and the underrepresentation of women (the volumes published up to 1988 each had between 1.74 and 12.89 per cent female subjects).[13] Such criticisms led to editorial board members Beverley Kingston, Stephen Garton, and Jill Roe's successful bid in 2001 to fund *A Supplementary Volume of the Australian Dictionary of Biography, 1770–1980*.[14] With Chris Cuneen

---

11 Chris Cuneen, 'Bede Nairn and Geoffrey Serle: A Fine Partnership, 1973–1987', in Nolan and Fernon, *The ADB's Story*, 138. doi.org/10.22459/ADBS.10.2013.04.
12 Table 1.2 in Nolan, '"Insufficiently Engineered"', 26.
13 Nolan, '"Insufficiently Engineered"', 24–25.
14 Stephen Garton, 'Staff Profile', University of Sydney, accessed 15 July 2017, sydney.edu.au/arts/history/staff/profiles/stephen.garton.php.

as managing editor, they produced the *ADB*'s 2005 'missing persons' supplementary volume, comprising 565 new biographies, including 167 on women and 50 on Indigenous people (8.9 per cent). However, the result of this initiative was not unanimously praised; for example, some critics argued that in attempting to include more women the volume merely proliferated entries on 'community and charity workers', nurses in particular, amplifying how the *ADB* already represented Australian women's experience.[15]

During the same period, there were increasing calls to not only include more Indigenous people in the *ADB*, but also to change the *ADB*'s editorial protocols to better accommodate Aboriginal and Torres Strait Islander interests. Frances Peters-Little, a Kamilaroi and Uralarai film-maker and historian, and Gordon Briscoe, a Marduntjara historian, criticised the *ADB* for 'failing to identify and include enough indigenous subjects', and for not adapting its editorial processes to acknowledge 'Indigenous conventions of narration and remembrance'.[16] Briscoe also objected to the *ADB*'s 'out-dated criterion of only including those who had been dead for at least 20 years'.[17]

Consequently, in 2004 an Indigenous working party was created, comprising Peters-Little as the chair, and eight other Canberra-based scholars, including Aboriginal members Dawn Casey, Margo Neale, and Kaye Price. Unlike the state working parties, their role was mainly limited to providing advice on Indigenous cultural protocols to the then general editor Di Langmore, and to ensuring that Indigenous sensitivities concerning deceased persons were respected.[18] However, the Indigenous working party voluntarily disbanded in late 2008 because it did not have the same purpose, responsibilities, and autonomy as the other working parties. Further, the then chair, Samantha Faulkner, who has family connections to the Wuthuthi/Yadhaigana peoples of Cape York Peninsula

---

15   Mark McGinness, 'Assessing the *ADB*: A Review of the Reviews', in Nolan and Fernon, eds, *The ADB's Story*, 305. doi.org/10.22459/ADBS.10.2013.10. I thank Malcolm Allbrook for drawing my attention to this point.
16   'Profile: Gordon Briscoe (b. 1938) and Frances Peters-Little (b. 1958)', in Nolan and Fernon, eds, *The ADB's Story*, 244.
17   Gordon Briscoe, *Racial Folly: A Twentieth Century Aboriginal Family* (Canberra: ANU E Press, 2010), 218–19. doi.org/10.22459/RF.02.2010.
18   'Profile: Gordon Briscoe (b. 1938) and Frances Peters-Little (b. 1958)', in Nolan and Fernon, eds, *The ADB's Story*, 244.

as well as Badu and Moa Islands in the Torres Strait, and I recommended that the membership be opened to Indigenous academics from across Australia to better reflect Indigenous communities and concerns from across the nation.[19]

In 2008 Melanie Nolan was appointed as the new general editor, and her previous experience with the *Dictionary of New Zealand Biography* made her especially attentive to Indigenous issues. In 2014 she recommended that the *ADB* appoint the acclaimed Miriwoong writer and scholar Steve Kinanne and myself to the editorial board, and in 2016, with her support, we reconstituted a new Indigenous working party, enlisting Aboriginal and Torres Strait Islander scholars from across Australia, with Gurreng Gurreng nursing academic Odette Best serving as the inaugural chair.[20] Moreover, the new Indigenous working party now had the same function and autonomy as the other working parties, with the added role of advising the *ADB* on Indigenous ethical concerns and cultural sensitivities.

While not all of the *ADB*'s attempts to redress the representation of Aboriginal and Torres Strait Islander people since the 1990s were entirely successful, there was a significant increase in Indigenous inclusion in the volumes published from 1996 to 2012 (numbers 14–18). These volumes, covering individuals who passed away between 1940 and 1980, each had between 15 (2.2 per cent) and 26 (3.8 per cent) Indigenous entries. And the most recent volume, number 18, actually exceeded the Indigenous proportion of the population (3.8 per cent).

Yet there is still much work to do. Today there are only 210 biographies of Aboriginal and Torres Strait Islander people amongst the approximately 13,000 *ADB* entries. This represents only 1.5 per cent of all entries, nearly half the current Indigenous proportion of the population (2016 census). Furthermore, these 210 entries are unevenly distributed throughout the volumes: only 17 out of 359 online entries covering those who passed away before 1840 are of Indigenous people (4.7 per cent), even though, according to Boyd Hunter and John Carmody's recent demographic study, the Aboriginal population outnumbered the non-Indigenous

---

19 Briscoe echoed this point in 2010. Briscoe, *Racial Folly*, 218–19.
20 The other inaugural members are Len Collard, Linda Ford, Natalie Harkin, Barry Judd, Jakelin Troy, and John Whop.

population during this time.[21] Moreover, in line with the inclusion rate of women in the *ADB* overall, only 46 out of the 210 Indigenous subjects are women (21.9 per cent). Thus, Indigenous Australians are not only vastly underrepresented in the *ADB*, they are also unevenly represented, with the *ADB* depicting a skewed snapshot of Indigenous historical experience. So, who are the Aboriginal and Torres Strait Islander people already represented in the *ADB*?

Indigenous Representation in the Current *ADB*

The first two volumes of the *ADB* covered the period 1788 to 1850, and, as previously mentioned, only included nine Aboriginal people: Arabanoo, Bennelong, Biraban, Bungaree, and Colebe in volume one, and Jackey Jackey, Wylie, Yagan, and Yuranigh in volume two.[22] Moreover, the online *ADB*, which includes entries from the 2005 supplement, still only lists 20 Aboriginal people for the years 1788–1850. In addition to those mentioned above are Broger and Broughton (who share a single entry), Calyute, Eumarrah, Mokare, Daniel Moowattin, Mullawirraburka, Musquito, Pemulwuy, Tarenorerer, and Windradyne. This group is not only small in number, but also reflects a narrow spectrum of Aboriginal society at the time. All except the Palawa (Indigenous Tasmanian) woman Tarenorerer are men, and 13 lived in what is now New South Wales, four in Western Australia, two in Tasmania, and Mullawirraburka was from Willunga in South Australia. Moreover, these 20 individuals are primarily defined as Aboriginal leaders (nine), Aboriginal guides (six), 'Aborigines' (four), and one as an Aboriginal warrior. The individuals in this group are further divided into a mere nine occupational categories, with some individuals ascribed multiple vocations: six leaders, seven guides, five resistance fighters, three executed criminals, two cultural informants, two murderers, one stockman, two trackers, and one duellist. Significantly, these descriptors suggest that these men, and one woman, were only significant because of their interaction with the British; be it

---

21 They convincingly argue that the non-Indigenous population would have first exceeded the Indigenous population in the mid-1840s. Boyd H. Hunter and John Carmody, 'Estimating the Aboriginal Population in Early Colonial Australia: The Role of Chickenpox Reconsidered', *Australian Economic History Review* 55, no. 2 (2015): 112–38, 135. doi.org/10.1111/aehr.12068.
22 Note that Jackey Jackey is said to have passed away in 1854 so should be in volume three. Edgar Beale, 'Jackey Jackey (?–1854)', *Australian Dictionary of Biography*, National Centre of Biography, The Australian National University, adb.anu.edu.au/biography/jackey-jackey-2264/text2897, published first in hardcopy 1967, accessed online 14 July 2017.

through seemingly positive contributions to colonial enterprises such as exploration, or due to their hostility to British colonists and as transgressors of British law.

Yet it is not only the narrow conceptualisation of the Aboriginal subjects' *noteworthy* qualities that is problematic, but also the interests and tone of the biographical narratives, which reflect now outdated representational practices. In volume one, Arabanoo, Bennelong, and Colebe are all primarily discussed as British captives. While Arabanoo passed away from smallpox before returning to his people, Bennelong and Colebe eventually became mediators between the British and the Eora, with the latter serving as a guide for Governor Arthur Phillip's excursions to the Nepean. The biographies also overemphasise the Aboriginal men's seemingly tragic, degraded, and brutal proclivities. Despite being the first Indigenous intermediary, Bennelong was portrayed as '"so fond of drinking that he lost no opportunity of being intoxicated"' because he 'no longer [found] contentment or full acceptance either among his countrymen or the white men'. Likewise, Bungaree's biography focuses on his role as a leader of the Sydney Aboriginal people, a 'pathetic remnant of their people, [who] spent their days giving exhibitions of boomerang throwing, doing odd jobs, and begging for bread, liquor, tobacco and cash'. '"Len' it bread"', was said to be 'Bungaree's favoured approach'. And finally, Colebe's entry describes his 'quarrelsome' behaviour, and details his 'particularly violent' treatment of women.[23] While the Aboriginal men included in volume one might have been deemed noteworthy as mediators and guides or leaders of their people, they are ultimately portrayed as victim, alcoholic, beggar, and abuser.

The next *ADB* period, 1851 to 1890, differs significantly from the earlier one. First, it includes a more diverse group, with seven Indigenous men and six women: Walter George Arthur, Lucy Beeton, Dick Cabadgee, Mary Ellen Cuper, Dolly Dalrymple, Dundalli, Cora Gooseberry,

---

23   Eleanor Dark, 'Arabanoo (1759–1789)', *Australian Dictionary of Biography*, National Centre of Biography, The Australian National University, adb.anu.edu.au/biography/arabanoo-1711/text23943, published first in hardcopy 1966, accessed online 14 July 2017; Eleanor Dark, 'Bennelong (1764–1813)', *Australian Dictionary of Biography*, National Centre of Biography, The Australian National University, adb.anu.edu.au/biography/bennelong-1769/text1979, published first in hardcopy 1966, accessed online 14 July 2017; F. D. McCarthy, 'Bungaree (?–1830)', *Australian Dictionary of Biography*, National Centre of Biography, The Australian National University, adb.anu.edu.au/biography/bungaree-1848/text2141, published first in hardcopy 1966, accessed online 14 July 2017; and F. D. McCarthy, 'Colebe (?–?)', *Australian Dictionary of Biography*, National Centre of Biography, The Australian National University, adb.anu.edu.au/biography/colebe-1909/text2263, published first in hardcopy 1966, accessed online 14 July 2017.

Kaarwirn Kuunawarn, Maria Lock, Nathaniel Pepper, Trugernanner, Tulaba, and Tommy Windich. Almost all of the states are represented by this group, which comprises four Tasmanians, three Victorians, two from New South Wales, two Western Australians, and one each from the Northern Territory and Queensland. They are also defined more broadly: in addition to leaders, guides, Aborigines, or Aboriginal women/matriarchs as we saw in the earlier period, the individuals in this group include teachers, landowners, cultural brokers, and evangelists. Their occupations also include the titles 'rights activist', 'postmistress', 'telegraphist', 'farmer', 'explorer', and 'Moravian lay preacher', as well as 'resistance leaders', 'cultural informants', and 'executed criminals' as per the earlier period.

In some respects, this broader spectrum of Indigenous lives included in the 1850–90 volume reflects the evolving history of colonisation, as Aboriginal people became more entangled with Western society and institutions, forming intimate relationships with colonists and former convicts, and engaging more actively with colonial ministries, governments, and commercial interests. Lucy Beeton, for example, was born on Gun Carriage Island in the Bass Strait in 1829, the daughter of a Palawa woman, Emmerennam or 'Bet Smith', and a Jewish sealer, Thomas Beeton. Shayne Breen explains that when George Augustus Robinson evicted the sealers to establish an Aboriginal settlement there, Thomas Beeton was removed, but soon gained permission to reunite with his family, and together they eventually returned to Gun Carriage Island when Robinson relocated his settlement to Flinders Island. Lucy Beeton served as the island's teacher, after the government rejected their request to appoint one, providing religious instruction for the local community children. This work was eventually recognised, and she was given a lifetime lease of Badger Island, and became a prominent and influential trader of mutton-bird products, and advocate of Indigenous interests.[24]

While the historical context of the second half of the nineteenth century had some considerable differences from the earlier period, arguably the key reason why these entries differ so significantly is due to changing historiographical approaches. Tellingly, only two of these 13 entries were published in the original volumes: the Tasmanian 'cultural informant'

---

24 Shayne Breen, 'Beeton, Lucy (1829–1886)', *Australian Dictionary of Biography*, National Centre of Biography, The Australian National University, adb.anu.edu.au/biography/beeton-lucy-12790/text23079, published first in hardcopy 2005, accessed online 14 July 2017.

Trugernanner and West Australian guide and tracker Tommy Windich were included in volume six. Volume four had no Indigenous entries, and the three Aboriginal biographies published in volumes five and six were of people who passed away at a later date: William Barak (1824–1903), Johnny Mullagh (1841–1891), and Pumpkin (1850–1908).[25] Consequently, 11 of the 13 entries for this period, including Lucy Beeton's, result from the 2005 supplement, and reveal a stronger commitment to Indigenous inclusion and attentiveness to culturally sensitive representational practices.

The next *ADB* period is 1891 to 1939 (known in *ADB* parlance as 'period 3'). There are 30 Indigenous biographies from this period, 19 of which were included in the original six volumes (numbers 7–12, published between 1979 and 1990). This represents 0.78 per cent of the 3,813 *ADB* entries from this period. In contrast to the more even gender balance in the 1850–90 entries, this period includes 24 Indigenous men and six women. The geographic spread is also more skewed towards New South Wales (nine or 30 per cent) and Victoria (eight or 26.6 per cent); Western Australia, Queensland, and South Australia each have three entries (10 per cent), and Tasmania and the Northern Territory have two entries (6.6 per cent). Whereas the concentration of entries on people from Sydney and the Swan River Colony (Western Australia) for the first period (1788–1850) bears some correspondence to the pattern of cross-cultural contact and establishment of settlements at the time, the uneven distribution for this third period is a product of the *ADB*'s arbitrary new editorial policy. Nolan explains that in 1975 the *ADB* editorial board decided to draw on 'weighted population figures' from the census (most likely the most recent 1971 figures) to determine quotas for each of the working parties. This meant that the more populous states—New South Wales and Victoria—received the lion's share of biographical entries with 27 and 24 per cent respectively, followed by the Armed Services working party with 14 per cent. Next were Queensland (9 per cent), South Australia (8 per cent), Commonwealth (8 per cent), Western Australia (5 per cent), Tasmania (3 per cent), New Guinea (1 per cent), and Miscellaneous (1 per cent).[26] Yet the Aboriginal and Torres Strait Islander population of 1971 did not correlate with the broader state populations: Queensland, 27.9 per cent; New South Wales, 22.6 per cent; Western Australia, 18.2 per cent; the Northern Territory,

25   See Table 1.2 'Representation of Women and Aboriginal Subjects in the ADB', in Nolan, '"Insufficiently Engineered"', 26.
26   Table 1.1 'Number and Proportion of Entries in Period 3 (1891–1939) Allocated to Each Working Party', in Nolan, '"Insufficiently Engineered"', 24.

17.3 per cent; South Australia, 5.9 per cent; Victoria, 5.5 per cent; Tasmania, 1.8 per cent; and the Australian Capital Territory, 0.4 per cent.[27] Thus, for Indigenous people the *ADB*'s quotas are very misleading as they bear little relationship to the 1971 Indigenous population, nor the contemporary populations in period 3. More significantly, they do not reflect the spread of Aboriginal language groups, or locations of key historical events and experience, so only offer a partial view from a window, to borrow Stanner's evocative metaphor.

The next period covered people who passed away between 1940 and 1980, and the *ADB* currently has entries on 87 Aboriginal and Torres Strait Islander people relating to this period. This represents 1.6 per cent of the 5,422 total entries, which is a significant increase on the earlier periods. More significantly, 79 of these were published in the original volumes (13–16, published between 1993 and 2002), illustrating the impact that changing historiography was starting to have on the *ADB* working parties and editorial board as they consciously included more Indigenous subjects in the initial planning. Moreover, for this period, the *ADB* seemed to have relaxed its quota system in relation to Indigenous entries, as there were 34 from New South Wales (39 per cent), 18 from Queensland (20.7 per cent), 14 from the Northern Territory (16 per cent), 10 from Western Australia (11.5 per cent), nine from South Australia (10.3 per cent), and five from Victoria (5.7 per cent).[28] This geographic distribution of Indigenous entries seems to better reflect both the 1990s Indigenous population, with New South Wales and Queensland having the highest concentration of Aboriginal and Torres Strait Islander people, followed by Western Australia and the Northern Territory, then Victoria and South Australia, with Tasmania and the Australian Capital Territory having the smallest populations.[29] However, the gender division remains unbalanced, as only 19 of the 87 subjects are women (21.8 per cent). More so than in the earlier periods, these biographies appear to reflect broader 'samples of the "Australian experience"', part of the *ADB*'s goal to not only commemorate Australian luminaries, but also the nation's

---

27 Alan Gray and Leonard Smith, 'The Size of the Aboriginal Population', *Australian Aboriginal Studies*, no. 1 (1983): 7.
28 These figures are based on the state of the individual's birth, so are not completely representative due to people's increased mobility at this time: 13 passed away in a different state, and two defence force personnel overseas.
29 See '4102.0—Australian Social Trends, 1994: Population Composition: Aboriginal and Torres Strait Islander people', Australian Bureau of Statistics, 27 May 1994, accessed 17 July 2017, www.abs.gov.au/AUSSTATS/abs@.nsf/2f762f95845417aeca25706c00834efa/2420d4dd8069 c743ca2570ec007853cb!OpenDocument.

'ordinary people'.[30] This period includes Indigenous people from a wider array of occupations, such as factory worker, carpenter, wharf labourer, soldier, public servant, police officer, nurse, and teacher. Yet this also partly reflects the historic policies of assimilation in the mid-twentieth century, which enabled, and even coerced, more Indigenous people to move from missions to rural centres and cities and engage in 'ordinary' paid employment (as opposed to the largely unpaid or underpaid labour conditions in the pastoral and maritime industries that Indigenous people who were subject to Protection Acts had experienced). More significantly, 16 of the Indigenous individuals included in the *ADB*'s period 4 are also defined as 'leaders', and 12 as 'activists' or 'resistance leaders', highlighting the political demands for equality and self-determination made by Indigenous activists in protests ranging from the Day of Mourning (1938) through to the Tent Embassy (1972), as well as the historiography of the 1990s, which commemorated this political history and introduced it to a broader audience.

The most recently published period of the *ADB* covered people who passed away between 1981 and 1990 (volumes 17 and 18, published in 2007 and 2012). Of the 1,336 entries, 44 are Indigenous, making period 5 the period of greatest Indigenous inclusion (3.29 per cent). The geographic distribution echoes the previous period, although the gender balance is worse with only 15 per cent of the Indigenous entries pertaining to women. This period has less of a focus on depicting the lives of the Indigenous 'everyman' than the previous one, with 25 of the subjects being defined as leaders or activists/campaigners, as well as 'footballer, pastor, activist and governor' Sir Douglas Nicholls. Yet, this group also includes Lloyd James Boney (1959–1987), Edward James Murray (1959–1981), and John Peter Pat (1966–1983), who all tragically died whilst in police custody, or at the hands of the police. As Tim Rowse notes in his biography of Boney, the 1980s saw a series of cases 'in which police were suspected of murder or, at best, manslaughter', which led to the Commonwealth Government appointing a Royal Commission into Aboriginal Deaths in Custody in 1989.[31] Such biographies reveal that the *ADB* is not focused just on celebrating the nation and its elite, but over time has also embraced its role of shining a light on the nation's dark histories.

---

30 Nolan, '"Insufficiently Engineered"', 22.
31 Tim Rowse, 'Boney, Lloyd James (1959–1987)', *Australian Dictionary of Biography*, National Centre of Biography, The Australian National University, adb.anu.edu.au/biography/boney-lloyd-james-12229/text21935, published first in hardcopy 2007, accessed online 17 July 2017.

'TRUE BIOGRAPHIES OF NATIONS?'

An Indigenous Australian Dictionary of Biography

In 2017 we embarked on a new project which aims to redress the historic underrepresentation of Indigenous Australian people in the *ADB* by producing some 190 new biographies of Aboriginal and Torres Strait Islander people. This will elevate the overall inclusion rate of Indigenous people to 3 per cent of the approximately 13,000 entries published in the *ADB*'s 19 volumes, a figure which roughly corresponds with the current Indigenous population. Yet we do not simply want to amplify the kinds of biographies that already exist, and proliferate 190 new entries on Aboriginal and Torres Strait Islander guides, cultural informants, community leaders, and rights activists. Instead, we want to ensure that the new biographies we produce are more emblematic of the demographic makeup of Indigenous communities, past and present. This means increasing the proportion of Indigenous women, ensuring more language groups and communities from across Australia are represented, and considering the kinds of figures who are important to our people, and not only those who are nationally recognised for their noteworthy contributions to mainstream society.

In order to ensure that the new biographies meet this broader remit, we will adopt a more systematic approach to selecting new biographical subjects than the *ADB*'s usual 'organic' approach.[32] This will entail three key preliminary stages. The first is to analyse other biographical dictionaries in order to understand the general criteria thus far used in selecting individuals, both Indigenous and non-Indigenous, for inclusion. We will draw inspiration from other national dictionaries such as the *Dictionary of New Zealand Biography*, which also published a stand-alone two-volume Māori dictionary of biography,[33] as well as the *American National Biography Online*, which has an American Indian Heritage special collection comprising 294 biographies, and the *Dictionary of Canadian Biography/Dictionnaire biographique du Canada* (*DCB/DBC*). Yet we

---

32 Nolan, '"Insufficiently Engineered"', 21.
33 *The People of Many Peaks: The Maori Biographies from* The Dictionary of New Zealand Biography, *Volume 1, 1769–1869* (Wellington: Bridget Williams Books and Dictionary of New Zealand Biography, 1991); and *The Turbulent Years: 1870–1900: The Maori Biographies from* The Dictionary of New Zealand Biography, *Volume Two*, Introduction by Claudia Orange (Wellington: Bridget Williams Books and Dictionary of New Zealand Biography, 1994).

can also look closer to home for inspiration, for instance, the *Northern Territory Dictionary of Biography*, which, proportionately, includes a higher percentage of Indigenous subjects (8.7 per cent).[34]

The second stage of the project involves consulting broadly with Aboriginal and Torres Strait Islander communities in order to ascertain grassroots visions of who should be included, and identify Indigenous cultural protocols in terms of how we research and write the biographical entries. We will do this through online surveys asking Indigenous people to reflect on the importance of a range of different qualities and criteria (identified from the current *ADB* and other dictionaries), and also ask people to nominate figures who are well remembered in their local communities, but who may not yet be nationally known, or who are still to have their life histories researched.

The final stage will investigate new biographical methods in order to identify cutting-edge life-writing approaches in Australia and elsewhere, with the intention of broadening our understanding of how Indigenous biography can be conceived. We are considering several new lines of inquiry. First, we are exploring how short-form biographies exemplified by the *ADB* might better acknowledge and accommodate Indigenous protocols, interests, and sensitivities. This is not only a matter of being sensitive to how we represent individuals who have passed on, but also of working out how we might better accommodate the communal sensibilities of many Indigenous cultures. This includes how we might produce collective Indigenous biographies of families, clans, and organisations, and how, in addressing the ostensible achievements of the Indigenous individual, we might also be more attentive to the instrumental role played by skin groups and Indigenous networks, for example in establishing the Pindan Mining cooperative following the 1946 Pilbara strike. It involves also developing an awareness of the cultural protocols concerning who might be identified as a 'leader' versus a 'spokesman' or 'scribe', as Penny Van Toorn found in her study of Coranderrk.[35]

---

34 David Carment, ed., *Northern Territory Dictionary of Biography* (Darwin: Charles Darwin University Press, 2008). The *NTDB* features 54 Indigenous biographies out of 618 entries. I thank Robyn Smith for providing a list of all Indigenous biographies in the *NTDB*.
35 Penny Van Toorn, *Writing Never Arrives Naked: Early Aboriginal Cultures of Writing in Australia* (Canberra: Aboriginal Studies Press, 2006).

We might also consider titles, positions, and occupations of significance to Indigenous world views. For example, the *Dictionary of New Zealand Biography*'s online advanced search page includes in the occupation field 'tohunga', which translates to priest or expert; 'woman of mana', that is, a woman with significant spiritual power; as well as carver, a role which is highly esteemed and significant in Māori society.[36] The closest approximation to the title 'tohunga' that the *ADB* currently uses is the term 'carradhy', an Eora word for a person who performed important ceremonies and mediated between the spiritual and mundane worlds. But this term only appears once, in the biography of Pemulwuy, and it is as a descriptor in the body of the biography, and not used as a title, or keyword in the search interface.[37] Four other *ADB* entries use the analogous term 'clever man', and five entries use 'lawman', that is, someone who has been initiated into tribal law and possesses the knowledge to conduct ceremonies. *Carradhy* is also the only Indigenous term used as a title descriptor in the *ADB*, whereas other biographical encyclopedias have employed other such terms. The National Museum of Australia's online biography of 'Old Masters', for example, describes Barraba artist Wally Mandarrk as a *marrkdijbu*, or clever man.[38] So perhaps we could emulate this example to incorporate Indigenous language titles in the *ADB* where they are known and appropriate.

Another question to consider is how to broaden interest in the lives of Indigenous individuals beyond the question of colonial impact. The constraints of using Western documentary sources have led to many Indigenous biographies turning on the question of how the state intervened in Indigenous lives, be it through interventionist protection policies, the removal of children from their Indigenous families, or, for historical biographies, how Indigenous people physically and politically resisted colonialism and asserted their rights. How might we write the lives of Indigenous people on their own terms, and frame Indigenous lives within their own cultural milieus? For example, the *DCB/DBC* includes an entry on the legendary figure Dekanahwideh, an Iroquois cultural hero who is commemorated as the founder of the Five Nations

---

36   See 'DNZB Search', *Te Ara: The Encyclopaedia of New Zealand*, accessed 17 July 2017, www.teara.govt.nz/en/biography_search.
37   J. L. Kohen, 'Pemulwuy (1750–1802)', *Australian Dictionary of Biography*, National Centre of Biography, The Australian National University, adb.anu.edu.au/biography/pemulwuy-13147/text 23797, published first in hardcopy 2005, accessed online 17 July 2017.
38   'Wally Mandaark', in 'Old Masters: Australia's Great Bark Artists', National Museum of Australia, accessed 17 July 2017, www.nma.gov.au/exhibitions/old_masters/artists/wally_mandarrk.

Confederacy.³⁹ Dekanahwideh was born amongst the Huron at what is now Thayendanaga or Deseronto Reservation, and before his birth his mother had a vision that he would 'plant the Tree of Peace at Onondaga'. He travelled around the Five Nations—Mohawks, Oniedas, Onondagas, Cayugas, and Senecas—performing miracles to inspire each to join his mission of peace. He then planted the Tree of Peace, and delivered to the chiefs of the Five Nations the 'Great Law'. He soon departed, promising to return if they faced extreme danger, and called his name. Dekanawideh's legend charts the origins of the confederacy, and predates all colonial accounts; in 1654 the Jesuit missionary Le Mercier reported that the legend had been in existence 'since the earliest times'.⁴⁰ This case suggests we could look to include Aboriginal and Torres Strait Islander people whose lives lie entirely outside of colonial contact and concern.

The example of Dekanahwideh also suggests we might be able to draw on Aboriginal and Torres Strait Islander lore and in the *ADB* include biographies of ancestral beings, or 'legendary' figures who shaped the landscapes across the continent and created the natural world as we know it. An example of a particular ancestral being is the Rainbow Serpent, an important figure for many Aboriginal groups across Australia who is closely associated with waterways and billabongs and is known by many names, including the Wagyl for the Noongar people of the south-west. Another is Baiame, a Sky God widely known to language groups across south-eastern Australia such as 'the Kamilaroi, Eora, Darkinjung, Wonnaruah, Awabakal, Worimi and Wiradjuri'.⁴¹ According to Warraimay historian Vicki Grieves, 'Baiame is important for creating people themselves and when he completed his creative work he returned to the sky behind the Milky Way'.⁴²

Another question to consider is the lives of non-Indigenous people who might have been incorporated within Indigenous communities. The *American National Biography Online* includes in its American Indian Heritage list Abraham, also known as Prophet, an early nineteenth-century runaway slave who was taken in by the Seminole of Florida. The Seminole

---

39   Paul A. W. Wallace, 'Dekanawideh (Deganawidah, Dekanahouideh, the Heavenly Messenger)', in *Dictionary of Canadian Biography*, vol. 1, University of Toronto/Université Laval, 2003– , accessed 17 July 2017, www.biographi.ca/en/bio/dekanahwideh_1E.html.
40   Wallace, 'Dekanawideh'.
41   Vicki Grieves, *Aboriginal Spirituality: Aboriginal Philosophy, the Basis of Aboriginal Social and Emotional Wellbeing*, Discussion Paper no. 9 (Darwin: Cooperative Research Centre for Aboriginal Health, 2009), 9.
42   Grieves, *Aboriginal Spirituality*, 9.

were once part of both the Muscogee Nation, who had been driven out of their lands in Georgia, and the Oconee and Yamasee tribes who had fled the Carolinas in the early eighteenth century. In Florida, they had taken in many runaway slaves, adopting them into their society, and faced many skirmishes with slave owners seeking to recapture runaways. After the 1830 Indian Removal Act was passed, Abraham was involved in the Seminole's resistance to being removed to the Indian Territory, and then upon his surrender in 1837 served as a translator between the government and the Seminole.[43] Although Abraham was not Indigenous, Native American historians such as Ashley Glassburn Falzetti argue that it is imperative for such historical figures to be acknowledged within Indigenous histories. In her work on Frances Slocum, a settler woman captured by Miami people who spent the rest of her life in their society and had a number of Miami children, Falzetti suggests Slocum be recognised as Miami for she is the only significant Miami historical figure commemorated in local histories in Indiana. Yet her Miami identity is never acknowledged, a process which Falzetti sees as the archival equivalent of the settler-colonial logic of elimination.[44]

The example of Abraham and Falzetti's argument suggests that the *ADB* could even consider the lives of non-Indigenous people who lived amongst Indigenous groups differently. For example, Worimi historian John Maynard and Victoria Haskins have written a series of biographical portraits of such individuals, *Living with the Locals: Early Europeans' Experience of Indigenous Life*. While not as explicit as Falzetti, their account of the escaped convict William Buckley, who spent 32 years amongst the Wathawurrung people of Victoria, suggests that his biography could be reinterpreted significantly. The *ADB* already has an entry on Buckley, but Marjorie Tipping's biography only briefly mentions his Aboriginal life:

> [he] was befriended by Aboriginals of the Watourong tribe, who believed the big white stranger to be a reincarnation of their dead tribal chief. He learnt their language and their customs, and was given a wife, by whom, he said, he had a daughter.[45]

---

43 Kenny A. Franks, 'Abraham', *American National Biography Online*, February 2000, accessed 23 February 2017. doi.org/10.1093/anb/9780198606697.article.2000002.
44 Ashley Glassburn Falzetti, 'Archival Absence: The Burden of History', *Settler Colonial Studies* 5, no. 2 (2015): 128–44. doi.org/10.1080/2201473X.2014.957258.
45 Marjorie J. Tipping, 'Buckley, William (1780–1856)', *Australian Dictionary of Biography*, National Centre of Biography, The Australian National University, adb.anu.edu.au/biography/buckley-william-1844/text2132, published first in hardcopy 1966, accessed online 18 July 2017.

In contrast, Maynard and Haskins argue that Buckley had been incorporated into a Wathawurrung family who had renamed him Murrangurk. They suggest that his reticence to discuss significant details of Wathawurrung society, in particular their beliefs and ceremonies, was not an artefact of his ignorance, or their absence of spiritual beliefs, as was often assumed by earlier commentators and historians. Instead, they argue his silence was a sign of his deep respect for maintaining the integrity of secret-sacred knowledge, and his implied incorporation as a Wathawurrung, who renamed him.[46]

At this stage of the project we are just beginning to open up how we might address biography in innovative new ways, and to consider a wide array of questions. Some further possible lines of inquiry are whether we can broaden our conceptions of Indigenous biography beyond the Indigenous person? Inspired by Cherokee scholar Daniel Heath Justice's work on the badger, can we write the biographies of nonhumans such as particular animals which have a special significance for some Indigenous communities, like Leah Lui-Chivizhe's research on the turtle in the Torres Strait or the significant characteristics that totemic animals symbolised for different communities?[47] Or can we take inspiration from the recent legal recognition of the Whanganui River in New Zealand as an ancestor, and its being given human status as a way of including the biographies of significant landforms in the *ADB*?[48] Further, could we explore the lives of individuals who lived in the deep past, and write biographies of individuals such as Mungo Lady, who lived 42,000 years ago?[49] All of these questions suggest new ways in which the *ADB* might explore Indigenous biography, and possibilities for considering new measures of noteworthiness for the nation.

---

46 John Maynard and Victoria Haskins, *Living with the Locals: Early Europeans' Experience of Indigenous Life* (Canberra: National Library of Australia, 2016), 26–59.
47 Daniel Heath Justice, *Badger* (London: Reaktion Books, 2014); Addie Leah Lui-Chivizhe, 'Le op: An Islander's History of Torres Strait Turtle-Shell Masks' (PhD thesis, University of Sydney, 2016).
48 Eleanor Aingie Roy, 'New Zealand River Granted Same Legal Rights as Human Being', *The Guardian*, 16 March 2017, accessed 18 July 2017, www.theguardian.com/world/2017/mar/16/new-zealand-river-granted-same-legal-rights-as-human-being.
49 Malcolm Allbrook and Ann McGrath, 'Collaborative Histories of the Willandra Lakes', in *Long History, Deep Time: Deepening Histories of Place*, eds Ann McGrath and Mary Anne Jebb (Canberra: ANU Press, 2015), 241–52. doi.org/10.22459/LHDT.05.2015.14. In 2019 Malcolm Allbrook published his *ADB* entry on Mungo Lady, which was the first biography published under the IADB project. Malcolm Allbrook, 'Mungo Lady (?–?)', *Australian Dictionary of Biography*, National Centre of Biography, The Australian National University, adb.anu.edu.au/biography/mungo-lady-27703/text35292, published online 2019, accessed 3 April 2019.

Conclusion

Over the course of its 60-year history, the *ADB* has arguably come to be recognised as a key repository of Australia's story. It provides an overview of the lives of influential figures who have shaped our nation, and has proven to be an invaluable resource for Australian scholars, teachers, journalists, writers, and students, as well as a general public increasingly fascinated with biography and family history. The *ADB*'s user base has increased over the years, especially since the online *ADB* was launched. The online *ADB* regularly receives around 60 million hits each year,[50] and its biographies are republished on or linked to a range of other educational, governmental, and commercial websites. Thus, increasing the number of Aboriginal and Torres Strait Islander biographies in the *ADB* will provide a means for ensuring that more Aboriginal and Torres Strait Islander people are better included in the 'Australian story'. Yet we want to ensure that we are included in the national story on our own terms. This means the *ADB* needs to diversify the kinds of Indigenous people included, accommodating both what matters to Indigenous communities, and new biographical approaches which better accord with cultural protocols. Our hope is that the new IADB will enhance Indigenous people's pride in our people, past and present, by identifying and recognising significant and interesting figures from across our communities, and enhance our sense of national recognition and belonging. Finally, given the national scale of the *ADB*'s readership, we also hope it will contribute to improving non-Indigenous understandings of the lives, experiences, cultures, and contributions many Aboriginal and Torres Strait Islander people have made throughout our history.

---

50 Information provided by Christine Fernon, online manager, National Centre of Biography, The Australian National University, 27 July 2018.

9
WRITING THE NATION IN TWO LANGUAGES: THE *DICTIONARY OF WELSH BIOGRAPHY*

DAFYDD JOHNSTON

Wales was the first of the four nations of the British Isles to establish its own separate national biographical dictionary, distinct from and yet necessarily modelled on the *Dictionary of National Biography*. The Welsh project was publicly announced in 1938, and the first volume, *Y Bywgraffiadur Cymreig hyd 1940*, was published in the Welsh language in 1953, followed by its English counterpart, *The Dictionary of Welsh Biography Down to 1940*, in 1959.[1] This chapter on the relationship between the two languages in the project, from the print volumes through to the current website,[2] will argue that bilingual publication has been vital both as a representation of the lived experience of the Welsh people, and as an assertion of distinctive national identity. First, however, a brief historical survey will highlight the multilingual nature of life writing in Wales from the earliest times, and its deployment at key points in the relationship between Wales and England.

---

1   John Edward Lloyd and R. T. Jenkins, eds, *Y Bywgraffiadur Cymreig hyd 1940* (Llundain: Anrhydeddus Gymdeithas y Cymmrodorion, 1953); John Edward Lloyd and R. T. Jenkins, eds, *The Dictionary of Welsh Biography Down to 1940* (London: The Honourable Society of Cymmrodorion, 1959).
2   *Dictionary of Welsh Biography/Y Bywgraffiadur Cymreig*, National Library of Wales and the Honourable Society of Cymmrodorion of London, biography.wales/ and bywgraffiadur.cymru/ [henceforth *DWB*].

'TRUE BIOGRAPHIES OF NATIONS?'

The History of Life Writing in Wales

The very earliest biographical work by a Welsh person, Asser's Latin life of King Alfred of Wessex up to the year 895, belongs to a period before either Wales or England existed as political entities, but it does record a crucial point in the formation of the English nation, if not the Welsh. Asser was a member of the clerical community of St David's in south-west Wales who had been invited to raise standards of learning at Alfred's court.[3] Asser's political allegiance cut across ethnic divisions, one of his main aims in his dealings with Alfred being to enlist his support for St David's against an oppressive local ruler. His biography promoted the Carolingian ideal of the learned Christian king, as expressed in the lives of Charlemagne and his son Louis the Pious, and its hermeneutic Latinity was an integral part of the work's message proclaiming loyalty to an international scholarly community. What is particularly interesting about this work when considered in the context of the history of biographical writing in and from Wales is that it reverses what later became the dominant flow of cultural influence, since St David's was evidently a centre of learning capable of providing the scholarship and literary skills necessary for the meaningful shaping of an English life. When Asser in his turn became the subject of biography in the Enlightenment period, his case was used to support belief in the antiquity of Welsh learning.

A key driver in the development of a Welsh national consciousness was the external threat posed by the Norman invasions from the late eleventh century onwards, and it is surely no coincidence that the first biographies—both religious and secular—to be composed in Wales relate to resistance to the Normans. The earliest life of a secular ruler is that of Gruffudd ap Cynan (c. 1055–1137), composed in Latin probably before 1148 and translated into Welsh by 1170, which is the earliest Welsh-language biography.[4] Gruffudd was king of Gwynedd in north-west Wales, and is primarily remembered for establishing his kingdom as a bastion

---

[3] See Patrick Wormald, 'Asser (d. 909)', *Oxford Dictionary of National Biography*, Oxford University Press, 2004; online edn, September 2004, accessed 29 June 2017, www.oxforddnb.com/view/article/810. doi.org/10.1093/ref:odnb/810; D. P. Kirby, 'Asser and His Life of King Alfred', *Studia Celtica* 6 (1971): 12–35.

[4] The Latin original was long thought to be lost, but was recently discovered and edited by Paul Russell, *Vita Griffini Filii Conani* (Cardiff: University of Wales Press, 2005). For the Welsh text, see D. Simon Evans, ed., *Historia Gruffud vab Kenan* (Cardiff: University of Wales Press, 1977); and D. Simon Evans, trans., *A Medieval Prince of Wales: The Life of Gruffudd ap Cynan* (Felinfach: Llanerch Enterprises, 1990).

of Welsh independence which stood firm against the Normans under his descendants until the late thirteenth century, and which continues to be a source of inspiration to Welsh nationalists to this day. However, Gruffudd's ethnic background was more complex than this teleological view might suggest. Born and brought up in Ireland, the son of a Welsh father and an Irish Viking mother, he could justifiably have been included in the *Dictionary of Irish Biography*, and his early military exploits were against Welsh rivals as much as against the Normans.

It has been argued that the Latin life was composed not in Gwynedd, as one might expect, but at St David's in the south-west, with the aim of bolstering the aspirations of that diocese—which were supported by Gruffudd's son Owain Gwynedd—as a metropolitan see. One feature suggestive of a St David's provenance is the use of the term *Cambria* for Wales (derived from Camber, son of Brutus, ancestor of the Welsh people according to Geoffrey of Monmouth's *Historia Regum Britanniae*), a neologism which is indicative of a new national consciousness, later taken up by Cambro-Latin writers of the Renaissance.[5] The Welsh translation appears to have been written in Gwynedd, and this is an early example of translation being associated with a change in perspective.

Opposition to Norman ecclesiastical reforms motivated the earliest hagiography in Wales, promoting the claims of the dioceses of Llandaff and St David's against encroachment by Canterbury. Two twelfth-century manuscripts contain collections of Latin lives celebrating local saints, the most significant of which is the life of St David, composed about 1094 by Rhigyfarch of Llanbadarn Fawr, another notable centre of ecclesiastical learning.[6] This was translated into Welsh in the fourteenth century as the spread of David's cult established him as patron saint of Wales. Numerous other translations of the lives of local and international saints made hagiography the most prominent form of biographical writing in Welsh in the premodern period.[7]

The earliest biography of a Welsh person in English is the *Life* of Sir Rhys ap Thomas, composed in the early seventeenth century by Henry Rice, a direct descendant of the subject, and thus belonging to the genre of family

---

5   See Huw Pryce, 'British or Welsh? National Identity in Twelfth-Century Wales', *English Historical Review* 116, no. 468 (2001): 775–801 (at 797–98). doi.org/10.1093/ehr/CXVI.468.775.
6   J. W. Evans and J. M. Wooding, eds, *St David of Wales: Cult, Church and Nation* (Woodbridge: Boydell and Brewer, 2007).
7   For texts and translations, see 'Seintiau', www.welshsaints.ac.uk/.

history.[8] Again we find biography linked to a key turning point in Welsh history, the purpose of the work being to celebrate the role played by Sir Rhys in Henry Tudor's victory at Bosworth in 1485 (Rhys is claimed to have slain Richard III himself), and in the establishment of the Tudor state which led in due course to the Acts of Union between England and Wales.

The gap in Wales's political history between the age of the independent princes and the Tudor union was eventually bridged by an account of the life of Owain Glyndwr (c. 1359–c. 1415) in Thomas Pennant's *A Tour in Wales* (1778).[9] Glyndwr was a descendant of the princes who led a rebellion against the English crown in 1400, and although ultimately unsuccessful he has been a potent figure in Welsh folklore and nationalist mythology ever since. Pennant drew on a wide range of sources, including Crown records, and his account can be seen as the first attempt at a scholarly and objective biography in the Welsh context. In so doing he created a fully shaped life worthy of a national hero to counter the English chroniclers' portrayal of a rabble-rouser whose career began and ended in obscurity. Short biographical sketches had already been a feature of Pennant's travel writing from his Scottish tours, depicting lives as an aspect of the history of place, but this lengthy excursion covering 69 pages stretched the genre to its limits.[10]

The development of Welsh biographical writing in the eighteenth century was a product of an antiquarian revival which sought to repossess or recreate Wales's past. It was in this period that London began to play a leading role in Welsh culture, and publications were aimed as much at a metropolitan readership as at the inhabitants of Wales. In the absence of civic institutions in Wales itself, London Welsh societies such as the Honourable Society of Cymmrodorion (literally 'earliest inhabitants') made a crucial contribution to the formation of a national consciousness. The first biographies to be published were in the *Cambrian Register*, a London-

---

8   Ralph A. Griffiths, *Sir Rhys ap Thomas and His Family: A Study in the Wars of the Roses and Early Tudor Politics* (Cardiff: University of Wales Press, 2014). The *Life* was first published in 1796 in the *Cambrian Register*, and as the original manuscript is lost that text is now the primary source.
9   Thomas Pennant, *A Tour in Wales, MDCCLXXIII* (London: Henry Hughes, 1778; 2nd edition, London: Benjamin White, 1784). For discussion, see D. Johnston, 'Shaping a Heroic Life: Thomas Pennant on Owen Glyndwr', in *Enlightenment Travel and British Identities: Thomas Pennant's Tours in Scotland and Wales*, eds Mary-Ann Constantine and Nigel Leask (London and New York: Anthem Press, 2017), 105–21.
10 In the three-volume edition of the *Tour* published in 1810 the section on Glyndwr is relegated to an appendix.

based journal devoted to Welsh antiquities and edited by William Owen under the auspices of the Gwyneddigion society. The first two issues, published in 1796 and 1799, contained a section entitled 'Biography', which was clearly intended to show English readers that Welsh lives were worthy of interest.[11] Owen was the first to produce a volume of collective biography with his *Cambrian Biography* of 1803, although in fact this is more of an encyclopedic index to Welsh history, literature, and legend, including numerous characters exemplifying romantic origin myths.[12]

The first collection of Welsh biographies to aim at historical objectivity was *The Cambrian Plutarch* (1824) by John H. Parry, another member of the Gwyneddigion Society. As the title implies, these are discursive essays emphasising the moral value of lives fit to be emulated (although sadly the author himself was killed in a brawl at the Prince of Wales tavern in Pentonville the following year). The 22 lives (all men) present an image of the Welsh as a people of warriors, statesmen, divines, poets, and men of letters—in short, a civilised nation worthy of its place in the British Empire. In what was to become a topos of Welsh biographical writing, the four nations of the British Isles are invoked both to claim historical priority for the Welsh and to lament their contemporary neglect:

> It is a fact not to be questioned, that a remarkable degree of ignorance prevails respecting the literature and history of that portion of our island, in which such of the aboriginal race, as had survived the repeated shocks of foreign invasion, sought their last asylum from the swords of their enemies. While the national peculiarities, whether in manners or literature, of Scotland and Ireland, have been industriously explored, and, in many instances, successfully developed, Wales has been regarded with an indifference not easily to be reconciled with that spirit of enterprise, by which the literary republic of Great Britain is known to be animated.[13]

It was in the nineteenth century that the Welsh language began to be used for biography as an alternative to English. Conflicting allegiances are apparent in the publishing career of Robert Williams (1810–1881),

---

11   Including that of Sir Rhys ap Thomas, see note 8 above.
12   Foremost in Owen's pantheon of mythic nation builders was 'Hu Gadarn, or Hu the Mighty, the patriarch of the Cymry, who first established them in a civil community, taught them agriculture with other useful arts, and conducted them to the West of Europe'. William Owen, *The Cambrian Biography: Or Historical Notices of Celebrated Men Amongst the Ancient Britons* (London: E. Williams, 1803), 178–80.
13   John H. Parry, *The Cambrian Plutarch: Comprising Memoirs of Some of the Most Eminent Welshmen, From the Earliest Times to the Present* (London: W. Simpkin and R. Marshall, 1824), [iii]–iv.

an Anglican clergyman who first ventured into the field of biography with a slim volume in Welsh, *Coviant Byr, am rai o'r dynion enwocav a aned yn Nghymru er amser y diwygiad*, published by the Cymmrodorion Society in London in 1833. This was followed by an English version of the same work,[14] and then by a much more ambitious collection which paid only lip-service to the Welsh language with the first two words of its title, *Enwogion Cymru: A Biographical Dictionary of Eminent Welshmen From Earliest Times to the Present*.[15] The decisive shift towards English can be explained not only by the desire to reach an audience outside Wales, but also by the commonly held utilitarian belief that the Welsh language belonged to the past and that English was essential for the progressive education of the people of Wales.

Nevertheless, the Welsh language continued to be used for a wide range of publications, including biography. The main reason for this was the rise of Nonconformism, in particular the Methodist movement, in eighteenth-century Wales. Nonconformists put great emphasis on literacy, promulgated through Sunday schools, in order to read the Bible which had been available in Welsh since 1588. Because the vast majority of the population were monoglot Welsh-speakers, this had the unintended consequence of creating a reading public with a voracious appetite for Welsh-language printed books and periodicals. The most distinctive literary genre of the nineteenth century was the *cofiant*, the biography of a minister of religion, weighty tomes celebrating the new cultural elite of Welsh society. From the root *cof* ('memory'), *cofiant* is still the normal Welsh term for a biography, with much more positive connotations than the calque *bywgraffiad*, implying a life worthy of memorial, indeed originally a manifestation of God's providence. These individual lives then fed into collective biographical volumes published in Welsh,[16] and they constitute one reason for the predominance of ministers in modern collections.

---

14 Robert Williams, *A Biographical Sketch of Some of the Most Eminent Individuals Which the Principality of Wales Has Produced Since the Reformation* (London: H. Hughes, 1836).
15 Robert Williams, *Enwogion Cymru: A Biographical Dictionary of Eminent Welshmen From Earliest Times to the Present* (Llandovery: William Rees, 1852). This title is clearly modelled on that of the four-volume work by Robert Chambers, *A Biographical Dictionary of Eminent Scotsmen* (London: Blackie and Son, 1835).
16 For instance Josiah Thomas Jones, *Geiriadur bywgraffyddol o enwogion Cymru* (Aberdare: J. T. Jones a'i Fab, 1867–70); and Isaac Foulkes, *Geirlyfr bywgraffyddol o enwogion Cymru* (Liverpool: I. Foulkes, 1870).

Welsh-language culture was also promoted by the Eisteddfod, a cultural festival of medieval origin which was reinvented and popularised by London Welsh societies from the late eighteenth century. Heavily influenced by romantic antiquarianism, the Eisteddfod was a site of contention between the Welsh and English languages for much of the nineteenth century, but Welsh eventually won out and the festival is today a bastion of the language. Before the advent of higher education in Wales, the Eisteddfod did much to promote scholarship by its competitions in a wide range of fields, including biography. A prize was offered in 1904 and again in 1906 for the best list of famous Welsh people between 1700 and 1900, which resulted in a flurry of publications in both languages over the following years.[17]

Genesis of the *Dictionary of Welsh Biography*

However, by the turn of the twentieth century the amateurism of the Eisteddfod was already outdated as a result of the new standard set by the British *Dictionary of National Biography* (*DNB*), and the development of national institutions laid the necessary foundations for an undertaking of a similar standard in Wales. The University of Wales, established in 1893 as a federal university with colleges at Aberystwyth, Bangor, and Cardiff, provided the research base of professional historians (some of whom contributed to the *DNB*), whilst the National Library of Wales, founded in Aberystwyth in 1907, brought together the necessary source materials. It is interesting to note that those two institutions did set up a project which is quite comparable to the biographical one; namely, a historical dictionary of the Welsh language, modelled on the *Oxford English Dictionary*, which the University of Wales Board of Celtic Studies established at the National Library in 1920.[18]

But the stimulus for a biographical dictionary came a generation or so later, and once again it was the London Welsh who took the lead. W. Jenkyn Thomas (1870–1959), a schoolteacher from Merionethshire, broadcast an appeal on West Regional Radio in May 1936 which shows clearly the impulse to emulate the English model in a spirit of national pride:

---

17 T. R. Roberts, *Eminent Welshmen: A Short Biographical Dictionary of Welshmen Who Have Attained Distinction From the Earliest Times to the Present*, vol. 1, *1700–1900* (Cardiff: Educational Publishing Company, 1908) is a notable predecessor to *The Dictionary of Welsh Biography*.
18 Published in print as *Geiriadur Prifysgol Cymru* (Cardiff: University of Wales Press, 1950–2002), and now available online at www.geiriadur.ac.uk/.

> I want to see published a Dictionary of Welsh Biography which will do for Wales what that magnificent English publication, unequalled even in Germany, the Dictionary of National Biography, the D.N.B as it is usually called, has done for the British Isles as a whole.[19]

Whilst admitting that the *DNB* did include 'a very large number of biographies of Welshmen and Welshwomen', Thomas claimed that 'the editors did not know as much about Wales as about England, Scotland and Ireland, and they did not apply their principles of admission as adequately to Wales as they did to the other three countries'.[20] He went on to give examples of Welsh contributions to British and world history, and concluded with an appeal for finance and organisation:

> Here is a glorious opportunity for the leaders of Welsh national life to get together with a view to providing the necessary finance, organising the work, and thereby rendering an inestimable service to their nation.
>
> What individual or society will take the initiative?[21]

The age of the heroic individual was past, and this enterprise clearly required the support of a society. The challenge was duly taken up by the Honourable Society of Cymmrodorion, which was still an influential force in Welsh cultural life. Planning and fundraising took place in 1937, and the project was announced by John Edward Lloyd (1861–1947), professor of history at the University College of North Wales, Bangor, in a meeting of the Cymmrodorion at the National Eisteddfod in Cardiff on 1 August 1938. As Wales's foremost academic historian, a fellow of the British Academy, author of a seminal study of early nation building (*A History of Wales to the Edwardian Conquest* (1911)), and contributor of over 100 entries to the *DNB*, Lloyd was the natural choice as editor of the proposed biographical dictionary.[22] He was to be assisted by another Bangor historian, R. T. Jenkins, and thus the University of Wales can be seen to have given academic credibility to the project.

---

19 The text of Thomas's broadcast was published by Brynley F. Roberts as an appendix to his article on the history of Welsh biographical writing, 'Dechreuadau'r *Bywgraffiadur Cymreig*', *Y Traethodydd* CLXVII, no. 703 (2012): 246–58.
20 Roberts, 'Dechreuadau'r *Bywgraffiadur Cymreig*', 253.
21 Roberts, 'Dechreuadau'r *Bywgraffiadur Cymreig*', 255.
22 See Huw Pryce, *J. E. Lloyd and the Creation of Welsh History: Renewing a Nation's Past* (Cardiff: University of Wales Press, 2011).

The text of Lloyd's speech announcing the project was published in the Cymmrodorion *Transactions* for that year,[23] and the view he expressed on the question of language is somewhat surprising. Faced with the choice between English and Welsh, he held that 'the argument in favour of an English work is decisive'. Whilst admitting that the Welsh language was appropriate for works dealing with Welsh literature, he argued that 'the history of the country is on a different footing'. But he grudgingly accepted the possibility of subsequent publication in Welsh: 'The fact that the work is issued in English does not preclude its issue in Welsh, for the research work will have been done'.[24]

Until I read the texts of Thomas's radio appeal and Lloyd's speech, I had assumed that one reason for establishing a separate Welsh biography was in order to ensure bilingual publication. However, Thomas made no mention of language at all, and for Lloyd Welsh seems to have been a secondary issue. Lloyd's attitude towards the Welsh language was typical of the Victorian Wales of his youth, in that he saw its value as limited to certain domains, primarily religion, literature, and the home, excluding the practical and public domain of history. This is borne out by his own publication practice; although he published some articles in Welsh-language journals, all his major historical works were in English, which he clearly regarded as the language of serious scholarship.

However, Lloyd's statement does not reflect the actual publication history, since as already noted the Welsh-language volume preceded the English one by six years, and two supplementary volumes were published in Welsh in 1970 and 1997 covering the period 1941–70, before a single English volume covering the same period was published in 2001.[25] I am not aware of any evidence of a change in official policy on the question of language, and it may be that others did not consider the argument in favour of English to be as 'decisive' as Lloyd thought. It must also be noted that

---

23 J. E. Lloyd, 'A Dictionary of Welsh Biography', *Transactions of the Honourable Society of Cymmrodorion* (1938): 67–75.
24 Lloyd, 'Dictionary of Welsh Biography', 74–75.
25 R. T. Jenkins and E. D. Jones, eds, *Y Bywgraffiadur Cymreig 1941–1950* (Llundain: Anrhydeddus Gymdeithas y Cymmrodorion, 1970); E. D. Jones and Brynley F. Roberts, eds, *Y Bywgraffiadur Cymreig 1951–1970* (Llundain: Anrhydeddus Gymdeithas y Cymmrodorion, 1997); R. T. Jenkins, E. D. Jones, and Brynley F. Roberts, eds, *The Dictionary of Welsh Biography 1941–1970* (London: The Honourable Society of Cymmrodorion, 2001).

Lloyd's period as editor was relatively short; due to the outbreak of World War II work did not begin in earnest until late 1943, and Lloyd died less than four years later in 1947, to be succeeded as editor by R. T. Jenkins.

The change in attitude towards the Welsh language, if such there was, may also have been a result of the National Library's involvement in the project, since Welsh was the main working language of that institution. When J. E. Lloyd died in 1947 the national librarian, Sir William Llywelyn Davies, was appointed assistant editor to Jenkins, and several members of the library's staff undertook to write entries. Two subsequent national librarians served as editors of the *DWB* for almost 50 years between them, Dr E. D. Jones from 1965 to 1987, and Dr Brynley Roberts from 1987 until the end of 2013, both working on a voluntary basis long after their retirement from the library. Since 2014 the project has been a partnership between the National Library and the University of Wales Centre for Advanced Welsh and Celtic Studies.

On the other hand, it may be a mistake to assume that precedence in publication necessarily meant a higher status for the Welsh language in the project. There was undoubtedly an element of pietas involved, and possibly also commercial considerations since there was a more dependable market amongst Welsh speakers at that time, but the truth is that the English volumes are more accurate than the Welsh ones simply because of the opportunity provided by later publication to correct errors and include new information.

An example of the kind of differences that can arise between Welsh and English articles is the treatment of the extramarital affairs of the politician David Lloyd George (1863–1945). In the Welsh article, written before 1955 (the date of the death of its author, the journalist E. Morgan Humphreys) and published in 1970 in the first supplementary volume, these are ignored completely, and his marriage to Frances Stevenson in 1943 after the death of his first wife is simply noted without any explanation that she had been his long-term mistress.[26] The English article, published in 2001, does at least explain that Stevenson was 'his long-serving personal assistant and companion', employing a fairly transparent euphemism.[27] Whether this difference was the work of the

---

26   Edward Morgan Humphreys, 'Lloyd George, David', in Jenkins and Jones, *Y Bywgraffiadur Cymreig 1941–1950*, 39–40.
27   Edward Morgan Humphreys, 'Lloyd George, David', in Jenkins, Jones, and Roberts, *The Dictionary of Welsh Biography 1941–1970*, 176–77.

original author or of later editors cannot now be ascertained, but in any case the reluctance to besmirch the good name of this national hero seems to have been at its most acute in the Welsh language. The need for a new article giving a full picture of the public and private life of Lloyd George is obvious.

Publication of parallel print volumes in Welsh and English presented considerable financial and logistical challenges, and due credit must be given to the role of the Cymmrodorion Society in raising the necessary funds and managing the project for over 60 years. Despite time lags in publication and minor discrepancies between the versions, the crucial thing was that biographies of people who died up to 1970 were available in both languages by the time that digital technology made it possible to combine the two in a single online resource. *Welsh Biography Online/Y Bywgraffiadur Ar-lein* was launched in 2007 on the National Library of Wales website,[28] containing digitised and searchable versions of all the articles from the five print volumes, with the facility to switch directly from one language to the other. Since then, all new articles have been published online only, and in Welsh and English simultaneously, in accordance with the strict bilingual policy maintained by the National Library for all its online resources.

Bilingualism in Wales

Full bilingualism of this kind has become normalised since the establishment of the National Assembly for Wales following the referendum on devolution in 1999. All public bodies are now required to operate bilingually, monitored by the Office of the Welsh Language Commissioner. In terms of language policy, the general consensus since devolution has been in favour of a bilingual country in which speakers can use the language of their choice, with a substantial proportion capable of working in both Welsh and English. In its 'National Action Plan for a Bilingual Wales' of 2003 the Assembly Government set out its aspiration for:

---

28   National Library of Wales, yba.llgc.org.uk/en. The title was changed in 2014 to *Dictionary of Welsh Biography/Y Bywgraffiadur Cymreig*, since there is no longer any intention to publish further print versions.

a truly bilingual Wales, by which we mean a country where people can choose to live their lives through the medium of either or both Welsh or English and where the presence of the two languages is a source of pride and strength to us all.[29]

This aspiration has to be set against a background of continuous decline in the percentage of Welsh speakers over the last 200 years. At the beginning of the nineteenth century it is estimated that about 72 per cent of the population of Wales were Welsh speakers, many of them monoglot, and although the proportion decreased gradually during the century there was an increase in absolute numbers to around a million due to population growth, which explains the existence of a thriving Welsh-medium print culture in nineteenth-century Wales.[30] By the census of 1891, which was the first to require information on language in Wales, the proportion of Welsh speakers was 54.5 per cent, and by 1931 this had decreased to 36.8 per cent, of which just under a third were monoglot speakers.[31] The decline continued over the following decades, but numbers stabilised towards the end of the twentieth century at just over half a million, or 20 per cent of the population, mainly as a result of activist campaigns in support of the language, particularly through Welsh-medium education, which led to an increase in the number of young people able to speak Welsh. The Welsh Government recently issued a strategy paper setting out its vision for a million Welsh speakers by 2050, an extremely ambitious target that could only be realised by further growth in Welsh-medium education at all levels.[32]

As a fully bilingual source of information about the history of Wales, the *DWB* is a vital component in any strategy using education to promote the Welsh language, not only in practical terms but also for its symbolic value as one of a small but growing number of online resources which demonstrate to young people that Welsh has not been left behind by the digital revolution. Considerable effort is also being put into the

---

29 'Iaith Pawb [Everyone's Language]: A National Action Plan for a Bilingual Wales', March 2003, accessed 14 November 2016, gov.wales/topics/welshlanguage/publications/iaithpawb/?lang=en.
30 Dot Jones, *Statistical Evidence Relating to the Welsh Language 1801–1911* (Cardiff: University of Wales Press, 1998), 211–25. For a useful general survey, see Janet Davies, *The Welsh Language: A History* (Cardiff: University of Wales Press, 2014).
31 Geraint H. Jenkins and Mari A. Williams, eds, *Let's Do Our Best for the Ancient Tongue: The Welsh Language in the Twentieth Century* (Cardiff: University of Wales Press, 2000), 34.
32 'Cymraeg 2050: Welsh Language Strategy', accessed 27 March 2019, gweddill.gov.wales/topics/welshlanguage/welsh-language-strategy-and-policies/cymraeg-2050-welsh-language-strategy/?lang=en.

development of a Welsh-language version of Wikipedia, which now has over 80,000 articles,[33] and collaboration with the *DWB* has recently begun to contribute data and authoritative source references.

The *DWB* itself was never intended for use by schoolchildren, and the fact that most of its articles have not been revised for over 50 years makes its language and style even less accessible. Separate versions of selected articles for use in schools would be desirable, and this is under consideration. As it stands, the *DWB* is of value for Welsh-medium education primarily at university level. Demand for courses through the medium of Welsh in the universities of Wales was a natural consequence of the success of Welsh-medium secondary schools, and provision has been supported since 2011 by a national Welsh college, Y Coleg Cymraeg Cenedlaethol. Source material in Welsh is valuable not just to those studying Welsh history and literature, but also to students across a wide range of science and humanities subjects seeking information on pioneers of their fields from Wales. And staff appointed to strengthen Welsh-medium provision in the universities are now in a position to contribute articles in their specialist areas.

Although Welsh is spoken by only one in five of the population, the existence of the language is an important marker of national distinctiveness for a much greater proportion of the people of Wales. And those who are active in Welsh-language culture tend to gain the prominence which justifies inclusion in a national biographical dictionary, as writers, preachers, politicians, musicians, and even rugby players. A good example is Richard (Dic) Jones (1934–2009), a farmer and *bardd gwlad* (country or community poet), one of the finest exponents of the modern bardic craft, who won the Chair at the National Eisteddfod in 1966.[34] Another, particularly relevant to Welsh in education, is T. Llewelyn Jones (1915–2009), best known as a children's writer who did a great deal to encourage Welsh-speaking children to delight in reading their own language.[35] Given his fame in Wales, it is interesting to note that T. Llew, as he is always known, has not been included in the new *Oxford Dictionary of National*

---

33   'Wicipedia: Y Gwyddoniadur Rhydd', cy.wikipedia.org/wiki/Hafan.
34   Idris Reynolds, 'Jones, Richard Lewis ('Dic')', *Dictionary of Welsh Biography/ Y Bywgraffiadur Cymreig*, accessed 8 January 2019, bywgraffiadur.cymru/article/c10-JONE-LEW-1934.
35   Idris Reynolds, 'Jones, Thomas Llewelyn', *Dictionary of Welsh Biography/ Y Bywgraffiadur Cymreig*, accessed 8 January 2019, bywgraffiadur.cymru/article/c8-JONE-LLE-1915.

Biography, which just goes to show how important the *DWB* is in ensuring a record of those whose contribution did not extend beyond the Welsh context.

It is perfectly natural that Welsh should be the primary language for recording lives such as these. But in a bilingual dictionary Welsh must encompass all aspects of national life, including spheres in which it has traditionally played little role, such as business and science. This has been facilitated by the development of terminology for Welsh-medium education, which has occurred largely since the publication of the first volumes of the *DWB*. A straightforward example is to be found in the article on the Tudor mathematician Robert Recorde (c. 1512–1558) from Tenby, inventor of the equals sign. The original English article states that 'to him is due the invention of the sign of equality (=)', but the Welsh gives no term for the mathematical concept of equality, referring simply to 'y simbol ='. When a new article was published in 2016 the Welsh version was able to use *hafaledd*, which is now the standard term for that concept.[36] There was in any case a tendency in the early volumes to gloss over technical details of subjects' achievements, particularly those of women. A case in point is Frances Hoggan (1843–1927), the first Welsh woman to qualify as a doctor. The original article on her is very brief and gives no details about her work in either language. A fuller article has just been published, to coincide with the establishment by the Learned Society of Wales of the Frances Hoggan Medal to recognise Welsh women's contribution to science, and the Welsh-language version of that article copes easily enough with terms such as 'progressive muscular atrophy'.[37]

Not the least of the *DWB*'s contributions to widening the vocabulary of contemporary Welsh is its one-word term for a biographical dictionary, *bywgraffiadur*, coined in 1952 by one of its committee members, the scholar and author T. H. Parry-Williams, just in time to be used in its

---

36   James Frederick Rees, 'Recorde, Robert', in Lloyd and Jenkins, *Y Bywgraffiadur Cymreig hyd 1940*, 822; Lloyd and Jenkins, *The Dictionary of Welsh Biography Down to 1940*, 773; Gordon Roberts, 'Recorde, Robert', *Dictionary of Welsh Biography/ Y Bywgraffiadur Cymreig*, accessed 8 January 2019, bywgraffiadur.cymru/article/c11-RECO-ROB-1558.

37   R. T. Jenkins, 'Hoggan, Frances Elizabeth', in Lloyd and Jenkins, *Y Bywgraffiadur Cymreig hyd 1940*, 338; Lloyd and Jenkins, *The Dictionary of Welsh Biography Down to 1940*, 359; Beth Jenkins, 'Hoggan (née Morgan), Frances Elizabeth', *Dictionary of Welsh Biography/ Y Bywgraffiadur Cymreig*, accessed 8 January 2019, bywgraffiadur.cymru/article/c11-HOGG-ELI-1843.

Welsh title. Formed by adding the suffix of the Welsh term for dictionary, *geiriadur*, to the root of the calque *bywgraffiad* ('biography'), this is an extremely handy term which has no equivalent in English.

Other Bilingual Biographical Dictionaries

The *DWB* is by no means the only national biographical dictionary to be published in more than one language. Two others within the English-speaking world are the *Dictionary of Canadian Biography/Dictionnaire biographique du Canada* in English and French, and the *Dictionary of New Zealand Biography* with its parallel series in the Māori language, *Ngā Tāngata Taumata Rau*. In both cases the two languages were originally published in separate print editions, and have recently been integrated into online resources that demonstrate the potential of digital technology to facilitate bilingual dissemination. Both also offer interesting contrasts to the *DWB*, which perhaps reflect the relationship between the language communities in the respective countries. Whereas the *DWB* has one general editor dealing with contributions submitted in either English or Welsh (or both), Canada's dictionary is produced by separate teams at two collaborating institutions: the University of Toronto being responsible for the English version and l'Université Laval for the French version.[38] The New Zealand dictionary provides a selective form of bilingualism along ethnic lines, the user interface being available in both languages but, apparently, only Māori people having entries in both Māori and English.[39]

Translation Issues

When a minority language coexists in a bilingual situation with a majority language there is a tendency for the former to adjust its vocabulary towards a one-to-one correspondence with that of the latter. That tendency is certainly evident in the *DWB* articles, particularly those published since the launch of the website, and makes it possible to achieve a good degree of equivalence between the two languages. Nevertheless, there are still plenty of resonances unique to Welsh which are resistant to direct translation.

---

38   'About Us', *Dictionary of Canadian Biography/Dictionnaire biographique du Canada*, accessed 14 November 2016, www.biographi.ca/en/about_us.php.
39   *Te Ara—The Encyclopedia of New Zealand*, accessed 14 November 2016, teara.govt.nz/en/biographies.

These can be seen in some key words relating to the sense of place and belonging, which serve to illustrate how language can encapsulate 'ways of thinking'.[40]

A highly positive term for region or neighbourhood, with strong connotations of organic community, is *bro*. A measure of the importance of this word for Welsh identity is the fact that it is the root of the ethnic identifier *Cymro* ('Welshman', literally 'fellow-countryman'), the plural of which gave the name of the country itself, *Cymru*. An example of one of many significant uses of the word in the *DWB* occurs in the article on William John Gruffydd (1881–1954) by Sir Thomas Parry, one of the finest Welsh prose writers of the twentieth century. Speaking of Gruffydd's memoirs, Parry stated that they reflected 'the men and women of his native parish and the Welsh people at a crucial time in their history', a translation which conveys the meaning but not the positive resonance of the Welsh 'o'r fro lle magwyd ef, ac o genedl y Cymry mewn cyfnod pwysig yn ei hanes'. There is a similar flattening in the rendering of *cenedl* (originally 'kin' and now 'nation') as 'people', and the progression within that Welsh sentence from *bro* (in its mutated form *fro*) to *cenedl* has political significance in itself which is entirely lost in the English.[41]

Losses in translation are not confined to words of native origin. A phrase which has taken on cultural resonance as a result of its use by the modern author D. J. Williams (1885–1970) of his own neighbourhood of Rhydcymerau in Carmarthenshire is *milltir sgwâr* (literally 'square mile', the second word being an English borrowing). This is used in the article on Richard (Dic) Jones referred to above, who is described in English as 'a countryman whose feet were firmly rooted in the land to which he belonged', and in Welsh with a stronger sense of solid foundation as 'gwladwr â'i draed yn gadarn ar ddaear ei filltir sgwâr'.[42]

The Welsh used in the *DWB* is of necessity a combination of traditional and contemporary, with the new terminology of recent decades alongside a lexical core with connotations accrued over centuries. As in

---

40   James Walter claimed in 'Seven Questions about National Biography' that 'arguably "the national" is most truly alive in ways of speaking, ways of thinking', in *National Biographies and National Identity: A Critical Approach to Theory and Editorial Practice*, eds Iain McCalman with Jodi Parvey and Misty Cook (Humanities Research Centre, The Australian National University: Canberra, 1996), 19–34 (at 21).
41   Thomas Parry, 'Gruffydd, William John', in Jones and Roberts, *Y Bywgraffiadur Cymreig 1951–1970*, 67; Jenkins, Jones and Roberts, *The Dictionary of Welsh Biography 1941–1970*, 86.
42   Reynolds, 'Jones, Richard Lewis ('Dic')'.

any biographical dictionary, many of the articles now being added deal with people brought up before World War II, when monoglot Welsh communities in rural Wales preserved forms of speech extending back across generations. As the poet D. Gwenallt Jones (1899–1968) said of his family connections in the iconic Rhydcymerau, with reference to the great Methodist hymnwriter of the eighteenth century: 'I remember my grandmother … the Welsh on her lips the Welsh of Pantycelyn'.[43]

Whilst in one sense the Welsh language constitutes an element of continuity which makes it essential to any true representation of the history of the Welsh people, this chapter has also shown that its significance is more than just backward-facing. Within the 80 years of the *DWB*'s existence the condition of the Welsh language has changed enormously—for the worse in terms of number of speakers but very much for the better in terms of usage and official status. The new language policy resulting from political devolution coincided with the development of digital technology, making it possible to bring together the contents of the print volumes to form an integrated resource which will be of enormous practical and symbolic value as Wales seeks to fulfil the aspiration to become a truly bilingual country.

---

43 'Rwy'n cofio am fy mam-gu … a'r Gymraeg ar ei gwefusau oedrannus yn Gymraeg Pantycelyn'. D. Gwenallt Jones, 'Rhydcymerau' in *Eples* (Gwasg Gomer: Llandysul, 1951). The translation quoted is by Joseph Clancy, *Twentieth Century Welsh Poems* (Gomer Press: Llandysul, 1982), 100. On the eighteenth-century hymnwriter Williams Pantycelyn, see Gomer Morgan Roberts, 'Williams, William', *Dictionary of Welsh Biography/ Y Bywgraffiadur Cymreig*, accessed 8 January 2019, biography.wales/article/s-WILL-WIL-1717.

PART III: THE TRANSNATIONAL DIMENSION

10
WRITING A DICTIONARY OF WORLD BIOGRAPHY

BARRY JONES

For more than 60 years I have worked in short bursts on a major project, known in its current iteration as the *Dictionary of World Biography* (*DWB*). It reflects my preoccupation, even obsession, about making sense of the world to myself and sharing my insights to others. The work, inevitably, is highly personal, even semi-autobiographical, projecting my involvement in politics, teaching history, extensive travel, and absorption in music, literature, the arts, religion, philosophy, ethics, and the relief of human suffering, through decades of work with a disaster relief organisation and campaigns to reduce blindness. It reflects the influence of Bertrand Russell, whom I observed in Melbourne at close quarters as a student in 1950. He said: 'Three passions, simple, but overwhelmingly strong, have governed my life: the longing for love, the search for knowledge, and unbearable pity for the suffering of mankind'.[1]

Produced in various incarnations since 1981, the *DWB* began to be published by ANU E Press (later ANU Press) in 2013. What began as a personal project has become a popular reference work. The *DWB* is not objective; biased in several ways, it is nevertheless accurate and well researched. Unlike many national biographical dictionary projects, it includes living as well as dead subjects. Long, at over 900 printed pages, I aimed to ensure it had an engaging, readable style. In a world of Wikipedia and large-scale collaborative national biographical dictionary

---

1 Bertrand Russell, *Autobiography*, with an introduction by Michael Foot (London and New York: Routledge, 1998), 9.

projects there is still a place for a sole-authored dictionary of world biography. It has been proposed that the work be renamed *Barry Jones' Dictionary of World Biography*, and for years I resisted the idea because it seemed egotistical. But it seems quite appropriate now, given the work's personal and idiosyncratic nature, when alternative sources of information, great masses of it, are available on Wikipedia and a range of websites. The project calls into question, perhaps, some of the standard templates of biographical dictionaries—above all, the national perspective—and shows how varied and popular the genre is.

Background of the *Dictionary of World Biography*

In the mid-1950s I had been puzzled that no comprehensive biographical dictionary was available in paperback at a modest price. I determined to fill the gap. As a university law student I had been concerned that so many contemporaries had either a sketchy, or nonexistent, grasp of recent political history, let alone familiarity with great composers, or philosophers, or of discoverers in other disciplines, such as medicine. References to my heroes Bertrand Russell, Albert Schweitzer, or Albert Einstein drew a blank. Important and controversial Australians, such as Billy Hughes, John Thomas Lang, or Percy Grainger, were forgotten, or had never been known. I was trying to pursue the concept of 'the abundant life' and I felt pained that so many had no access to the unfamiliar. If they knew nothing of Bach or Michelangelo, they were missing something significant. I always planned that my *DWB* would be more than a collected list of names, dates, and places. It was always intended to provide a hook, something that encouraged the reader to pursue the subject: in effect, sharing my enthusiasms.

It was hubris of a high degree to embark on something so ambitious for my first book, but I could see that there was a gap to be filled. The two generally available major works in the field—*Chambers Biographical Dictionary* and *Webster's* (later *Merriam-Webster's*) *Biographical Dictionary*—both had significant weaknesses. One was too British, with a poor representation of names outside of Europe (a deficiency corrected somewhat in later editions), and the second, while far more comprehensive, offered short entries, little more than concise lists of dates, offices held, or works produced, providing no, or rare, interpretation or context. Both were heavy and expensive, while I planned a book that students could carry around.

While I was teaching history and literature at Dandenong High School, I typed away furiously on my old Olivetti. I retain three bound volumes of my first draft bearing the final date of 5 May 1959, when I was only 26. The text runs to 837 foolscap pages, with about 430,000 words and 6,000 entries. Amendments and new entries over the next 20 years were pasted in. Much of the original text survives in later, much expanded, editions, now about double in length.

Several significant elements were integral to my project. It proved to be an important teaching tool, giving me confidence and communicating enthusiasm, making sense of the great religions, the Renaissance, Reformation, revolutions in America, France, Russia, and China, World Wars I and II, Communism and Fascism, Australian Federation, opening up scientific method, philosophy, music, architecture, and the visual arts. Another factor was the development of my collection of autographed letters and documents. I bought many specimens of subjects who were out of reach (Napoléon, Darwin, Lincoln, Dickens, Wagner, Queen Victoria, Tolstoy), but if I sent copies of my draft entries to those who were living—for example, Igor Stravinsky, Ezra Pound, Oskar Kokoschka, E. M. Forster, Francis Crick, or Noam Chomsky—I was likely to receive a significant reply. This was an incentive to get it right, although I did not invariably accept their self-assessment.

Between 1960 and 1968, while I was refining the *DWB*, I appeared 208 times on the television quiz show *Pick-a-Box*, far more than any other contestant. This conferred an immediate, uncomfortable, and at times embarrassing, celebrity on me, comparable to minor sporting heroes. Some saw me as a role model, others as an irritating, overconfident, overexposed know-all. The work on my first draft was a central factor in my success on *Pick-a-Box*. I was also heavily involved in Labor Party politics, research, and public advocacy on many causes, especially the abolition of capital punishment, and educational reform. So I read voraciously on the history of criminal law, and thought endlessly about creativity and exposure to the arts.

I worked on my project on and off for decades. While largely relying on instinct, I would have backed my own judgment on the choice of names, and their relative length, against all comers. My selections were influenced by my constant reading of biographies, noting how often a particular name would have multiple references in indexes in a random sample of books about, say, twentieth-century politics. If Winston Churchill was in all of them he received a far longer entry in the *DWB* than, for example, his Labour contemporary Herbert Morrison, quite apart from Churchill's intrinsic interest and versatility as historian and painter. However, I could check my judgment objectively by referring to the *Biography Index*, a cumulative list of biographical material in books and magazines, published quarterly by the H. W. Wilson Company, New York. (This was long before the internet revolutionised the ranking of name frequency.) I set my entries in the broad context of history, pointed to relationships and influences between major characters and their times, and challenged entries in other reference books. I was making judgments all the time. I included cross references (*) and a bibliography to encourage discursive reading.

I wrote to Penguin Books in Harmondsworth, London, and received a thoughtful and encouraging letter from A. S. B. Glover, a classical scholar and editor. In January 1961 I took my first draft to London and arranged a meeting with Penguin Books. Charles Clarke, a senior editor, began by reviewing my entry on the psychiatrist Carl Gustav Jung, and this impressed him enough to offer me a contract and a generous advance. Unfortunately, soon after the contract was signed, Clarke left Penguin for the Tavistock Institute, and years of uncertainty and confusion followed. There were deep divisions within Penguin Books, and very strong differences of opinion about whether they should be publishing general reference books at all. After both Glover and Clarke had departed, the project drifted for years and there was obvious concern about the credibility of a young antipodean author, of whom they knew nothing. An attempt to break up the text and send it off to specialist editors ended in high farce. In 1969 I received the first page proofs only to find that many entries in the letters B (Bach, Beethoven, Brahms, Bruckner, Byrd) and H (Händel, Haydn, Heine, Hemingway, Herodotus, Homer, Horace, Victor Hugo) had gone missing. Confucius and Goya had dropped out too. In 1977 the project was abandoned, and Penguin paid me off, but it was soon taken up by Macmillan.

The Macmillan Dictionary of Biography was published in London in 1981 and by Rutledge (1981) and the St Martin's Press (1986) in New York. In 1994 a much expanded edition, under the title *Dictionary of World Biography*, was published by Michael Wilkinson at Information Australia, in association with the *Age*, Melbourne. In 2013 ANU E Press produced the work, revised and rewritten again, in paperback and online. Then Michael Wilkinson published a handsome hard-cover version in 2016 in conjunction with ANU Press.

Sourcing Entries

Inevitably, my work is semi-autobiographical, reflecting my own experience, understanding, attempts to grasp a world view, dealing with diversity, and trying to neutralise prejudice. I was always a very rapid and—more important—efficient reader and over the decades I have consumed thousands of books, including novels, biographies, plays, and poetry, as well as being an assiduous visitor to art galleries and museums, a modest collector of art works and archaeology, and a concert hall habitué. Travel was also a very important factor. In Paris in May 1958, I had witnessed the collapse of the Fourth French Republic, and this, followed by years in France as Australia's representative to the United Nations Educational, Scientific and Cultural Organization (UNESCO: 1991–95) and the World Heritage Committee (1995–96), fuelled my interest in French history, especially the French Revolution, art, music, politics, science, and architecture. I have visited France more than 40 times. My obsessions included revolutionary and political history, Montaigne and Pascal, Debussy and Ravel, Proust, films, churches and cathedrals, Cavaille-Coll organs, menhirs and dolmens in Brittany, and prehistoric cave art in the Dordogne. Entries on de Gaulle, Mitterrand, Chirac and Macron, Simone Veil and Viollet-le-Duc have been enlarged as I better understand complexities.

My book *Sleepers, Wake!: Technology and the Future of Work* (1982) reflected my growing preoccupation with the information technology revolution; I observed the impact of globalisation through work with the Organisation for Economic Co-operation and Development; saw the collapse of the Soviet Union at first hand; was an early advocate of international action on global warming; and became involved with medical researchers. As science minister and thereafter I had close contact with eminent scientists: Burnet, Medawar, Crick, Nossal, Doherty, Oliphant, Perutz, Denton, Miller, Stanley, May, and Williamson. I revised interminably, after discussions with Isaiah Berlin, Michael Tippett, Karl Popper, Henry Moore, Ernst Gombrich, and Benoît Mandelbrot.

I was exhilarated by the challenge to rethink and rewrite my positions on great historical figures after many years of deep reading, travel, and reflection. Time in Egypt, Spain, Turkey, Brazil, Peru, and Cambodia led to fresh insights, major revisions, and expansions of many entries—for example, Tutankhamun, Pol Pot, Dilma Roussef, and Fujimori. Visits to Rome in 2013 and 2014, followed by reading Mary Beard's *SPQR: A History of Ancient Rome* (London: Profile, 2015), fed my obsessions about the Caesars, the papacy, early church architecture, and Caravaggio, resulting in significant revision and expansion of many entries. Similarly, nine days in Iran in 2015 led to a reconsideration of Ferdowsi, Hāfez, Sa'di, Rumi, Omar Khayyam, al Ghazāli, and the Shi'ite/Sunni schism. Access to Nobel Prize archives provided insight into the selection (and rejection) process. Time in Bourges, Chinon, Blois, and Canterbury led to rethinking about Jacques Coeur and early capitalism, Eleanor of Aquitaine, the Dukes of Guise, Thomas Becket, and Geoffrey Chaucer; rereading Homer, Dante, Dostoevsky, Tolstoy, Proust, and Joyce demanded expanded entries, as did deep exposure to Shakespeare, Beethoven, Wagner, and Mahler.

Dramatic changes in 2016, including the Brexit vote in the United Kingdom and Donald Trump's election as president of the United States of America, led to significant rethinking and revision, especially the significance of the rise of populism and hostility to globalism. Visiting New Zealand in 2017 gave me the opportunity to see Richard Serra's great sculpture *Te Tuhirangi Contour* and inspect Sir George Grey's astounding collection of medieval manuscripts. That led to revision of entries on Grey and Serra. Since turning 85 my writing and revision for the *DWB* has been stimulated by a sense of urgency, with time running out.

In comparison to national dictionaries of biography, my attempt has been an overview, analogous to what H. G. Wells had attempted, if that does not sound too pretentious, admittedly limited by my lack of expertise in some areas and remoteness from primary sources, but fortified by the (small c) creator's knowledge and experience. The *DWB* makes no pretence at objectivity, but it aims at accuracy, so far as possible.

Living and the Dead?

I always intended to include entries on the living in my *DWB*. When I finished my first draft in 1959, while Hitler, Mussolini, Tojo, Franklin Roosevelt, and Josef Stalin were dead, Churchill, de Gaulle, Chiang, Eisenhower, MacArthur, Tito, and Zhukov were still alive. It would have given a very lopsided account of World War II and the postwar world to have eliminated the quick in favour of the dead. Postponing treatment of subjects still living, and presumably not eager to be eligible, gives future biographers space and time to reflect instead of rushing to judgment. Presumably any attempt to institute a major international biographical reference work would founder if the living were to be included (think Donald Trump and Vladimir Putin). I had no such inhibition with my *DWB* and emphasised linkages between past and current subjects. Publishing serious entries on the living may inhibit discussion of sensitive issues such as sexuality, mental and physical health, addictions and obsessions, or financial links, and much primary source material will be inaccessible or embargoed. Inevitably, not having a cut-off date means that I need to check recent deaths or changes in status and attempt some revision. (Less than an hour before writing this paragraph I noted that ex-king Michael (Mihai) of Romania had died in December 2017, unremarked in the Australian press. This will require some attention.)

Wikipedia and the Digital Revolution

The information technology revolution has been described as a 'digital hurricane'. Reference books were early victims. The creation of Wikipedia, by Jimmy Wales and Larry Sanger, completely transformed reference publishing: few hard- or soft-cover references survived. Wikipedia went online in January 2001 and is available, free, in 292 languages, with 5.3 million entries and 2.8 million biographies (many of them 'stubs'). So there is already a dictionary of world biography of unparalleled scope, available for free on a screen near you, written by enthusiasts, but checked and challenged by readers. There are claimed to be 27,842,261 'registered editors', suggesting an average of five for each entry. *Nature* examined Wikipedia's science entries and concluded that they were almost as accurate as *Encyclopædia Britannica*.² While the opportunity for fake and distorted entries exists, so does opportunity for immediate challenge and correction. However, Wikipedia will be a major disincentive to embarking on a very large, expensive project on world biography, written by professional scholars.

In the *Times Literary Supplement*, Peter Thonemann commented that 'Wikipedia does just fine at uncontroversial factual information, but as soon as a topic demands critical discrimination or a bit of intelligent digging, its quality control goes completely haywire'.³ He points out that 'none of the major British reference works—the *OED*, the *DNB* [now *ODNB*], *Grove* [*The New Grove Dictionary of Music and Musicians*], *Encyclopedia Britannica*—began life within the academy, though some have ended up there'.⁴ The same comment could be made about my *Dictionary of World Biography*. Jack Lynch, in his admirable *You Could Look It Up: The Reference Shelf from Ancient Babylon to Wikipedia*, comments: 'Wikipedia, despite being non-commercial, still poses many of the dangers of a traditional monopoly, and we run the risk of living in an information monoculture'.⁵ When I check a reference, it can be disconcerting to find in Wikipedia that I am the reference myself.

Language

My *DWB* has an inevitable bias towards the Anglophone world. It is the principal world language, virtually all my readers will have English as a first or second language, and the sources used in my research will have been overwhelmingly published in the United Kingdom, the United States, or Australia. And my own experience outside Australia is predominantly in Europe, then in the United States, and—far behind—Asia, South America, and Africa. Of the 30 longest entries in the *DWB*, 10 are of English-speaking subjects (Shakespeare, Franklin Roosevelt, Lincoln, Churchill, Joyce, Dickens, Ford, Cromwell, Washington, Margaret Thatcher), seven German (Wagner, Mozart, Bach, Beethoven,

---

2   Jim Giles, 'Internet Encyclopaedias Go Head to Head', *Nature* 438 (15 December 2005): 900–901, accessed 12 December 2018. doi.org/10.1038/438900a.
3   Peter Thonemann, 'The All-Conquering Wikipedia', *Times Literary Supplement*, 25 May 2016, accessed 18 October 2018, www.the-tls.co.uk/articles/public/encyclopedic-knowledge/.
4   Thonemann, 'All-Conquering Wikipedia'.
5   Jack Lynch, *You Could Look It Up: The Reference Shelf from Ancient Babylon to Wikipedia* (New York and London: Bloomsbury, 2016), quoted in Thonemann, 'All-Conquering Wikipedia'.

Hitler, Goethe, Marx), three Italian (Michelangelo, Dante, Columbus), two each are French (Napoleon, Proust), Russian (Tolstoy, Stalin), and Spanish (Picasso, Cervantes), and one each is Greek (Homer), Aramaic (Jesus), Chinese (Mao), and Hindi (Gandhi). In recent editions of the *DWB* I have made significant changes in the names for entries, moving away from or adding to the familiar Anglophone versions to the spelling in the original language, or, with Chinese entries, the nearest equivalent, for example **Samuel** (Shmu'el), or **Jinnah, Muhammad Ali** (originally Mahomedali Jinnabhai) or **Yongle** ('perpetual happiness': personal name Zhu Di).

Gender Bias

As with other reference books, women are scandalously underrepresented in the *DWB*, due to their historic exclusion from major areas of activity, such as science or politics. Exceptions have been saints (Mary, Catherine, Teresa, Frances, Elizabeth), rulers (Hatshepsut, Cleopatra, Elizabeth I, Maria Theresia, Catherine the Great, Victoria, Cixi), writers (Sappho, Aphra Behn, Jane Austen, George Sand, Emily Dickinson, George Eliot, Agatha Christie, Simone Weil, Iris Murdoch, Oodgeroo Noonuccal, Judith Wright, Tony Morrison, Hilary Mantel), artists (Angela Kauffman, Louise Bourgeois, Georgia O'Keeffe, Barbara Hepworth, Bridget Riley), musicians (Hildegard of Bingen, Clara Schumann, Melba, Sutherland, Ferrier, Callas, Argerich), actors (Greta Garbo, Edith Evans, Grace Kelly, Catherine Deneuve, Cate Blanchett), or dancers (Pavlova, de Valois, Fonteyn, Ulanova). Later, female politicians and scientists gained international recognition, but it was a slow process: Eleanor Roosevelt, Jiang Qing, Eva Peron, Margaret Thatcher, Theresa May, Angela Merkel, Hillary Clinton, Julia Gillard, Marie Curie, Dorothy Hodgkin, Rosalind Franklin, Rosalyn Yalow, Elizabeth Blackburn, and Fiona Stanley are among the exceptions. Of my 30 longest entries, only one (Thatcher) is female. She played a very significant role in ending the bipartisan consensus in British, and, later, world politics. Angela Merkel is an admirable and courageous figure but her impact has been less. I estimate that women take up barely 15 per cent of the *DWB*'s length. *Chambers Biographical Dictionary* has a higher proportion of female entries because of its emphasis on contemporary entertainers and athletes, such as the Spice Girls, Amy Winehouse, and the controversial ice-skater Tonya Harding.

'TRUE BIOGRAPHIES OF NATIONS?'

National Bias

Of my 30 longest entries, five are German, five English, four American, three Italian, two each French, Spanish and Russian, one each Greek, Austrian, Chinese, Indian and Irish, with Jesus and Marx too hard to classify. I was careful about the relative balance of entries. Certain categories were automatically included: all the Roman Caesars, most Holy Roman Emperors, all British sovereigns and prime ministers, French kings and presidents, United States presidents, and prime ministers of Canada, Australia, New Zealand, India, and South Africa (presidents after 1984). Of the 266 Popes, I have included more than 60: all who held the papal tiara since the eighteenth century, and earlier Popes who left a lasting influence. The numbers of entries on Jews, Irish, Scots, and Hungarians, despite their relatively small populations, reflect their exceptional contributions to music, literature, philosophy, mathematics, physics, medicine, and engineering. Inevitably, Israel and Ireland had and have a disproportionate political and cultural significance globally, with more representation in the *DWB*, say, than the more populous New South Wales and Victoria.

I tried to be careful not to overload the *DWB* with Australians. If I included a contemporary Australian poet or composer, should there be a Canadian of equal standing? The intention was to keep some balance but I may have overdone it. It is striking how many Australians are included in the *Chambers Biographical Dictionary*, many of whom I would not have chosen. However, *Chambers* omits some major figures: Redmond Barry, Peter Lalor, the Myer family, Herbert Vere Evatt, Essington Lewis, Edward 'Weary' Dunlop, Phillip Law, Frank Fenner, Donald Horne, Don Dunstan, John Olsen, Brett Dean, William Deane, Michael Kirby, Gareth Evans, Peter Singer, and Tim Winton.

Contemporary and Political Bias

It was inevitable that there would be some bias in entry selection towards the twentieth and twenty-first centuries—the lifetime of my readers, reflecting their desire for information to understand the context of how we live now, the impact on politics, revolutions, ideology, technology, science, World Wars I and II, the Cold War, literature, art, film, music, and media. Of my 30 longest entries, 11 subjects were active in the twentieth or twenty-first centuries. I have made some attempts to write about The Beatles, who have had (I am told) a continuing influence. Despite my long (and increasingly unhappy) career in politics, I tried to be clinically detached in my entries on public figures, and would immodestly point to entries on Harold Macmillan, Margaret Thatcher, and Richard Nixon. However, I have not disguised my loathing of totalitarian systems, whether Left or Right, and entries on Hitler, Stalin, Mussolini, and Mao are obvious examples. I felt that my explanation of ideologies was a strength and over many years I have tried to cover my areas of weakness, such as sport, popular music, ballet, ornithology, gardening, and fourteenth-century Islamic tiles.

Proportionality

The latest edition of my *DWB* (2018) has the equivalent of 920 full pages of text, more than 8,000 entries, and 840,000 words. Four factors determined entry length: likelihood that the entries would be frequently consulted, availability of resource material, degree of influence that the subjects exerted on how we live (language, theatre, catharsis, humour, tragedy, and so on), and the extent of cross-referencing to other subjects in the *DWB*. Thus, Shakespeare is by far my longest entry. Of the 30 longest entries in the *DWB*, nine are of writers, 12 political leaders, four composers, two artists, and one each are religious (Jesus), political philosopher (Marx) and manufacturer (Ford). It is a matter for regret that only Jesus, Mao, Gandhi, and possibly Homer were not of European ancestry, and that reflects the cultural biases that influence me and my potential readers. I try to compensate, but it is a formidable task.

The *Merriam-Webster* entry on William Shakespeare covers his life in nine lines (94 words), followed by a list of plays and dates, making 29 lines (single column) in total. *Chambers* devotes two full pages to Shakespeare, the second mostly a chronological list, about 2,000 words in total. My Shakespeare entry has 2,386 words, with 56 cross-references (indicated by *), emphasising his life, his sources, the context of his work in the times of Elizabeth I and James I, and his influence on later writers, as well as including a bibliography. Thirty-seven plays are referred to, but in context, not set out in tabular form.

'TRUE BIOGRAPHIES OF NATIONS?'

The *Chambers* Case Study

Chambers Biographical Dictionary is in direct competition with my *DWB*, so I can hardly claim objectivity. Nevertheless, I am puzzled by its contents and have failed to coax *Chambers*'s editors to explain their rationale. *Chambers* has serious problems of balance and proportionality, being variable, and often weak, in politics, literature, music, painting and sculpture, architecture, science and technology, and exploration. It is exceptionally strong in sport, film and television, and pop music and other performing arts, including murder. Murderers are well represented: Ted Bundy, Rosemary and Fred West, Ruth Ellis, James Hanratty, John Christie, Albert Desalvo, Edith Thompson, Myra Hindley, Peter Sutcliffe, Peter Manuel, and Donald Neilson, but not the American terrorist Timothy McVeigh. Many of its subjects are famous for being famous.

Chambers operates at three levels: serious, popular, and local. There are significant numbers of subjects, some quite lengthy, who appear to have been included only because, until 2009, *Chambers* operated from Edinburgh. Classic examples are retired newspaperman Sir Alastair Dunnett and his wife Dorothy, with 32 lines between them. Sir Alastair was 'intensely committed to his native country' and 'served … on the board of several national bodies'.[6] Lady Dunnett was a member of the Scottish Society of Women Artists, and has written several novels. Good for them, but who outside Edinburgh will look them up?

The longest entries in *Chambers* are Shakespeare, Hitler, Mozart, Dickens, Scott, Napoléon, Wagner, Mary Queen of Scots, Jesus, and the Wesleys. Margaret Thatcher is well ahead of Winston Churchill or Elizabeth I of England (not to mention Elizabeth I of Australia). George Washington has the longest entry for any United States president, followed by Abraham Lincoln and Ronald Reagan. The Dunnetts are slightly behind Franklin D. Roosevelt but well ahead of Jefferson, Madison, or Monroe. Four central figures of the second Industrial Revolution—Edison, Bell, Ford, and Marconi—have very short entries in *Chambers*. Elton John's entry is longer than Gustave Flaubert's, and the poet Ted Hughes has more than Keats, Kafka, Proust, Pound, Joyce, or Beckett.

---

6   *Chambers Biographical Dictionary*, 9th ed. (London: Chambers Harrap Publishers, 2013), 465.

Australia is well represented, suggesting a zealous national working party without central direction. There are surprises. Elizabeth Evatt, a distinguished judge and campaigner for social change, is there, rightly, but not her eminent and controversial uncle Herbert Vere Evatt, who was a historian, Australia's youngest High Court judge, minister for external affairs and attorney-general, an architect of the United Nations, president of the UN General Assembly, Labor leader, central figure in the Australian Labor Party split (1954–55), chief justice of New South Wales, and the subject of five biographies. Judith Wright, poet and environmentalist, has a longer entry than the Wright brothers. Ita Buttrose, the journalist, publisher, and broadcaster, has slightly fewer words than Michel de Montaigne but more than President Woodrow Wilson. In *Chambers* 2013 edition many Australian athletes and entertainers, including Rolf Harris, are there but seven prime ministers are missing: Chris Watson, Joseph Cook, James Scullin, Earle Page, Frank Forde, John McEwen (admittedly, the previous three only for short periods), and Julia Gillard. (Tony Abbott was elected later in 2013 and Malcolm Turnbull displaced him in 2015.) The Australian soprano Nellie Melba (née Helen Porter Mitchell), the pride of Melbourne, and of Scottish descent, has more words in her entry than Palestrina, Monteverdi, Telemann, Händel, Haydn, Rossini, Berlioz, Chopin, Liszt, Bruckner, Brahms, Dvořák, Puccini, Mahler, Debussy, Richard Strauss, Sibelius, Rachmaninoff, Ravel, Bartók, or Stravinsky. Even odder, her entry exceeds the length of Franklin and Theodore Roosevelt combined, and is more than Homer, Muhammad, Galileo, Columbus, Cervantes, Velázquez, Goya, Dostoevsky, or Einstein. They shook the world; she had a lovely voice.

Chambers has a foreword, not by a scholar but by a television presenter, Dame Jane Bakewell, who begins: 'I'm always alarmed when people tell me that there are more individuals alive on the planet right now, than the sum total of all those who ever lived throughout history'.[7] (The punctuation is presumably hers.) She is right to be alarmed, but it simply is not true. The current estimate of world population is 7.4 billion: credible estimates of total population throughout history are in the range of 95 to 105 billion. That *Chambers* begins with such a serious error is a concern. Has this delusion shaped the selection of names with its emphasis on the twenty-first century? It may have been a marketing strategy too, emphasising the second Elizabethan era rather than the first.

---

7   *Chambers Biographical Dictionary*, 9th ed., vii.

Conclusion

The *DWB* means a great deal to me because I have poured more into it, over a longer period, than any other work. *Sleepers, Wake!: Technology and the Future of Work* (Oxford University Press, 1982) was my most important book, a textbook for a generation, and having some impact in China and Korea: a prophetic work in some ways. But many of the ideas that I wrote about which seemed wild speculation (people having hand-held computers, for example) are now a central factor in contemporary life. But my *DWB* is a guidebook for the abundant life and I am touched by the number of couples who say that they take turns in reading it to each other. They value the book—and here some immodesty bursts out—because they hear my voice, detect my enthusiasms, and value its authenticity (and accuracy, I hope).

11

BRITISH NATIONAL BIOGRAPHY AND GLOBAL BRITISH LIVES: FROM THE *DNB* TO THE *ODNB*— AND BEYOND?[1]

DAVID CANNADINE

The *Oxford Dictionary of National Biography* (*ODNB*), like the original *Dictionary of National Biography* (*DNB*) from which it has evolved and developed, has rightly been described as a recent culmination of several centuries of collective biographical efforts, which have taken three distinct and different forms. The oldest is group biography, which was of classical origins, was widely practised in Renaissance Italy, and thrived in eighteenth-century Britain, where many professionals sought to establish their own occupational pedigrees, and where competing religious denominations sought to create their own canon of heroes and martyrs. The second was so-called 'universal biography', which was an essentially Enlightenment enterprise, as philosophes and polymaths produced multivolume works aspiring to contain the lives of all the notable people who had ever lived. The third genre was national biography, which flourished across much of the Western world during the nineteenth century, and it is scarcely a coincidence that this was also the first European

---

1   I am, as ever, deeply grateful to former and present colleagues at the *ODNB* for their help and support in the preparation of this essay: to Jo Payne, Philip Carter, Mark Curthoys and Alex May; and to the writings of previous editors, the late Colin Matthew, Sir Brian Harrison, and Lawrence Goldman.

era of nationalist sentiment and state creation. Many of these works, most notably in Germany after its unification in 1870, were sponsored by government, which saw the production of such biographical dictionaries, commemorating great figures from an heroic (and sometimes mythical) national past, as a way of promoting unity, identity, consciousness, and pride across the varied regions, languages, religions, and ethnicities which in reality made up many of these new countries. Yet from a different perspective, such national biographies were also regarded as progressive and improving agents of moral uplift, public education, and individual entertainment—as, indeed, was the nation state itself.[2]

* * *

Like the National Portrait Gallery (founded in 1856), and the Blue Plaques scheme for London (begun 10 years later), the original *DNB* (of which the first instalment appeared late in 1884, although it was dated 1885) may easily be presented as a classic instance of national self-regard, Victorian hero worship, and British patriotic veneration: in sum as a sort of 'Westminster Abbey in print'.[3] Yet in none of these three cases was this the whole truth of things, and perhaps least of all in regard to the *DNB*.[4] For unlike many such works that were being produced on the continent, it was a private rather than a state-sponsored enterprise, and if its begetter and publisher, George Smith, had had his way, the result would have been a much more wide-ranging *Dictionary of Universal Biography*, which would have harked back to those earlier Enlightenment publications, suffused with the ideals of internationalism and cosmopolitanism. Indeed, it was only on further reflection, and following the advice of his friend Leslie Stephen, who would become the *DNB*'s founding editor, that

---

2   Keith Thomas, *Changing Conceptions of National Biography: The* Oxford DNB *in Historical Perspective* (Cambridge: Cambridge University Press, 2005), 2–21. doi.org/10.1017/CBO97805 11497582; Colin Matthew, 'Dictionaries of National Biography', in *National Biographies and National Identity: A Critical Approach to Theory and Editorial Practice*, eds Iain McCalman with Jodi Parvey and Misty Cook (Canberra: Humanities Research Centre, The Australian National University, 1996), 3–4.
3   David Amigoni, 'Life Histories and Cultural Politics of Historical Knowing: The *Dictionary of National Biography* and the Late Nineteenth-Century Political Field', in *Life and Work History Analyses: Qualitative and Quantitative Developments*, ed. Shirley Drex (London: Routledge, 1991), 146, 163; David Amigoni, *Victorian Biography: Intellectuals and the Ordering of Discourse* (Hemel Hempstead: Harvester Wheatsheaf, 1993), 180, note 27; Iain McCalman, 'Introduction', in McCalman with Parvey and Cook, *National Biographies and National Identity*, ii, iv.
4   David Cannadine, *The Pleasures of the Past* (London: Collins 1989), 275–84; David Cannadine, *National Portrait Gallery: A Brief History* (London: National Portrait Gallery, 2007), 10–21; Emily Cole, 'Introduction', in *Lived in London: Blue Plaques and the Stories Behind Them*, ed. Emily Cole (London: Yale University Press and English Heritage, 2009), 1–11.

Smith narrowed down the scope of his multivolume publishing venture from global biography to national coverage. But Stephen's concern about Smith's original project was practical anxiety about its manageability, rather than chauvinistic disappointment at its lack of patriotism; indeed, one of the early names that was considered for what became the *DNB* was simply 'the new biographical dictionary'. And although the years during which the *Dictionary* appeared, from 1884 to 1900, were a time of unprecedented British overseas expansion and high Tory imperialism, its overall tone was documentary rather than celebratory, and, as befitted a multiauthored work, it displayed not only 'tranquil consciousness of Britain's world superiority', but also an element of *fin-de-siècle* cultural pessimism. Indeed, according to F. W. Maitland, the *DNB* reflected more the confusion than the confidence of what he termed the 'national mind'.[5]

Moreover, from the very beginning of the project, Stephen had disdained eulogy and hero-worship for *DNB* entries, urging contributors to eschew rhetoric, sentiment, and panegyric. As one of his colleagues later put it, the preferred style of the contributions was best summarised in the phrase 'no flowers by request', while some of them have rightly been described as 'remarkably disrespectful and at times rude'.[6] Stephen also settled on a brilliantly ambiguous title for the *Dictionary*, which put the adjective 'national' at the very centre of the enterprise, even as he refused to state precisely what, or where, or when, the 'nation' that was to be thus biographied had been, or what or where it was now. And since there was no preface or introduction to the first volume, setting out the aims or scope of the work, this meant 'the *DNB* asserted nationality but carefully avoided defining it', either in terms of identities or geographies.[7] This in turn meant that the criteria for inclusion were 'fluid and pragmatic', rather than rigid and confining, and as a result many of the original entries (as was also the case with the Blue Plaques scheme) recognised British nationals who had been active abroad, and foreign nationals who had played some part in British life. Indeed, neither the *DNB*'s first article (on the French

---

5   Thomas, *Changing Conceptions of National Biography*, 8–9, 26; Lawrence Goldman, 'A Monument to the Victorian Age? Continuity and Discontinuity in the Dictionaries of National Biography, 1882–2004', *Journal of Victorian Culture* 11, no. 1 (2006): 113–14, 129–30, note 53. doi.org/10.3366/jvc.2006.11.1.111; Frederick William Maitland, *The Life and Letters of Leslie Stephen* (London: Duckworth, 1906), 368.
6   Matthew, 'Dictionaries of National Biography', 7; H. C. G. Matthew and B. Harrison, 'Introduction and Other Preliminary Pages [to the *ODNB*]', issued separately (Oxford: Oxford University Press, 2004), x.
7   Matthew, 'Dictionaries of National Biography', 4; Matthew and Harrison, 'Introduction and Other Preliminary Pages', viii.

Protestant minister and writer, Jacques Abbadie, 1654?–1727), nor its penultimate entry (on the Dutch soldier and diplomat, Wilhelm Zuylestein, 1645–1709), was devoted to a person born in the British Isles; both of them had only later settled there.[8] Such an imaginative and integrative policy on inclusion also fitted well with the libertarian, free-trading, and internationalist outlook that was prevalent among late Victorian Liberals, of whom Stephen was undoubtedly one (even though he would split from the party when Gladstone took up Home Rule).[9]

As the original 63 volumes of the *DNB* appeared, responses to Stephen's capacious inclusionary criteria were mixed. Some commentators, such as Professor Richard Copley Christie, writing in the *Quarterly Review* in 1887, applauded the fact that the entries in the *Dictionary* 'illustrate the cosmopolitan character of our nation'.[10] But there were also critics, including an anonymous writer in the *Athenaeum*, in 1889, who could not understand why 'complete foreigners, such as De Baan the painter and some of the Dillons, are included'.[11] Others acclaimed the *DNB* for reasons that would have been anathema to Stephen and Smith, regarding its successful completion, and on schedule, as well as its funding by a private publishing enterprise rather than with any support from the state, as an impressive indication of the very national superiority that they themselves had disdained. Another writer in the *Athenaeum* claimed that 'our British lexicographers have had the satisfaction of administering a handsome beating to their most formidable competitors, the Germans'.[12] Sidney Lee, who had followed Stephen as full-time editor in 1891, but who was less cosmopolitan and more chauvinistic in his outlook, took a similar view, placing the *DNB* project explicitly within the context of such *fin-de-siècle* international rivalries, and declaring it a far more 'earnest endeavour' to satisfy 'the just patriotic instinct' of the 'British and Irish race' than the equivalent attempts in 'Germany, Holland, Belgium,

---

8   Matthew, 'Dictionaries of National Biography', 17; H. C. G. Matthew, *Leslie Stephen and the* New Dictionary of National Biography (Cambridge: Cambridge University Press, 1997), 36; Goldman, 'Monument to the Victorian Age?', 114.
9   Goldman, 'Monument to the Victorian Age?', 115.
10 R. Copley Christie, 'DNB vols 1–10', *Quarterly Review* 164 (1885): 367.
11 Unsigned review of DNB vols 14–18, *Athenaeum*, 20 April 1889, 500.
12 *Athenaeum*, 14 July 1900, 45. Quoted in Robert Faber and Brian Harrison, 'The *Dictionary of National Biography*: A Publishing History', in *Lives in Print: Biography and the Book Trade from the Middle Ages to the 21st Century*, eds Robin Meyers, Michael Harris, and Giles Mandelbrote (London: Oak Knoll Press and the British Library, 2002), 172; Goldman, 'Monument to the Victorian Age?', 116.

Austria, and Sweden'.[13] And with the publication of the twentieth-century *Supplements*, covering the more recently deceased, the *DNB* did become what Matthew would later describe (and regret) as 'a sort of establishment roll-call of national pre-eminence', to the exclusion of other different and more varied lives.[14]

Yet this was undoubtedly an aberration from the broader original remit that had been set by Smith and Stephen. To be sure, the original *DNB* was conspicuously lacking in entries on entrepreneurs (despite the fact that it was privately funded by a publisher), and also on women (for which the more than 90,000-word entry on Queen Victoria, which appeared in the first supplement, scarcely atoned). The nation that was being biographied was overwhelmingly male, not female, but the men were rarely businessmen (or trades union leaders), while those Britons who worked in Europe were largely ignored.[15] On the other hand, Stephen's *DNB* had accepted entries on 'second rate people' and 'obscure names'; it included lives of criminals, highwaymen, brothel-keepers, contortionists, gamblers, journalists, and actors; and one of its most striking entries was the 3,000-word biography of the eighteenth-century, French-born, transvestite, the Chevalier d'Eon.[16] Moreover, the extended chronological span meant the *DNB* encompassed significant periods of Roman, Anglo-Saxon, Danish, Norman, and Angevin dominion across much of the British Isles. From the outset, the *Dictionary* also included many lives, not only from England, but also from the separate nations of Ireland and Scotland (although less so from Wales), from the composite Kingdom of Great Britain, and from the United Kingdom of Great Britain and Ireland. (As a Liberal-turned-Unionist, Stephen was especially eager to integrate the history of Ireland into British national life, and all the leaders of the Irish Rebellion of 1798 were given entries.)[17] And the *DNB* also paid heed to the dramatic expansion of British rule overseas, especially the

---

13 S. Lee, 'The *Dictionary of National Biography*: A Statistical Account', preface to *Dictionary of National Biography*, vol. 63, *Wordsworth–Zuylestein* (London: Smith, Elder and Co., 1900), lxii.
14 Lee, 'A Statistical Account', x–xi, xxii; Brian Harrison, 'Comparative Biography and the *DNB*', *Comparative Criticism* 25 (2004): 11–12; Matthew and Harrison, 'Introduction and Other Preliminary Pages', vii.
15 Matthew, 'Dictionaries of National Biography', 8–11; Matthew, *Leslie Stephen and the* New Dictionary of National Biography, 14–19, 31.
16 Matthew, *Leslie Stephen and the* New Dictionary of National Biography, 13, 15, 18; Matthew, 'Dictionaries of National Biography', 8; Thomas, *Changing Conceptions of National Biography*, 23, 30; Goldman, 'Monument to the Victorian Age?', 117.
17 Matthew, *Leslie Stephen and the* New Dictionary of National Biography, 13; Matthew, 'Dictionaries of National Biography', 8.

settlement colonies and India. Under these circumstances, it was not only prudent, but also unavoidable to keep the definition of English nationality or British identity or British imperial reach implicit and undefined.

* * *

When, more than a century later, Colin Matthew came to consider these matters afresh as editor-designate of the new *Oxford Dictionary of National Biography*, he was eager to return to, and even to extend, Stephen's original definition of nationality and criteria of inclusion. To be sure, he carried over into the new version all the names that had originally appeared in the old *DNB*. But in addition, the number of women included more than trebled, the number of businessmen and labour leaders more than doubled, and the twentieth-century entries covered a much broader range of activity than the original *Supplements*, including such icons of popular culture as footballers, comedians, and pop musicians, as well as individuals branded 'rakes', 'wastrels', and 'swindlers'.[18] All subjects were chosen, not because they were deemed to be exemplary, and thus worthy of commemoration or celebration, or because they were exemplary instances of moral uplift, but on account of their historical importance and influence—whether for good or ill, or for good *and* ill. Matthew also adopted a working delineation of nationality which was 'fluid, practical and inclusive', and which followed and extended Stephen's original conception by treating the inhabitants of the British Isles and the British Empire as what he termed a 'nation-in-effect'.[19] This, in turn, enabled him to emphasise the inherent pluralism of the constituent and changing nationalities of the British Isles and the British Empire, and to enhance the *ODNB*'s coverage of people born, living in, working in, and sometimes leaving, Ireland, Scotland, Wales, the Isle of Man, and the Channel Islands; and he also gave greater prominence than the *DNB* had done to those who went out to, or were born in, many of the British colonial territories, as well as continental Europe.[20]

---

18 Thomas, *Changing Conceptions of National Biography*, 35; Harrison, 'Comparative Biography and the *DNB*', 11; Goldman, 'Monument to the Victorian Age?', 119–20, 122–23.
19 Thomas, *Changing Conceptions of National Biography*, 34–42; Matthew, 'Dictionaries of National Biography', 17; Matthew, *Leslie Stephen and the* New Dictionary of National Biography, 35–37; Matthew and Harrison, 'Introduction and Other Preliminary Pages', viii.
20 Matthew and Harrison, 'Introduction and Other Preliminary Pages', viii.

True to Stephen's founding vision, the original *Dictionary* had included many people who lived in British colonies, but who had never set foot in the British Isles. By allowing occasional entries on imperial and Commonwealth prime ministers and other leading figures, the *DNB Supplements* had continued this earlier practice, albeit diminishingly so, and largely confining themselves to the colonies of settlement, namely Australia, Canada, New Zealand, and South Africa, as well as the Indian Empire.[21] Matthew included all these colonial figures in the *ODNB*, and in assessing the claims of further potential entrants from the greater British overseas world, he was influenced by the extent to which, as he put it in another pragmatic and flexible working definition, they were 'known to Whitehall', as (for example) ruling chiefs, or British proconsuls, or nationalist leaders. On this basis, he increased the coverage of men and women who had lived in the former settlement colonies and South Asia, and he extended the 'known-to-Whitehall' principle to ex-colonial territories elsewhere in the British Empire, especially to other parts of Africa and to the Caribbean. He gave particular attention to those politicians who agitated and campaigned to end British colonial rule, and who oversaw the transition to independence, and who were thus the last imperial cohort who were 'known-to-Whitehall'. For the same reason, he also commissioned more articles on Irish lives for the years after 1922: partly because many nationalists had still been British subjects during the creation of the new, independent state, and partly because Eire formally remained a dominion within the British Empire until 1949.[22]

When the *ODNB* was published in 2004, it was prefaced by the sort of introduction which Stephen had conspicuously refused to provide, and it offered a more extended definition of these 'pragmatic and flexible' concepts of nationality, noting that the *Dictionary* included

> people who were born and lived in the British Isles, people from the British Isles who achieved recognition in other countries, people who lived in territories formerly connected to the British Isles at a time when they were in contact with British rule, and people born elsewhere who settled in the British Isles for significant periods or whose visits enabled them to leave a mark on British life.[23]

---

21 Harrison, 'Comparative Biography and the *DNB*', 5–6.
22 Matthew, *Leslie Stephen and the* New Dictionary of National Biography, 31–32; Matthew and Harrison, 'Introduction and Other Preliminary Pages', viii.
23 Matthew and Harrison, 'Introduction and Other Preliminary Pages', v.

Hence the entry on the earliest identifiable subject in the *ODNB*, who was not included in the original *Dictionary*, namely the Greek explorer Pytheas (floruit, fourth century BCE), who was the author of the first known account of the British Isles by a foreign observer. Hence the 150 biographies of notable Roman officials who had been active in Britain during the period of occupation, along with entries on the Viking and Scandinavian invaders of the ninth and tenth centuries, and the warriors and notables who accompanied William the Conqueror in 1066. Hence also the entries on 800 prerevolutionary colonial Americans, whose lives had found no place in the original *Dictionary*, but who were undoubtedly 'known to Whitehall', and separate entries on the first four American presidents. Hence, too, the greatly increased coverage and range of the twentieth-century biographies. And hence the fact that more than one-tenth of all the subjects in the *ODNB* had been born outside the British Isles.[24]

Across the years since its original hard-copy publication, the *ODNB* has routinely been described as providing 'the record of 60,000 men and women who shaped British history worldwide'. It is an apt summation of a collective biographical enterprise which in its scale and scope is national, yet also international, and in some ways world-encompassing. Many of the entries in the *ODNB* are on Britons who might also be deemed to be 'world figures', and they pay appropriate attention to the extended reach and resonance of such individuals' lives and labours: the entry on Shakespeare, for example, includes sections on his reception and influence in America, Russia, and Japan; while the biography of John Locke stresses his significance for the development of political thought in many parts of the Western world and beyond.[25] Other entries are on figures of major historical importance, but of foreign origin, who spent some time in Britain, among them Julius Caesar, Erasmus, Handel, Voltaire, George Washington, Benjamin Franklin, Mazzini, Marx, Gandhi, and King Farouk of Egypt—although many other such 'honorary Britons'

---

24 Harrison, 'Comparative Biography and the *DNB*', 6; Matthew and Harrison, 'Introduction and Other Preliminary Pages', viii; Goldman, 'Monument to the Victorian Age?', 115.
25 Peter Holland, 'Shakespeare, William (1564–1616)', *Oxford Dictionary of National Biography*, Oxford University Press, 2004; online edn, January 2013, accessed 16 August 2017. doi.org/10.1093/ref:odnb/25200; J. R. Milton, 'Locke, John (1632–1704)', *Oxford Dictionary of National Biography*, Oxford University Press, 2004; online edn, May 2008, accessed 16 August 2017. doi.org/10.1093/ref:odnb/16885.

were excluded.[26] The 'worldwide, collaborative' nature of the *ODNB*, as a project by turns both national and international, is also reflected in the global profile of its authors, of whom 9,804 contributed to the 2004 publication, either as writers of new entries or as revisers of previous lives. Nearly three-quarters of them were based in the British Isles: 7,026 in the United Kingdom and 252 in Ireland. Another 2,526 contributors were recorded in 49 other countries: 1,396 in the United States, and 391 in Canada; 302 in Australia, and 88 in New Zealand; then 52 in Germany, 50 in France, 32 in South Africa, 31 in Italy, 16 in India, and 12 in Japan. A further 96 lived elsewhere in Europe, while 60 were living in 20 other countries in the rest of the world.[27]

* * *

The 60 volumes of the *ODNB* included 50,113 substantive articles covering the lives of 54,922 people, all of them with a significant British connection, who had lived and died before 31 December 2000. But as always, the *Dictionary* remains a work in progress, and the continuing addition of new lives, whether from the distant past or of the more recently deceased, has been made much easier because the main form in which its text is now delivered and accessed is online. Since the beginning of 2005, the *Dictionary* has published updates in January, May, and September each year, and a significant number of these entries demonstrate the *ODNB*'s continuing commitment to explore earlier transnational British lives which, thanks to the IT revolution, can now be reconstructed and pieced together in ways that would previously have been impossible. Some of them present the findings of long-running research projects to extend the *ODNB*'s coverage in areas now deemed to be of great significance, including post-Reformation religious exiles leaving Protestant England for the comfort and reassurance of Catholic Europe; diplomatic representatives to London from the major continental courts, and visitors to Britain from much further afield; British merchants and traders working in the Middle East during the early modern period,

---

26   For example, Chateaubriand, King Louis-Philippe, Nathaniel Hawthorne, Giuseppe Garibaldi, Napoleon III, Robert Frost, and King Hussein of Jordan, all of whom also spent significant periods of time in Britain, have no entries: see James Raven, '*The Oxford Dictionary of National Biography*: Dictionary or Encyclopaedia?', *Historical Journal* 50, no. 4 (2007): 1000–1001. doi.org/10.1017/S0018246X07006474.
27   Matthew and Harrison, 'Introduction and Other Preliminary Pages', xiii, xviii; Goldman, 'Monument to the Victorian Age?', 127.

and in China and Japan during the nineteenth century and beyond; the Pilgrim Fathers and the Founding Fathers of the American Republic; the biographies of settlers, traders, and investors in nineteenth-century Latin America, where there was a very strong British presence; and the lives of men and women from South Asia, Africa, and the Caribbean who since World War II have transformed the British nation into a multifaith, multiethnic, and multicultural society.

The *ODNB* is also engaged in continuing efforts to explore international networks and cosmopolitan groups, among them the participants in the Third Crusade, those who took part in the Field of the Cloth of Gold, the Pilgrim Fathers, the Providence Island Company, the investors in the Darien scheme, the Anglo–South African 'Randlords', and the members of Lord Milner's 'Kindergarten'. Other lives that have recently emerged from research projects highlighting transnational themes are those of German- and East European–born directors and actors who were so important for the development of the British film industry from the 1920s. Many one-off transnational biographies have also been added to the online *ODNB*, among them overseas figures active in Britain, such as Theodoric Rood (floruit 1480–1484?), who was born in Germany and became the first named printer at the University of Oxford; John Blanke (floruit 1507–1512), a royal trumpeter, who was probably African-born, played for Henry VII and Henry VIII, and was the only identifiable black person portrayed in sixteenth-century British art; Pasqua Rosee (floruit 1652–1656), who grew up in the Greek community in Sicily, became a trader in Smyrna, and came to London in 1652 where he extolled the virtues of coffee and established London's first coffee house in the city; Francisco de Miranda (1750–1816), who originated in Venezuela, but spent much of his life in London, campaigning for Spanish American independence; Krishnabhabini Das (1864–1919), who was born in Bengal, came to England with her husband in 1876, and nine years later published *Englande Bangamahila* (*A Bengali Lady in England*)—an account of British manners based on her seven-year residence in London, much of it spent reading and researching in the British Library; and Georgi

11. BRITISH NATIONAL BIOGRAPHY AND GLOBAL BRITISH LIVES

Markov (1929–1978), a Bulgarian writer and dissident, who moved to Britain in 1971 and worked for the British Broadcasting Corporation and Radio Free Europe, but was assassinated in London in 1978.[28]

At the same time, many new lives have been added to the *ODNB* of Britons who were primarily active overseas rather than at home. William Weston (the precise dates of his birth and death are unknown) was a merchant and explorer, and the first Englishman to lead an expedition to North America, probably in 1499.[29] Margaret Clement (1539–1612) belonged to a Roman Catholic family, and she was compelled, like many of her faith, to leave England because of her religious beliefs, and eventually became a prioress of St Ursula's, in Louvain.[30] Henry Smeathman (1742–1786) was an explorer, who was born in Scarborough; he was a pioneer of African entomology and eventually settled in Sierra Leone.[31] John Hughes (c. 1816–1889) grew up in Merthyr Tydfil, and became an ironmaster and engineer; he was later employed from the 1860s by the Russian Government, and took with him 100 specialist ironworkers and miners, who were mostly recruited from the industrial valleys of south Wales.[32] William Lobb (baptised 1809, died 1863) was a Cornishman who devoted his life to collecting exotic plants; in southern Chile he found huge forests of *Araucaria*, which became popularly known in the

---

28   Kristian Jensen, 'Rood, Theodoric (*fl.* 1480–1484?)', *Oxford Dictionary of National Biography*, Oxford University Press, September 2014, accessed 16 August 2017. doi.org/10.1093/ref:odnb/106749; Miranda Kaufmann, 'Blanke, John (*fl.* 1507–1512)', *Oxford Dictionary of National Biography*, Oxford University Press, October 2014; online edn, April 2016, accessed 16 August 2017. doi.org/10.1093/ref:odnb/107145; Brian Cowan, 'Rosee, Pasqua (*fl.* 1651–1656)', *Oxford Dictionary of National Biography*, Oxford University Press, September 2006; online edn, October 2007, accessed 16 August 2017. doi.org/10.1093/ref:odnb/92862; Karen Racine, 'Miranda, (Sebastián) Francisco de (1750–1816)', *Oxford Dictionary of National Biography*, Oxford University Press, May 2006, accessed 16 August 2017. doi.org/10.1093/ref:odnb/89687; Jayati Gupta, 'Das [*née* Sarbadhikari], Krishnabhabini (1864–1919)', *Oxford Dictionary of National Biography*, Oxford University Press, September 2012, accessed 16 August 2017. doi.org/10.1093/ref:odnb/102847; R. J. Crampton, 'Markov, Georgi Ivanov (1929–1978)', *Oxford Dictionary of National Biography*, Oxford University Press, May 2005; online edn, January 2007, accessed 16 August 2017. doi.org/10.1093/ref:odnb/77434.
29   Evan T. Jones, and M. M. Condon, 'Weston, William (d. in or before 1505)', *Oxford Dictionary of National Biography*, Oxford University Press, May 2010, accessed 16 August 2017. doi.org/10.1093/ref:odnb/101082.
30   Victoria Van Hyning, 'Clement, Margaret (1539–1612)', *Oxford Dictionary of National Biography*, Oxford University Press, May 2014; online edn, April 2016, accessed 16 August 2017. doi.org/10.1093/ref:odnb/105818.
31   Starr Douglas, 'Smeathman, Henry (1742–1786)', *Oxford Dictionary of National Biography*, Oxford University Press, Oct 2005; online edn, October 2013, accessed 16 August 2017. doi.org/10.1093/ref:odnb/93969.
32   Susan Edwards, 'Hughes, John (*c.* 1816–1889)', *Oxford Dictionary of National Biography*, Oxford University Press, 2004, accessed 16 August 2017. doi.org/10.1093/ref:odnb/49171.

west as the monkey puzzle tree.³³ And Kathleen Drew (1901–1957) was a Manchester-born phycologist, whose work on red algae led Japanese scientists to cultivate seaweed artificially after the nori industry had been severely affected by typhoons in the 1940s. In gratitude, the Japanese set up a memorial to the 'Mother of the Sea' near Uto City, where an annual ceremony is held in her honour.³⁴

These global and transnational British connections are further illustrated in the annual updates, published every January, of those who have died in the years since 2001. Among the entries that were published in January 2016, recording the lives of men and women who had expired four years before, were many British-born figures who made their careers in the United States. One such was Alexander Cockburn, who had been born in Cromarty in Scotland, but who moved to America in 1972, where he established a reputation as a radical journalist and social critic, publishing much of his work in the *Nation*.³⁵ Another was the hairdresser Vidal Sassoon, who grew up in Whitechapel in the East End of London, but who spent his later business career in California.³⁶ Yet a third was the Manchester-born musician, Davy Jones, who lived in the United States from the 1960s, and was a member of the American pop group The Monkees.³⁷ In a similar category was the film director Tony Scott, who began life, like his brother Ridley, in Northumberland, but who made his breakthrough film, *Top Gun* (1986), in the United States.³⁸ But such transatlantic traffic has never been confined to those Britons heading west from the Old World to the New: it has also been in the opposite direction, as some Americans have made their lives and careers in the

---

33   Sue Shephard, 'Lobb, William (bap. 1809, d. 1863)', *Oxford Dictionary of National Biography*, Oxford University Press, May 2009; online edn, January 2010, accessed 16 August 2017. doi.org/10.1093/ref:odnb/59320.
34   Juliet Brodie, 'Drew [*married name* Baker], Kathleen Mary (1901–1957)', *Oxford Dictionary of National Biography*, Oxford University Press, May 2010, accessed 16 August 2017. doi.org/10.1093/ref:odnb/94193.
35   Godfrey Hodgson, 'Cockburn, Alexander Claud (1941–2012)', *Oxford Dictionary of National Biography*, Oxford University Press, January 2016, accessed 16 August 2017. doi.org/10.1093/ref:odnb/105283.
36   Caroline Cox, 'Sassoon, Vidal (1928–2012)', *Oxford Dictionary of National Biography*, Oxford University Press, January 2016, accessed 16 August 2017. doi.org/10.1093/ref:odnb/106626.
37   Johnny Rogan, 'Jones, David Thomas [Davy] (1945–2012)', *Oxford Dictionary of National Biography*, Oxford University Press, January 2016, accessed 16 August 2017. doi.org/10.1093/ref:odnb/104817.
38   Justin Smith, 'Scott, Anthony David Leighton [Tony] (1944–2012)', *Oxford Dictionary of National Biography*, Oxford University Press, January 2016, accessed 16 August 2017. doi.org/10.1093/ref:odnb/105447.

United Kingdom. Among those who died in 2012 were two women journalists: Eve Arnold, who had been born in Philadelphia, and who began her writing career in the United States, but moved to Britain in 1961; and Marie Colvin, who started out in New York, settled in London, became the *Sunday Times* Middle East correspondent in 1989, and was killed while covering the siege of Homs in Syria.[39]

Although lived out on opposite sides of the Atlantic, all these 'British' lives might properly be described as being Anglo-American, rather than as being bounded by one single nationality. Equally cosmopolitan, although more by necessity than by choice, were the religious and political exiles from Germany and Eastern Europe who settled in Britain during the 1930s. Among those who died in 2012, and whose lives were put up online four years later, were the historian Eric Hobsbawm, who was born in Alexandria in Egypt in 1917, moved from Berlin to London in 1933, and always felt himself to be an outsider, albeit one residing at the heart of the British establishment; he was, appropriately, a pioneer and practitioner of global histories.[40] Another such figure was the author and feminist Eva Figes, who arrived in Britain from Germany in 1938.[41] Yet a third was the actor Herbert Lom, who reached Britain from Prague in the following year; he appeared in many of the Ealing Comedies, and also played the part of Inspector Dreyfus alongside Peter Sellers's Inspector Clouseau in the *Pink Panther* films.[42] Many Britons have also lived global lives, not as émigrés or exiles, but by virtue of their professions: as soldiers, diplomats, proconsuls, or businessmen. One such figure who died in 2014 was Sir Rex Hunt, who was born in Redcar in Yorkshire, and after a succession of diplomatic postings, mostly in the Far East, served as governor of the Falkland Islands between 1980 and 1985. When the Argentinians invaded, he was expelled to Uruguay, but later returned once

---

39 Beeban Kidron, 'Arnold [née Cohen], Eve Deborah (1912–2012)', *Oxford Dictionary of National Biography*, Oxford University Press, January 2016, accessed 16 August 2017. doi.org/10.1093/ref:odnb/104539; Lindsey Hilsum, 'Colvin, Marie Catherine (1956–2012)', *Oxford Dictionary of National Biography*, Oxford University Press, January 2016, accessed 16 August 2017. doi.org/10.1093/ref:odnb/106518.
40 Martin Jacques, 'Hobsbawm, Eric John Ernest (1917–2012)', *Oxford Dictionary of National Biography*, Oxford University Press, January 2016; online edn, April 2016, accessed 16 August 2017. doi.org/10.1093/ref:odnb/105680.
41 Eva Tucker, 'Figes [née Unger], Eva (1932–2012)', *Oxford Dictionary of National Biography*, Oxford University Press, January 2016, accessed 16 August 2017. doi.org/10.1093/ref:odnb/105542.
42 Brian McFarlane, 'Lom, Herbert (1917–2012)', *Oxford Dictionary of National Biography*, Oxford University Press, January 2016, accessed 16 August 2017. doi.org/10.1093/ref:odnb/105645.

the islands had been recaptured by the British.[43] Some 'British' lives are yet more transnational, and are spent in several locations, as in the case of the cricketer Tony Greig: he grew up in South Africa, but played cricket for England, and later worked as a television commentator in Australia.[44]

* * *

The combined effects of the continuing and intensifying IT revolution, and of the academic turn towards global and transnational history, means that the *ODNB* now contains many more entries on lives that are simultaneously British and worldwide than Smith or Stephen could have conceived of in the 1880s—or even than Matthew might have foreseen more than 100 years later. This in turn means the *Dictionary* may now be used not only as a place to look up individual lives online, but also as a starting point for original research into global networks and transnational life-patterns. Here is one example: Magna Carta is invariably regarded as a defining English event, both in terms of royal politics and the common law; but the entries in the *ODNB* on those who were involved make plain that there was also an international dimension, not least on account of the overseas property interests of those English magnates who lost out through King John's failed campaigns. In the same way, the *Dictionary* has recently extended its coverage of the pre-Reformation episcopacy to provide entries on all medieval British bishops, and this makes possible comparative studies of their geographical origins, their movements from one bishopric to another across Europe, and their varied relations with papal and royal authorities. And although not comprehensive, the many entries on Britons employed in South Asia by the East India Company and later in the Indian Civil Service offer a starting point for comparative surveys of the social origins, educational backgrounds, and career development of those ruling imperial cadres and proconsular elites. Place-searching in the *ODNB* also makes it possible to identify some of those potential networks established in Britain by people born abroad: the *Dictionary* currently includes entries on more than 200 men and women who grew up in India but were resident in London between 1880 and 1920.

---

43 David Tatham, 'Hunt, Sir Rex Masterman (1926–2012)', *Oxford Dictionary of National Biography*, Oxford University Press, January 2016, accessed 16 August 2017. doi.org/10.1093/ref:odnb/105750.

44 Rob Steen, 'Greig, Anthony William [Tony] (1946–2012)', *Oxford Dictionary of National Biography*, Oxford University Press, January 2016, accessed 16 August 2017. doi.org/10.1093/ref:odnb/105873.

At the same time, the still-unfolding impact of IT holds out the exciting possibility of connecting data in the *ODNB* to online material generated in other national biographies which the *Dictionary* has spawned and stimulated across the English-speaking world, thereby linking up entries on particular lives—of notable Britons, Irish men and women, Americans, Australians, New Zealanders, and Canadians—as they travelled round the globe and settled in different places. A much more ambitious project would be to link up all the data on all the lives that are recorded in these Anglophone biographical dictionaries, so as to allow online searching across them by name or by a category such as a profession. It is now also possible to appreciate more fully the many historic links between the British Isles and mainland Europe, as so many men and women moved back and forth across the English Channel and the North Sea. To that end, the *ODNB* is beginning to work with the national dictionaries of Sweden, the Netherlands, and Austria, in the hope that similar online links and connections may be made. These partnerships, both Anglophone and European, based on 'the electronic combining of individual national biographical dictionaries', should eventually make it possible to assemble a modern-day version of the sort of 'universal or world biography' that was originally envisaged by Smith, and had been envisioned by the Enlightenment philosophes before him.[45]

Such fully comprehensive dictionaries, and such authentically world-encompassing works, were neither possible nor manageable in eighteenth-century France or in nineteenth-century Britain; but they were foreseen by Oxford University Press as early as 1987, and they were predicted and welcomed by Matthew eight years later. They are both possible and manageable now. But there is still a great deal that needs to be done to make this happen. The technologies and the politics of linking national biographical dictionaries are more complex and more challenging than might at first sight appear. Even if such obstacles can be overcome, would the end result in fact be a universal compendium of global lives? Many parts of the world have yet to produce any such dictionaries, which means the coverage would be overwhelmingly European and English-speaking, and far from universal. Would the gathering together of such national biographies as have been written do full justice to the transnational nature of many people's existences? Would an aggregated dictionary of pre-existing national biographies be an adequate substitute for a dictionary of

---

45 McCalman, 'Introduction', viii.

authentically global lives? And will the current reassertion of xenophobic nationalism in so many parts of the globe, and the backlash against globalisation, mean that global history and global biography seem less alluring projects and less appealing prospects than once they did?

These are sombre questions which are difficult to ignore in the era of Donald Trump and Brexit. The cosmopolitan vision and wide-angled perspective which informed the writings of Matthew and Keith Thomas on the *ODNB* and the greater compilations and combinations to which it might lead, now seem a long time ago and a distant world away. Yet adversity should be a stimulus to greater effort rather than an excuse for narrowing horizons or abandoning ambitions. The tenor and trend of our times may be less friendly to globalisation than it was during the 1990s, and before 9/11 and the financial crash of 2007. But the pursuit and practice of global biography remain important objectives and essential tasks in adding to knowledge and in helping us to better understand our planet and its peoples. 'Posterity', Matthew presciently warned, 'will think us negligent if we do not make what provision we can' for undertaking these tasks and achieving these objectives. More than 20 years on, we have not made as much provision, or as much progress, as we should have done, as we need to do—and as we ought to do.[46]

---

46 Faber and Harrison, '*Dictionary of National Biography*: A Publishing History', 189; Matthew, 'Dictionaries of National Biography', 17; Matthew, *Leslie Stephen and the* New Dictionary of National Biography, 35.

12

THE *DICTIONARY OF CANADIAN BIOGRAPHY* AND THE IRISH DIASPORA

DAVID A. WILSON

How do dictionaries of national biography fit into the context of transnational historical studies? This question is particularly apposite at a time when the very idea of transnationalism is being challenged by the resurgence of atavistic and frequently intolerant forms of nationalism, exemplified in varying degrees by the British withdrawal from the European Union, the election of Donald Trump as President of the United States of America, the politics of leaders such as Vladimir Putin, Tayyip Erdogan, and Viktor Orbán, and the rise of extreme right-wing parties in western Europe. As the post–World War II liberal order threatens to unravel, it is perhaps worthwhile remembering that there is nationalism, and then there is nationalism. 'When nationalism stunts the growth, and embitters the generous spirit which alone can produce generous and enduring fruits of literature', wrote the Irish Canadian politician and poet Thomas D'Arcy McGee in 1867, 'then it becomes a curse rather than a gain to the people among whom it may find favour, and to every other people who may have relations with such a bigoted, one-sided nationality.'[1] The kind of nationalism that McGee endorsed had been expressed by his mentor, Charles Gavan Duffy, more than two decades earlier:

---

1   *Montreal Gazette*, 5 November 1867. See also T. D. McGee, 'The Mental Outfit of the New Dominion', in *1825—D'Arcy McGee—1925; A Collection of Speeches and Addresses, Together with a Complete Report of the Centennial Celebration of the Birth of the Honourable Thomas D'Arcy McGee at Ottawa, April 13th, 1925*, ed. Charles Murphy (Toronto: MacMillan, 1937), 1–21.

> Nationality is broad, comprehensive, and universal; inspiring generous emotions, and encompassing noble ends. I, for one, will never consent to dwarf it down to the selfish schemes of a class in society, or the pedantic theories of a sect in politics.[2]

It was in this latter spirit that one of the generous and enduring fruits of Canadian literature was produced: the *Dictionary of Canadian Biography/ Dictionnaire biographique du Canada* (*DBC/DCB*). Founded in 1959, and inspired by the example of Britain's *Dictionary of National Biography*, it was conceived as a 'biographical reference work for Canada of truly national importance',[3] and intended to strengthen a sense of Canadian identity and unity. Although its promoters and funders sometimes spoke of its role in celebrating Canadian history, the *Dictionary* itself did not develop along such lines. With around 5,000 scholarly contributors writing in French and English, it has provided a multiplicity of viewpoints that are united by a desire to understand rather than praise Canada's past. It is, in short, a dictionary of national biography, not a dictionary of national hagiography.

Yet, in common with its counterparts in Britain, Ireland, the United States, Australia, New Zealand, and elsewhere, it also has a transnational dimension—and was intended to have one right from the start. James Nicholson, the English-born and Canadian-raised birdseed manufacturer whose bequest founded the *DBC/DCB*, stipulated in his will that 'the term "National" shall not be held to exclude ... those born in Canada who may have gained distinction in foreign lands, nor shall it exclude persons of foreign birth who have achieved eminence in Canada'.[4] And so, a project that was established with national objectives in mind immediately took on characteristics of an international source base. It could not have been otherwise, given the large number of people who came to Canada from away, and given the large number of Canadians who made their mark outside the country, from missionaries in China to entertainers in the United States.

---

2   Quoted in Thomas D'Arcy McGee, *Memoir of Charles Gavan Duffy, Esq., as a Student, Journalist, and Organizer* (Dublin: W. Hogan, 1849), 26–27.
3   Quoted in 'About Us', *Dictionary of Canadian Biography/Dictionnaire biographique du Canada*, www.biographi.ca/en/about_us.php.
4   Will of James Nicholson, in Dictionary of Canadian Biography, Robarts Library, University of Toronto.

12. THE *DICTIONARY OF CANADIAN BIOGRAPHY* AND THE IRISH DIASPORA

In considering the national and international aspects of the *DBC/DCB*, at least five factors must be kept in mind. First, the biographies are based upon primary sources, and are subjected to a rigorous fact-checking and stylistic editorial process. Second, the *DBC/DCB* makes every effort to include individuals who span the social spectrum—from prominent politicians such as John A. Macdonald to forgotten figures such as 'Alice G', who spent almost her entire life toiling in the laundry of Toronto's Asylum for the Insane. Third, the decision was made at the beginning to organise the biographies chronologically by death date, in a series of volumes beginning with the period from 1000 to 1700, and moving gradually towards the present. Fourth, the *DBC/DCB* is a fully bilingual project, in which all biographies are published in French and English; the general editor in Toronto works on an equal basis with the directeur general adjoint at Université Laval in Quebec. And fifth, a conscious effort is made to ensure that all regions of the country are fairly represented in the biographies.

As a result of its adherence to these principles, the *DBC/DCB* has secured a national and international reputation for its high standards. In Canada, it received in 2012 the Governor General's Award for Popular History; outside the country, it has been praised by historians such as David Hackett Fischer as 'superior in coverage, documentation, and quality of writing' to the first British *Dictionary of National Biography* and the original *Dictionary of American Biography*.[5] Fischer also drew attention to its accessibility. The *DBC/DCB* is freely available online, with the result that it now has around 1.5 million visits each year.

At the same time, the approach of the *DBC/DCB* poses several challenges that cannot easily be overcome. There is a tension, for example, between the insistence upon primary sources and the goal of including people from all walks of life. In practice, the biographies are heavily weighted towards those who were ensconced in the power structures of Canadian life, and for whom sufficient sources have survived; the lives of politicians, lawyers, and businessmen are far more numerous than those of farmers, fishers, and labourers. This has produced a severe gender imbalance. In the early volumes, up to 1900, women constituted between 3 and 6 per cent of the entries; the figure is currently running at 15 per cent for the 1930s, and will increase as the *Dictionary* moves closer to the present.[6]

---

5   David Hackett Fischer, *Champlain's Dream* (Toronto: Vintage Canada, 2009), 557.
6   See 'Women in the Dictionary of Canadian Biography/Dictionnaire biographique du Canada', *Dictionary of Canadian Biography*, www.biographi.ca/en/theme_women.html.

Another problem is that the emphasis on quality has come at the price of quantity. With thorough fact checking, stylistic editing, and translation procedures in the Quebec and Toronto offices, there can be a long delay between the original submission of a biography and its appearance online. Apart from publishing some 30 'out of synchronisation' biographies that include figures such as Prime Minister Pierre Elliott Trudeau and the ice hockey star Maurice 'Rocket' Richard, the *DBC/DCB* has not yet moved beyond those who died during the 1930s. The challenge has been compounded by severe government cutbacks that the *DBC/DCB* experienced between 1989 and 1994; although stable funding has been restored, it has not matched earlier levels. There is a striking contrast between the output of the *DBC/DCB* and that of the *Oxford Dictionary of National Biography* (*ODNB*). While the former has published just over 8,600 biographies, consisting largely of people who died before 1940, the latter has produced almost 60,000 biographies, including those of people who died as recently as 2013, such as the Northern Irish poet Seamus Heaney and the British politician Margaret Thatcher.

Inescapably, biographies that have been published over five decades reflect the dominant historiographical assumptions and levels of knowledge that existed at the time of writing. An unanticipated by-product is that the *DBC/DCB* is a valuable source for Canadian historiography, as well as Canadian history. This also presents some problems. Language that was deemed acceptable in an earlier period is offensive to many people today. Some of the biographies that were written during the 1960s and 1970s used words such as 'savages', 'squaws', 'Eskimos', and 'negroes' to describe native peoples, indigenous women, the Inuit, and black Canadians. Conflicts between Europeans and natives were sometimes couched in terms of courageous Christian missionaries versus superstitious and violent pagan Indians. It was decided to replace currently offensive words with neutral language; to avoid an Orwellian rewriting of history, links to the original biographies were included. But the deeper problem of ethnocentric assumptions is much more difficult to handle; the task of recommissioning, rewriting, and re-editing earlier biographies is simply impossible without a massive and sustained infusion of cash. As we shall see, some of the issues arising from historiographical shifts and the availability (or existence) of primary sources also affect the *DBC/DCB*'s coverage of Irish immigrants and their descendants in Canada.

12. THE *DICTIONARY OF CANADIAN BIOGRAPHY* AND THE IRISH DIASPORA

The Irish

In considering the relationship between the *DBC/DCB* and global history, it is important to remember Kevin Kenny's distinction between cross-national and transnational history. Cross-national history involves a comparative analysis of immigrant experiences in different nation states, or regions and towns within those states; it examines such questions as settlement patterns, social mobility, labour history, and attachments to Old Country nationalism. Transnational history, in contrast, focuses on the flow of people between and among different nation states, and the demographic, economic, political, and cultural movements and interactions that occur in the process. As Kenny argues, both approaches are needed to provide a comprehensive framework for the study of migration history.[7]

Dictionaries of national biography do not lend themselves to the kind of comparative analysis that Kenny recommends, but, precisely because of their focus on individuals, they can contribute to our understanding of transnational history. In Canada, the Irish are an ideal test case. They were the largest single ethnic group in English-speaking Canada for much of the nineteenth century, they had a significant impact on the country's political and religious history, and they were part of a broader transnational migration.[8] Because most of them arrived during the first half of the nineteenth century, the fact that the *DBC/DCB* does not currently venture much past 1940 is not a serious problem—although it does mean that some Irish immigrants and people of Irish ethnicity are still awaiting their turn.

Irish Canadian experiences were quite distinct from those of Irish Americans, and this difference can be discerned in the sequence and frequency of Irish entries in the *DBC/DCB*; the number of Irish-born Canadians in the dictionary picks up in the early nineteenth century, but starts to fall in the 1920s, as the mid-nineteenth-century migrants were dying out. In contrast to the United States, Irish migration to Canada was largely a pre-Famine phenomenon, and fell off sharply

---

7   Kevin Kenny, 'Diaspora and Comparison: The Global Irish as a Case Study', *Journal of American History* 90, no. 1 (2003): 134–62. doi.org/10.2307/3659794.
8   Donald Harman Akenson, *The Irish in Ontario: A Study in Rural History* (Kingston and Montreal: McGill-Queen's University Press, 1984); Cecil Houston and William J. Smyth, *Irish Emigration and Canadian Settlement: Patterns, Links, & Letters* (Toronto: University of Toronto Press, 1990).

during the mid-1850s. While Irish migrants in the United States were overrepresented in industrial parts of the country, those who came to Canada generally moved into the countryside rather than the towns and cities. A redaction of the 1871 census reveals that 60 per cent of the Irish Canadian ethnic group were Protestants, and that the Irish as a whole matched Canadian norms in terms of occupation, occupational success, and spatial distribution—although Irish Protestants had a significant edge over Irish Catholics.[9]

The major Irish institution in Canada was the Orange Order, which combined hyper loyalism with hyper anti-Catholicism, and which served as a mutual benefit society, a recreational outlet, and a well-oiled patronage machine. By the early twentieth century, one in three adult Protestant males in Canada was a member of the Order. Moving beyond its Irish origins, it included Scots, Welsh, English, and American Protestants; there were also Mohawk lodges. The most Orange place in the early twentieth-century world was not the north of Ireland, but Newfoundland; its members were not Irish Protestants, but descendants of west country English fishermen.[10]

On the other side of the religious line, there were Irish Catholic St Patrick's Day parades, and numerous Catholic religious and political societies, most of which operated within a constitutional nationalist frame of reference. In the mid-nineteenth century, though, there was also a revolutionary Irish nationalist underground, with a significant Fenian presence. And anyone who was going to be a Fenian in loyalist, Orange Ontario was likely to be a very serious Fenian indeed.[11]

The Irish, Protestants and Catholics alike, energised every level of Canadian society. The Ontario school system was strongly influenced by Irish models; the North West Mounted Police drew on the example of the Royal Irish Constabulary; the low church character of Canadian Anglicanism stemmed from its Irish Protestant roots; the English-speaking Catholic Church spoke with a pronounced Irish accent; the Knights of

---

9   Gordon A. Darroch and Michael D. Ornstein, 'Ethnicity and Occupational Structure in Canada in 1871: The Vertical Mosaic in Historical Perspective', *Canadian Historical Review* 61, no. 3 (1980): 305–33. doi.org/10.3138/CHR-061-03-02.
10 Cecil Houston and William J. Smyth, *The Sash Canada Wore: A Historical Geography of the Orange Order in Canada* (Toronto: University of Toronto Press, 1980).
11 See, for example, Peter M. Toner, '"The Green Ghost": Canada's Fenians and the Raids', *Éire-Ireland* 16, no. 4 (Winter 1981): 27–47.

12. THE *DICTIONARY OF CANADIAN BIOGRAPHY* AND THE IRISH DIASPORA

Labor had a strong Irish component; and Irish Protestants and Catholics made their mark in such fields as administration, journalism, business, and the law. The lawyer who defended Patrick James Whelan—an Irish Canadian Fenian who was accused of assassinating Thomas D'Arcy McGee in 1868—was John Hillyard Cameron, a grand master of the Orange Order. The Crown counsel who successfully prosecuted Whelan was James O'Reilly, a Catholic lawyer who was born in County Mayo.

The *DBC/DCB* captures much—but not all—of this reality. Of its more than 8,600 entries, around 800 have an Irish connection—ranging from St Brendan (who almost certainly never set foot in Canada) to William James Pentland, who migrated from County Down in 1911, founded the Dominion Grocery chain, and helped finance a stadium for Toronto's Ulster United football team.[12] It is in no sense 'representative' of the Irish in Canada, nor does it claim to be. Owing to a combination of earlier historiographical assumptions and its reliance on primary sources, the *DBC/DCB* contains more Irish Protestant colonial administrators than unskilled Irish Catholic labourers, and many more Irish men than Irish women. The *Dictionary* is particularly useful for its coverage of Irish Canadian politicians, soldiers, journalists, lawyers, businessmen, priests, and ministers—those who acquired prominence in their chosen fields. It is a rich resource for the principal personages in the Orange Order in Canada—a national variant of a transnational Orange network that operated within and beyond the British Empire.[13]

A good example is Ogle Gowan, the founder of the Grand Orange Lodge of British North America. Hereward Senior's biography in the *DBC/DCB* discusses the Irish origins of Gowan's Orangeism, and shows how his conflict with another Irish Orangeman who came to Canada, George Perkins Bull, was carried across the Atlantic. Gowan also appears in the *Dictionary of Irish Biography* (*DIB*). While the *DBC/DCB*'s entry comes in at 4,000 words and is heavily weighted to his Canadian career, Bridget Hourican's biography in the *DIB* is a quarter of the length and

---

12 T. J. Oleson, 'Brendan (Bréanainn), Saint', *Dictionary of Canadian Biography*, vol. 1, published 1966; revised 1979, University of Toronto/Université Laval, 2003– , accessed 1 October 2018, www.biographi.ca/en/bio/brendan_saint_1E.html; David Roberts, 'Pentland, William James', *Dictionary of Canadian Biography*, vol. 16, published 2016, University of Toronto/Université Laval, 2003– , accessed 1 October 2018, www.biographi.ca/en/bio/pentland_william_james_16E.html.
13 Donald M. MacRaild, 'Wherever Orange is Worn: Orangeism and Irish Migration in the 19th and early 20th Centuries', *Canadian Journal of Irish Studies* 28/29, no. 1 (Fall 2002–Spring 2003): 98–117. doi.org/10.2307/25515430.

is equally divided between his Irish and Canadian activities. Hourican was able to draw not only on Senior's biography, but also on the work of Donald Harman Akenson and Bruce Elliott, with the result that Gowan's conflict with George Perkins Bull is brought into much sharper focus. The biographies complement each other; what the *DIB* article lacks in length and Gowan's Canadian career, it gains in its fuller treatment of his Irish background and its engagement with more recent historiography.[14]

Cumulatively, the *DBC/DCB*'s biographies on Orangeism reveal not only a great deal about the individuals who joined the organisation, but also about its changing character. We can trace the personal and political divisions within the movement, and the strong reaction against Orangeism from traditional Canadian Tories, colonial administrators, liberal Protestants, and Catholics throughout the country. By examining the genealogical information in the biographies, we can see how the Orange Order came to transcend its Irish origins. George Benjamin, who took over from Gowan as grand master in 1846 (and subsequently fought and lost a battle with him over the political direction of the order), was born in England. Moving into the second half of the nineteenth century, we encounter the biography of Oronhyatekha, a Mohawk physician who joined the Orange Order during the 1870s. Among the later biographies, we find black Canadians joining the order, such as George Washington Smith, a Toronto barber and spellbinding orator with a reputation as the leader of the city's 'colored colony', and Alfred Shadd, a physician and farmer in Melfort Saskatchewan, who proudly called himself a 'black Orangeman'.[15]

Although the Order was open to any adult Protestant male, it was driven by an anti-Catholicism that was rooted in its Irish background, and articulated forcefully by Irish-born leaders such as D'Alton McCarthy.

---

14   Hereward Senior, 'Gowan, Ogle Robert', *Dictionary of Canadian Biography*, vol. 10, University of Toronto/Université Laval, 2003– , accessed 1 October 2018, www.biographi.ca/en/bio/gowan_ogle_robert_10E.html; Bridget Hourican, 'Gowan, Ogle Robert', *Dictionary of Irish Biography*, dib.cambridge.org.

15   Hereward Senior, 'Benjamin, George', *Dictionary of Canadian Biography*, vol. 9, University of Toronto/Université Laval, 2003– , accessed 1 October 2018, www.biographi.ca/en/bio/benjamin_george_9E.html; Gayle M. Comeau-Vasilopoulos, 'Oronhyatekha', *Dictionary of Canadian Biography*, vol. 13, University of Toronto/Université Laval, 2003– , accessed 1 October 2018, www.biographi.ca/en/bio/oronhyatekha_13E.html; Barrington Walker, 'Smith, George Washington', *Dictionary of Canadian Biography*, vol. 15, University of Toronto/Université Laval, 2003– , accessed 1 October 2018, www.biographi.ca/en/bio/smith_george_washington_15E.html; Colin Argyle Thomson, 'Shadd, Alfred Schmitz', *Dictionary of Canadian Biography*, vol. 14, University of Toronto/Université Laval, 2003– , accessed 1 October 2018, www.biographi.ca/en/bio/shadd_alfred_schmitz_14E.html.

12. THE *DICTIONARY OF CANADIAN BIOGRAPHY* AND THE IRISH DIASPORA

Applying to Canada the Orange principles that he had learned from his father in Ireland, he spoke of the need to destroy what he called 'French ascendancy', if not by the ballot box then by bayonets. He became a prominent figure in the Equal Rights Association that was founded in 1889 with the objectives of abolishing separate schools for Catholics and preventing the French language from spreading to the Canadian northwest. These goals struck a responsive chord with the Orange rank and file, and persisted well into the twentieth century, when they took the form of a 'one language, one flag and one religion' reaction to bilingual and multicultural policies.[16] Canadian Orangemen also played an active role in supporting Ulster Unionist resistance against Home Rule in Ireland, but these individuals are not represented in the *DBC/DCB*.

Surprisingly, given the *Dictionary*'s policy of including 'those born in Canada who may have gained distinction in foreign lands', the most famous Canadian of all in the anti-Home Rule movement was omitted from the *DBC/DCB*: Andrew Bonar Law. Born in New Brunswick in 1858, he lived there until he was 12 years old, and according to the entry in the *Oxford Dictionary of National Biography* he 'never completely lost the Canadian accent acquired in his youth'.[17] As the only British prime minister to have been born outside the United Kingdom, he naturally occupies a prominent place in the *ODNB*, yet for reasons unknown he was not included in the *DBC/DCB*. In striking contrast is Florence Lawrence, who was born to Irish parents in Hamilton, Ontario, left Canada at the age of four, and found fame as 'the Biograph Girl', the 'first movie star' in the world of silent films. She *is* included in the *DBC/DCB*.[18]

On the Irish nationalist side of the equation, a number of Irish Canadians who supported Irish Home Rule are included in the *Dictionary*. Three in particular stand out: Edward Blake, Charles Ramsay Devlin, and Katherine Hughes. None of them was born in Ireland, but all had Irish roots—thus illustrating the persistence of Irish nationalist thought and feeling among the second and third generations of Irish Canadians. Edward Blake, a Protestant who was born in Canada of Irish parents, served as the Liberal

---

16 See, for example, Jock V. Andrew, *Bilingual Today, French Tomorrow: Trudeau's Master Plan and How It Can Be Stopped* (Richmond Hill, Ont.: BMG Publications Ltd, 1977).
17 E. H. H. Green, 'Law, Andrew Bonar (1858–1923)', *Oxford Dictionary of National Biography*, Oxford University Press, 2004; online edn, January 2011, accessed 28 September 2018. doi.org/10.1093/ref:odnb/34426.
18 Or will be: Cecilia Morgan, 'Florence Lawrence', *Dictionary of Canadian Biography*, forthcoming, www.biographi.ca.

premier of Ontario and the leader of the federal Liberal Party; among other things, he fought against a bill to incorporate the Orange Order in Canada. (The bill passed.) After losing two general elections to the Conservatives, he left Canadian politics in 1892, moved to Ireland, and became a Home Rule MP for South Longford. At a time when the Irish Parliamentary Party was financially strapped and deeply divided, he raised Irish Canadian funds for the cause, donated a large amount of money himself, and played an important role in uniting the party's Parnellite and anti-Parnellite factions. But his attempts to apply Canadian and Australian examples of self-government to the Irish situation fell flat. In the words of his *DBC/DCB* biographers, 'His model of Irish nationalism, which was set within a federalist, imperial framework, lacked broad appeal in Ireland, and his limited grasp of British and Irish politics prevented much open leadership on his part, a role many had expected'.[19] One is reminded of another figure in the *DBC/DCB*, Goldwin Smith, who commented in the course of his attacks on Home Rule that 'Statesmen might as well provide the Irish people with Canadian snowshoes … as extend to them the Canadian Constitution'.[20] The *DIB* also has an entry on Blake; it is much shorter than the Canadian one, and spends equal time on his Canadian and Irish experiences.[21] As is the case with Ogle Gowan, the two biographies of Blake operate within distinct national frameworks, but together they illuminate the transnational character of his career.

Charles Ramsay Devlin's career not only underlines the importance of second-generation Irish Canadian nationalism, but also reveals the connections that could arise between French Canadian and Irish politicians. The common denominator was Catholicism. Devlin came from an Irish Canadian Catholic family with strong Irish nationalist convictions; his uncle, Bernard Devlin (who wound up as a federal Liberal MP during the 1870s), had urged Irish American revolutionaries in 1848 to aid and abet an Irish revolution by invading Canada. With French Canadian support, Charles Devlin in 1891 became a Liberal MP in Quebec, only to break with the party six years later for not taking a strong enough stand on the question of educational rights for Catholics in the province of Manitoba.

---

19   Ben Forster and Jonathan Swainger, 'Blake, Edward', *Dictionary of Canadian Biography*, vol. 14, University of Toronto/Université Laval, 2003– , accessed 1 October 2018, www.biographi.ca/en/bio/blake_edward_14E.html.
20   Ramsay Cook, 'Smith, Goldwin', *Dictionary of Canadian Biography*, vol. 13, University of Toronto/Université Laval, 2003– , accessed 1 October 2018, www.biographi.ca/en/bio/smith_goldwin_13E.html.
21   David Murphy, 'Blake, Edward', *Dictionary of Irish Biography*, dib.cambridge.org.

12. THE *DICTIONARY OF CANADIAN BIOGRAPHY* AND THE IRISH DIASPORA

Appointed Canada's first trade commissioner to Ireland, he became an Irish nationalist MP for Galway and the secretary of the United Irish League. On his return trips to Canada, he joined French Canadian politicians such as Henri Bourassa in attacking British imperialism and advocating Home Rule for Ireland. Devlin does not appear in the *DIB*, but his *DBC/DCB* entry is a valuable resource for anyone interested in the international dimensions of Irish nationalism.[22]

This is also true of Katherine Hughes, the only female Irish nationalist to appear in the *DBC/DCB*. Born in Prince Edward Island in 1876, she was a remarkable woman in many respects: a teacher, missionary to indigenous peoples, biographer, journalist, cofounder of the Canadian Women's Press Club, the first provincial archivist of Alberta, and assistant in the London office of the province's agent general. In London during the height of the Home Rule crisis, she converted from Canadian imperialism to Irish nationalism. After the Easter Rising of 1916, she brought the case for Irish independence to Canadian audiences, and during the Anglo-Irish war of 1919–21 she became a key organiser in the Self-Determination League for Ireland, travelling throughout Canada, the United States, Australia, New Zealand, and France in the service of Sinn Fein—a global figure if ever there was one.[23]

Although Irish Canadian nationalists such as Hughes, Devlin, and Blake generated intense controversy in Canada, and were pilloried by loyalists as traitors to the British Empire, they were not a direct threat to the Canadian state. It was a different story with the Fenians, who between 1866 and 1871 made four attempts to invade Canada. The treatment of the Fenians in the *DBC/DCB* demonstrates the way in which these transnational revolutionaries were viewed through a Canadian national (and sometimes implicitly nationalist) lens. When their biographies were written, the dominant view in Canadian historiography was that the Fenians were, in Donald Creighton's words, 'a crew of grandiloquent clowns and

---

22   Alexander Reford, 'Devlin, Charles Ramsay', *Dictionary of Canadian Biography*, vol. 14, University of Toronto/Université Laval, 2003– , accessed 1 October 2018, www.biographi.ca/en/bio/devlin_charles_ramsay_14E.html. See also J.-C. Bonenfant, 'Devlin, Bernard', *Dictionary of Canadian Biography*, vol. 10, University of Toronto/Université Laval, 2003– , accessed 1 October 2018, www.biographi.ca/en/bio/devlin_bernard_10E.html. For Bernard Devlin's support for an American Irish invasion of Canada in 1848, see *New York Daily Tribune*, 25 August 1848.

23   Pádraig Ó Siadhail, 'Hughes, Katherine (Catherine) Angelina', *Dictionary of Canadian Biography*, vol. 15, University of Toronto/Université Laval, 2003– , accessed 1 October 2018, www.biographi.ca/en/bio/hughes_katherine_angelina_15E.html. See also his award-winning book, *Katherine Hughes: A Life and A Journey* ([Newcastle, Ontario]: Penumbra Press, 2014).

vainglorious incompetents'.[24] It may not be entirely coincidental that, as Donald Wright points out in the *DBC/DCB* entry on Creighton, he was descended from Presbyterians in County Derry.[25]

This view comes across clearly in C. P. Stacey's entry on John O'Neill, leader of the Fenian attempt to invade Canada in 1866. 'It is hard to believe that O'Neill was a man of much intelligence,' wrote Stacey:

> for the idea of righting Irish wrongs by attacking Canada, of which he was the most active exponent, was essentially stupid. He was egotistical and credulous. He seems however to have been a brave soldier and a sincere Irish patriot. Unlike many Fenian leaders, he was ready to risk life and liberty for the cause he believed in.[26]

The Fenians were dismissed and mocked as Celtic cranks with a typically 'Irish' hare-brained scheme to liberate Ireland by invading Canada. Such an approach not only reveals a failure of historical imagination, but also reduces complex realities to the level of caricature; ultimately, it tells us more about Canadian historiography than about Fenian motivations and strategies. In contrast, Desmond McCabe's entry on O'Neill in the *DIB* points out that, rather than being 'essentially stupid', the idea of O'Neill and his fellow Fenians was to 'exploit Anglo-American tensions and perhaps spark a war between Britain and America'.[27]

At least O'Neill made it into the *DBC/DCB*. This was not the case with at least three Irish Canadians from Toronto who became prominent figures in international Fenianism: Edward O'Meagher Condon, William Mackey Lomasney, and Thomas Francis Bourke. Condon's speech from the dock in 1867, with its closing cry of 'God Save Ireland', became a source of inspiration for subsequent generations of Irish nationalists. His friend Lomasney conducted a guerrilla campaign in Cork after the failed Fenian rising of 1867, and in 1884 blew himself up while planting a bomb under London Bridge. Bourke led the Tipperary contingent of the 1867 rising; the speech he gave during his trial was widely regarded as one of the finest

---

24 Donald Creighton, *The Road to Confederation: The Emergence of Canada, 1863–1867* (Toronto: MacMillan, 1964), 304.
25 Donald Wright, 'Creighton, Donald Grant', *Dictionary of Canadian Biography*, vol. 20, University of Toronto/Université Laval, 2003– , accessed 1 October 2018, www.biographi.ca/en/bio/creighton_donald_grant_20E.html. See also his *Donald Creighton: A Life in History* (Toronto: University of Toronto Press, 2015).
26 C. P. Stacey, 'O'Neill, John', *Dictionary of Canadian Biography*, vol. 10, University of Toronto/Université Laval, 2003– , accessed 1 October 2018, www.biographi.ca/en/bio/o_neill_john_10E.html.
27 Desmond McCabe, 'O'Neill, John', *Dictionary of Irish Biography*, dib.cambridge.org.

12. THE *DICTIONARY OF CANADIAN BIOGRAPHY* AND THE IRISH DIASPORA

in the nationalist tradition. Although they are absent from the *DBC/DCB*, they all feature in the *DIB*. But the ways in which they were radicalised in Orange Toronto are absent in the *DIB*, and Lomasney's origins are misplaced in Cincinnati. Here we have good examples of the ways in which transatlantic figures in national biographies can fall between the cracks. Operating within a Canadian frame of reference, the *DBC/DCB* missed their Irish importance; operating with an Irish frame of reference, the *DIB* missed the significance of their Canadian background.[28]

For the most part, the Irish in the *DBC/DCB* were more engaged in the issues of Canada than events in the Old Country. Their Canadian careers, though, were often deeply rooted in their Irish origins. Early nineteenth-century harbingers of responsible government, such as Robert Thorpe and William Weekes, came out of an Anglo-Irish Whig tradition that was equally suspicious of popular radicalism and arbitrary power. As their biographer, Graeme Patterson, noted, they tended 'to understand local politics in terms of Irish analogies'.[29] Personal ambition was an equally powerful, or possibly an even more powerful, motivator as well. Part of the same circle was William Warren Baldwin, whose family had left Ireland to escape the 'horrors of domestic war' in 1798. His biographer, Robert Fraser, observed that Baldwin drew on 'Irish models for the question of the sovereignty of colonial legislatures', and that he played a leading role in

> the transition from the idea of ministerial responsibility (that is, the legal responsibility of the king's ministers to the legislature enforced by impeachment) to the idea of responsible government (which meant the political responsibility of individual ministers or the cabinet to the elected house).[30]

---

28   Owen McGee, 'Condon, Edward O'Meagher'; Desmond McCabe and Owen McGee, 'Lomasney, William Francis Mackey'; James Quinn, 'Bourke, Thomas Francis', *Dictionary of Irish Biography*, dib.cambridge.org.
29   G. H. Patterson, 'Thorpe, Robert', *Dictionary of Canadian Biography*, vol. 7, University of Toronto/Université Laval, 2003– , accessed 1 October 2018, www.biographi.ca/en/bio/thorpe_robert_7E.html; G. H. Patterson, 'Weekes, William', *Dictionary of Canadian Biography*, vol. 5, University of Toronto/Université Laval, 2003– , accessed 1 October 2018, www.biographi.ca/en/bio/weekes_william_5E.html.
30   Robert L. Fraser, 'Baldwin, William Warren', *Dictionary of Canadian Biography*, vol. 7, University of Toronto/Université Laval, 2003– , accessed 1 October 2018, www.biographi.ca/en/bio/baldwin_william_warren_7E.html.

William Warren's son, Robert Baldwin, carried on the tradition, retained a keen sense of Irishness, and would be a key figure in turning the idea of responsible government into reality during the 1840s.[31]

The *DBC/DCB* entries also shed light on the Irish contributions to Canadian Confederation. Among pro-Confederate Irish politicians, such as Edward Kenny in Nova Scotia and Edward Whelan in Prince Edward Island, by far the most important was D'Arcy McGee. 'Much of McGee's Canadian programme', notes his biographer Robin Burns, 'was derived from the nationalist theories of Young Ireland'.[32] But the Irish connection could cut both ways; some Irish Canadians attacked the proposed union of the Canadian provinces in the same language that they attacked the existing union of Great Britain and Ireland. They include the New Brunswick journalist and politician Timothy Warren Anglin, although his biography focuses on his practical objections to Confederation rather than his use or misuse of Irish analogies.[33]

Similar lines of inquiry could be pursued for Irishmen or their descendants who helped to shape colonial administration, religious life, the labour movement, and literary traditions in Canada. A major reason why the Irish Whig Lord Gosford was appointed governor-in-chief of British North America in 1835 was because the government 'hoped that he might be able to apply in Lower Canada the techniques of conciliation that he had employed so successfully in Ireland'. (The hope proved in vain; as his biographer Phillip Buckner tersely remarked, 'Lower Canada was not Ireland'.)[34] Irish Catholic bishops such as John Joseph Lynch, who viewed the Irish as 'a chosen people destined to preserve and extend the true faith throughout the world', brought Irish sensibilities to the English-speaking

---

31 Michael S. Cross and Robert Lochiel Fraser, 'Baldwin, Robert', *Dictionary of Canadian Biography*, vol. 8, University of Toronto/Université Laval, 2003– , accessed 1 October 2018, www.biographi.ca/en/bio/baldwin_robert_8E.html.
32 Robin B. Burns, 'McGee, Thomas D'Arcy', *Dictionary of Canadian Biography*, vol. 9, University of Toronto/Université Laval, 2003– , accessed 1 October 2018, www.biographi.ca/en/bio/mcgee_thomas_d_arcy_9E.html.
33 William M. Baker, 'Anglin, Timothy Warren', *Dictionary of Canadian Biography*, vol. 12, University of Toronto/Université Laval, 2003– , accessed 1 October 2018, www.biographi.ca/en/bio/anglin_timothy_warren_12E.html.
34 Phillip Buckner, 'Acheson, Archibald, 2nd Earl of Gosford', *Dictionary of Canadian Biography*, vol. 7, University of Toronto/Université Laval, 2003– , accessed 1 October 2018, www.biographi.ca/en/bio/acheson_archibald_7E.html.

Catholic Church in Canada.[35] A host of Irish Anglican, Presbyterian, and Methodist ministers in the *DBC/DCB* injected Protestant Irish traditions (frequently with large doses of anti-Catholicism) into the country. When it comes to the labour movement in Canada, the *Dictionary* has dozens of biographies on trade union leaders, some of whom combined labour activism with Orange politics. In the field of literature, the *DBC/DCB* has biographies of a dozen Irish poets whose work has largely been forgotten today. Interestingly, all of them were Protestant. Conspicuous by his absence was the poet laureate of Canadian Fenianism, James McCarroll. He was quietly and effectively written out of Canadian history during the nineteenth century, and was not included in the *Dictionary* because the sources seemed too thin.[36]

There are books waiting to be written on these subjects, and the biographies and bibliographies of the *DBC/DCB* are a rich resource for all of them. Anyone writing a general history of the Irish in Canada could also benefit enormously from the *Dictionary*, as could anyone working on the Irish diaspora—providing its limitations are kept in mind. Operating within a national framework, the *DBC/DCB* is naturally stronger on Irish contributions to Canadian life than on the transnational dimensions of Irish Canadian experiences. But it does not ignore those transnational dimensions (Andrew Bonar Law excepted), and it can point readers in diasporic directions. Perhaps, in the end, that is enough.

Some Irishmen and women with transnational careers can be traced through different national biographies. D'Arcy McGee, for example, appears in four of them: the *DBC/DCB*, the *DIB*, the *ODNB*, and the *American National Biography*. Others, such as Charles Ramsay Devlin and Katherine Hughes, are confined to one. Now that these dictionaries are online, with easy search functions, it is well worth considering how they can be made to speak to one another. Keith Thomas has written that 'One day perhaps we may have a database so vast that its claim to be a true national biography will be incontrovertible'.[37] There is no reason, in principle, why

---

35   Charles W. Humphries, 'Lynch, John Joseph', *Dictionary of Canadian Biography*, vol. 11, University of Toronto/Université Laval, 2003– , accessed 1 October 2018, www.biographi.ca/en/bio/lynch_john_joseph_11E.html.
36   More recently, Michael A. Peterman has done prodigious work in tracking down information on McCarroll, and rescuing him from obscurity. See his *Delicious Mirth: The Life and Times of James McCarroll* (Montreal and Kingston: McGill-Queen's University Press, 2018).
37   Keith Thomas, *Changing Conceptions of National Biography: The* Oxford DNB *in Historical Perspective* (Cambridge: Cambridge University Press, 2005), 56. doi.org/10.1017/CBO9780511497582.

this could not be extended to a true international biography—a high-tech revival of the seventeenth-century dreams of universal biography. In practice, however, the barriers to such a project are formidable. Not only do the various national biographies have different approaches, funding models, and degrees of accessibility; some of them operate under financial constraints that preclude such an initiative. A system of transnational cross-referencing is doubtless desirable. It would be useful, for example, for students of the Irish diaspora who read the biography of Katherine Hughes to get links to the prominent Irish cultural and political figures whom she met in London; two of them, Pádraic Ó Conaire and Arthur O'Brien, are in the *DIB*.[38] But the task of adding transnational references to all biographies in a national dictionary is truly daunting.

It comes down to a question of resources and priorities. In the case of the *DBC/DCB*, the staff in both the Toronto and Quebec offices are working to complete the current volume. Any increase in funds would be directed towards tasks of completing the next volume (dealing with those who died during the 1940s), and correcting or recommissioning earlier biographies. A zero-sum situation exists: time spent on transnational projects is time taken away from pressing current objectives. Having said that, there is no reason why the *DBC/DCB* and its counterparts elsewhere should not develop a greater consciousness of the international context in which their subjects lived, and within which the dictionaries themselves operate: in the case of the *DBC/DCB*, this can be done by placing more emphasis on the extra-Canadian activities of its subjects, highlighting transnational connections in the special thematic projects, and keeping lines of communication open with other dictionaries of national biography, to see what might be possible as events unfold. These are, without question, very modest goals. But at least they have the benefit of being realistic ones.

---

38   Lesa Ní Mhunghalle, 'Ó Conaire, Pádraic'; Kelko Inoue, 'O'Brien, Arthur Patrick Donovan', *Dictionary of Irish Biography*, dib.cambridge.org.

CONTRIBUTORS

Cannadine, David

Sir David Cannadine is Dodge professor of history at Princeton University and visiting professor of history at the University of Oxford, and since 2017 has been the president of the British Academy. He has been the general editor of the *Oxford Dictionary of National Biography* since 2014. A specialist in modern British history from 1800 to 2000, he has published widely on this period, focusing especially on questions of class, the British aristocracy, ceremony and cultural expression in Britain and the wider British empire, and urban development and hierarchy in towns. He has authored, edited, or co-edited numerous books, including *The Decline and Fall of the British Aristocracy* (1990), *Class in Britain* (1998), *Ornamentalism: How the British Saw Their Empire* (2001), *The Undivided Past: Humanity Beyond Our Differences* (2013), and *Victorious Century: The United Kingdom 1800–1906* (2017). He has published biographies of Margaret Thatcher, King George V, G. M. Trevelyan, and Andrew W. Mellon.

Carter, Philip

Philip Carter is senior lecturer and head of IHR Digital at the Institute of Historical Research in the School of Advanced Study, University of London. Until 2016 he was senior research and publication editor for the *Oxford Dictionary of National Biography*, and a member of the History Faculty at the University of Oxford. Philip's publications include more than 150 entries for the *Oxford DNB* as well as studies in eighteenth-century British social history and historical and national biography.

Ewan, Elizabeth

Elizabeth Ewan is university research chair and professor in history and Scottish studies at the University of Guelph, Canada. With Sue Innes, Siân Reynolds, and Rose Pipes, she co-edited *The Biographical Dictionary of Scottish Women: From Earliest Times to 2004* (2006). Her research focus is medieval and early modern Scotland, especially women's and gender history, urban history, and the history of crime. Elizabeth is the author of *Townlife in Fourteenth-Century Scotland* (1990), co-editor with Maureen Meikle of *Women in Scotland* c.*1100–*c.*1750* (1999), co-editor with Janay Nugent of *Finding the Family in Medieval and Early Modern Scotland* (2008) and *Children and Youth in Premodern Scotland* (2015), and co-editor with Lynn Abrams of *Nine Centuries of Man: Manhood and Masculinities in Scottish History* (2017). She has recently completed co-editing *The New Biographical Dictionary of Scottish Women* (2018).

Fox, Karen

Karen Fox is research fellow in the National Centre of Biography and research editor with the *Australian Dictionary of Biography* at The Australian National University. A historian of Australia and New Zealand, her research interests include famous lives, reputations, and biographies; media history; women's, gender, and feminist history; and imperial and colonial history. She is particularly interested in the history of fame and celebrity, and in the ways in which representations of heroes—national and otherwise—shift over time. Karen is the author of *Māori and Aboriginal Women in the Public Eye: Representing Difference, 1950–2000* (2011), and has published in a range of journals, including *Women's History Review*, *History Australia*, and the *Journal of Imperial and Commonwealth History*.

Johnston, Dafydd

Dafydd Johnston is professor and director of the Centre for Advanced Welsh and Celtic Studies at the University of Wales. He has been co-editor of the *Dictionary of Welsh Biography* since 2014, and is chief editor of the journal *Studia Celtica*. His research focuses upon Welsh literature, with a particular focus on medieval Welsh poetry. He has edited three major editions—*Gwaith Iolo Goch* (1988), *Gwaith Lewys Glyn Cothi* (1995), and *Gwaith Llywelyn Goch ap Meurig Hen* (1998)—and two thematic collections, *Medieval Welsh Erotic Poetry* (1991) and *Poets' Grief* (1993). He is the author of *Llên yr Uchelwyr: Hanes Beirniadol Llenyddiaeth Gymraeg 1300–1525* (2005) and *The Literature of Wales* (2017).

Jones, Barry

Barry Jones is a professorial fellow at the University of Melbourne. He was a member of the Victorian parliament 1972–77, of the federal House of Representatives 1977–98, Minister for Science 1983–90, and National President of the Australian Labor Party 1992–2000 and 2005–06. He represented Australia at UNESCO and the World Heritage Committee in Paris 1991–96. He is the only person to have been elected as a Fellow of four of Australia's five learned academies and was appointed AC in 2014. He is the author of *Sleepers, Wake!: Technology and the Future of Work* (1982), *A Thinking Reed* (2006), and *The Shock of Recognition: The Books and Music That Have Inspired Me* (2016), among others. The most recent edition of his *Dictionary of World Biography*, which he has been updating since the 1950s, was published by the National Centre of Biography and ANU Press in 2019.

Konishi, Shino

Shino Konishi is an Australian Research Council research fellow in the School of Humanities and the School of Indigenous Studies at the University of Western Australia. A descendant of the Yawuru people, she is a member of both the *Australian Dictionary of Biography*'s editorial board and of its Indigenous working party. Her research interests focus upon early encounters between Indigenous Australians and European explorers, and in particular the ways that early European representations of Indigenous Australian individuals and cultures have continued to influence understandings of Indigenous societies and politics. Shino is the author of *The Aboriginal Male in the Enlightenment World* (2012). With Malcolm Allbrook and Tom Griffiths, she is leading an Australian Research Council Discovery Indigenous project to produce an Indigenous Australian Dictionary of Biography.

Nolan, Melanie

Melanie Nolan is professor of history and director of the National Centre of Biography, and general editor of the *Australian Dictionary of Biography*, at The Australian National University. She is the chair of the editorial committee of the ANU Press series in biography, ANU.Lives. Specialising in Australian and New Zealand history and biography, she is a labour historian, with a particular interest in the role of the state in Australasian history. Melanie is the author of *Breadwinning: New Zealand Women and the State* (2000) and *Kin: A Collective Biography of a New Zealand Working-Class Family* (2005), and the co-editor with Christine Fernon of *The* ADB*'s Story* (2013).

O'Riordan, Turlough

Turlough O'Riordan is online and editorial administrator for the *Dictionary of Irish Biography*. He has worked for the *DIB* for over 18 years, and is the author of numerous entries, particularly in the areas of architecture, medicine, religion, print culture and publishing, science, and sport; he also focuses on Irish figures with distinct overseas careers. After taking a BA in history and politics, he completed an MA in early modern history (University College Dublin), an MPhil in European studies (University of Cambridge), and an MSc in computer science (Dublin Institute of Technology). Interested in the evolution of the digital humanities, especially with regard to name authority services and onomastics, he occasionally reviews resources and publications for journals.

Phillips, Jock

Jock Phillips was chief historian at the Department of Internal Affairs in New Zealand from 1989 to 1997 and 2000 to 2002, and acting general manager (heritage) from 1997 to 2000. He was the general editor of *Te Ara: The Encyclopedia of New Zealand*—incorporating the online version of the *Dictionary of New Zealand Biography*—from 2002 to 2011, and senior editor in charge of content from 2011 to 2014. A historian of New Zealand, Jock is the author of a number of books, including *A Man's Country? The Image of the Pakeha Male—A History* (1987), *Settlers: New Zealand Immigrants From England, Ireland and Scotland 1800–1945* (2008, with Terry Hearn), and *To the Memory: New Zealand's War Memorials* (2016).

Ware, Susan

Susan Ware has served as the general editor of *American National Biography* since 2012. She is an accomplished historian and editor, and the author of eight books, including biographies of Billie Jean King, Amelia Earhart, Molly Dewson, and Mary Margaret McBride. In 2015, Oxford University Press published her *American Women's History: A Very Short Introduction*. Susan is the editor of several documentary collections and of the most recent volume of *Notable American Women*, published in 2004, which contains biographies of 483 women from over 50 fields. Educated at Wellesley College and Harvard University, she has taught at New York University and Harvard. She has long been associated with the Schlesinger Library at the Radcliffe Institute for Advanced Study, where she is currently the honorary women's suffrage centennial historian, and is active in a variety of professional organisations.

Wilson, David A.

David A. Wilson is professor of history at the University of Toronto. The general editor of the *Dictionary of Canadian Biography*, he is an expert in modern Irish history and the history of the Irish in North America. David is the author of *Paine and Cobbett: The Transatlantic Connection* (1988); *Ireland, a Bicycle and a Tin Whistle* (1995); *United Irishmen, United States: Immigrant Radicals in the Early Republic* (1998); *The History of the Future* (2000); *Thomas D'Arcy McGee, Volume 1: Passion, Reason, and Politics 1825–57* (2008); and *Thomas D'Arcy McGee, Volume 2: The Extreme Moderate 1857–1868* (2011), as well as a number of edited or co-edited volumes.

www.ingramcontent.com/pod-product-compliance
Lightning Source LLC
Chambersburg PA
CBHW040624240426
43666CB00020BA/2910